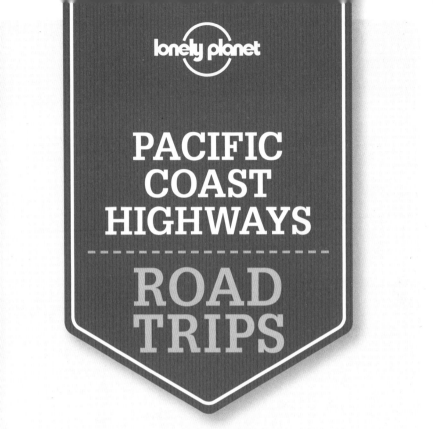

lonely planet

PACIFIC
COAST
HIGHWAYS

ROAD
TRIPS

D0180746

Brett Atkinson, Andrew Bender, Sara Benson, Alison
Bing, Cristian Bonetto, Jade Bremner, Ashley Harrell,
Josephine Quintero, John A Vlahides

HOW TO USE THIS BOOK

Reviews

In the Destinations section:

All reviews are ordered in our writers' preference, starting with their most preferred option. Additionally:

Eating and Sleeping reviews are ordered by price range (budget, midrange, top end) and, within these ranges, by writer preference.

Symbols In This Book

✔	Top Tips	🍷	Food & Drink
📎	Link Your Trips	🌳	Outdoors
💬	Tips from Locals	📷	Essential Photo
➡	Trip Detour	🚶	Walking Tour
📖	History & Culture	✕	Eating
👪	Family	🛏	Sleeping

👁	Sights	🛏	Sleeping
⛱	Beaches	✕	Eating
🏃	Activities	🍷	Drinking
🎓	Courses	☆	Entertainment
👉	Tours	🔒	Shopping
✳	Festivals & Events	ℹ	Information & Transport

These symbols and abbreviations give vital information for each listing:

☎	Telephone number	🚢	Ferry
⊙	Opening hours	🚋	Tram
P	Parking	🚊	Train
⊖	Nonsmoking		apt apartments
❄	Air-conditioning		d double rooms
@	Internet access		dm dorm beds
📶	Wi-fi access		q quad rooms
🏊	Swimming pool		r rooms
🥗	Vegetarian selection		s single rooms
			ste suites
👨‍👧	Family-friendly		tr triple rooms
🐾	Pet-friendly		tw twin rooms
🚌	Bus		

Map Legend

Routes

	Trip Route
	Trip Detour
	Linked Trip
	Walk Route
	Tollway
	Freeway
	Primary
	Secondary
	Tertiary
	Lane
	Unsealed Road
	Plaza/Mall
	Steps
)= =	Tunnel
	Pedestrian Overpass
---	Walk Track/Path

Boundaries

---	International
----	State/Province
⌐⌐⌐	Cliff

Hydrography

	River/Creek
	Intermittent River
	Swamp/Mangrove
	Canal
	Water
	Dry/Salt/ Intermittent Lake
	Glacier

Route Markers

97	US National Hwy
5	US Interstate Hwy
44	State Hwy

Trips

1	Trip Numbers
9	Trip Stop
🔷	Walking tour
🔷	Trip Detour

Population

✪	Capital (National)
◉	Capital (State/Province)
●	City/Large Town
○	Town/Village

Areas

	Beach
	Cemetery (Christian)
	Cemetery (Other)
	Park
	Forest
	Reservation
	Urban Area
	Sportsground

Transport

✈	Airport
Ⓑ	BART station
Ⓣ	Boston T station
Cable Car/	Funicular
Ⓜ	Metro/Muni station
Ⓟ	Parking
Ⓢ	Subway station
	Train/Railway
Tram	
Ⓤ	Underground station

Note: Not all symbols displayed above appear on the maps in this book

CONTENTS

WELCOME TO

PACIFIC COAST HIGHWAYS

Starry-eyed newbies head to the Golden State to find fame and fortune, but you can do better. Come for the landscapes, stay for the farm-fresh and global fusion food, and glimpse the future in the making on America's creative coast.

The trips in this book will take you along the breezy, wildlife-rich Pacific Coast highways, from the famed Southern Californian beaches of Orange County and San Diego and the open roads of Big Sur, through to the towering redwoods of Northern California. Take time out to explore the vineyards of the Napa and Sonoma Valleys, the chilled-out beach cities of Monterey and Santa Cruz, and the big-city lights of San Francisco and Los Angeles.

From backcountry lanes to beachside highways, we've got something for you.

Golden Gate Bridge (p85)

PACIFIC COAST HIGHWAYS

★

2 **Bay Area Culinary Tour**
Taste the source of California's phenomenal farm-to-fork cuisine.
2–3 DAYS

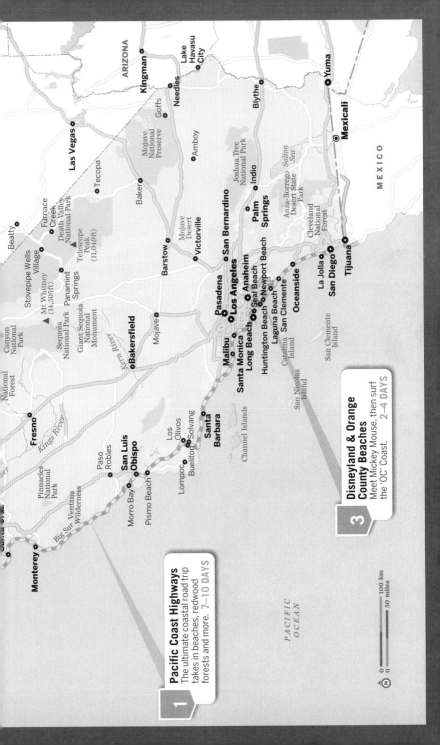

ARIZONA

Kingman

Lake Havasu City

Needles

Goffs

Mojave National Preserve

Amboy

Blythe

Joshua Tree National Park

Indio

Salton Sea

Anza-Borrego Desert State Park

Cleveland National Forest

Tijuana

Mexicali

Yuma

MEXICO

Las Vegas

Beatty

Furnace Creek

Death Valley National Park

Stovepipe Wells Village

Telescope Peak (11,049ft)

Panamint Springs

Tecopa

Baker

Mt Whitney (14,505ft)

Sequoia National Park

Giant Sequoia National Monument

Kern River

Mojave Desert

Barstow

Victorville

San Bernardino

Palm Springs

Bakersfield

Mojave

Pasadena

Los Angeles

Anaheim

Seal Beach

Malibu

Santa Monica

Long Beach

Huntington Beach Newport Beach

Laguna Beach

San Clemente

Oceanside

La Jolla

San Diego

Catalina Island

San Nicolas Island

San Clemente Island

Fresno

Canyon National Park

Kings River

Pinnacles National Park

Paso Robles

San Luis Obispo

Los Olivos

Lompoc Solvang

Buellton

Santa Barbara

Channel Islands

Morro Bay

Pismo Beach

Big Sur Ventana Wilderness

Monterey

PACIFIC OCEAN

1 Pacific Coast Highways
The ultimate coastal road trip takes in beaches, redwood forests and more. **7–10 DAYS**

3 Disneyland & Orange County Beaches
Meet Mickey Mouse, then surf the 'OC' Coast. **2–4 DAYS**

0   100 km
0   50 miles

PACIFIC COAST HIGHWAYS
HIGHLIGHTS

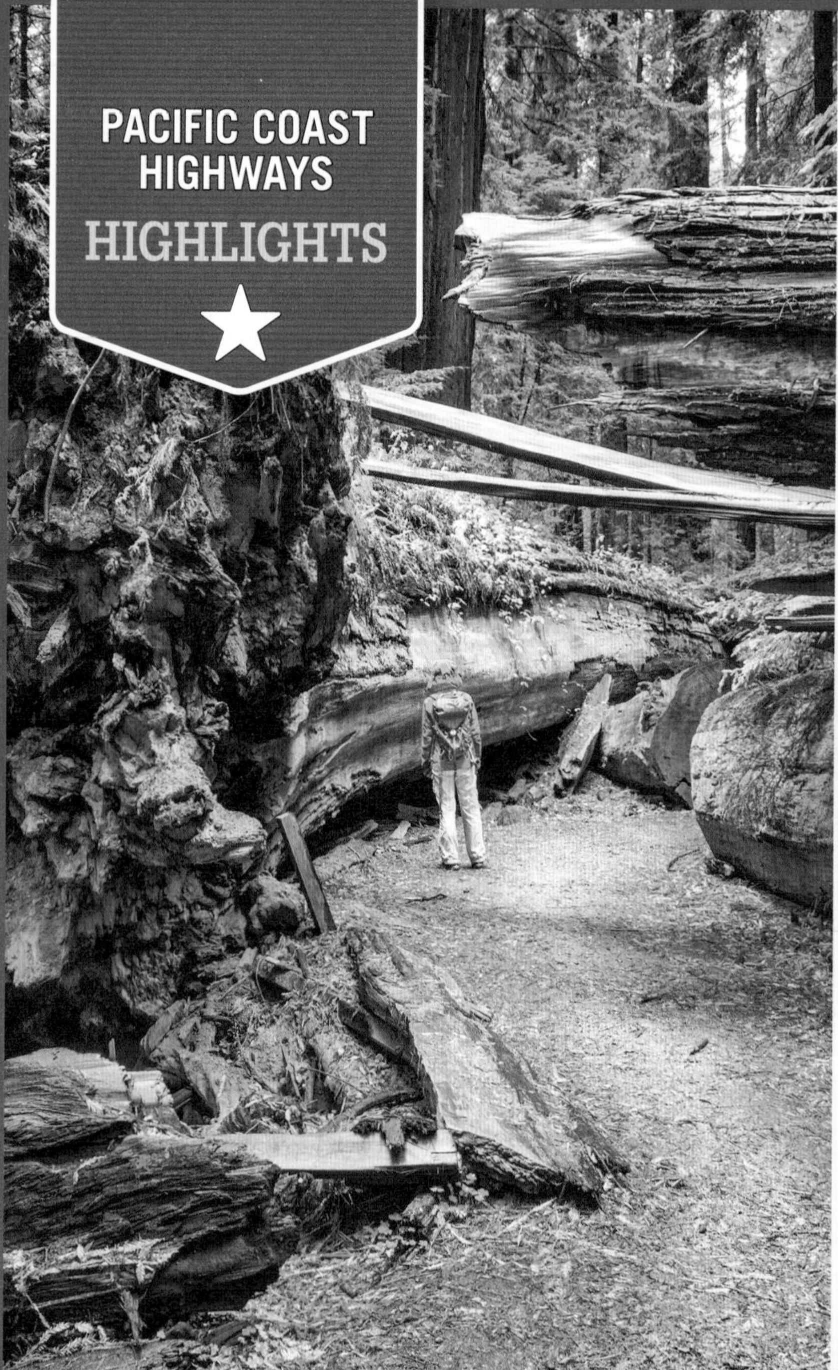

Redwoods (left) Nothing compares to the awe you'll feel while walking underneath these ancient trees.
See it on Trip **1**

San Francisco (above) Marvel at the twinkling lights across the Bay Bridge from the Ferry Building, the city's monument to trailblazing local, sustainable food.
See it on Trip **1**, **2**

Hearst Castle (right) Stop and stare at the sprawling landmark to eccentricity known as Hearst Castle. Pictured left is the Doges Suite Sitting Room at Hearst Castle.
See it on Trip **1**

CITY GUIDE

Lombard Street (p90)

SAN FRANCISCO

Ride the clanging cable cars up unbelievably steep hills, snake down Lombard St's famous hairpin turns, cruise through Golden Gate Park and drive across the arching Golden Gate Bridge. Then go get lost in the creatively offbeat neighborhoods of California's capital of weird.

Getting Around

Avoid driving downtown. Cable cars are slow and scenic (single ride $7). Muni streetcars and buses are faster but infrequent after 9pm (fares $2.25). BART (tickets from $1.95) runs high-speed Bay Area trains. Taxis cost $2.75 per mile; meters start at $3.50.

Parking

Street parking is scarce. Meters take coins, sometimes credit or debit cards; central pay stations accept coins or cards. Overnight hotel parking averages $35 to $55; downtown parking garages start at $2.50 per hour or $30 per day.

Where to Eat

The Ferry Building, Mission District and South of Market (SoMa) are foodie faves. Don't miss the city's outdoor farmers markets. Head to North Beach for Italian, Chinatown for dim sum and the Mission District for Mexican flavors.

Where to Stay

The Marina is near the family-friendly waterfront and Fisherman's Wharf. Union Square and SoMa are most expensive, but conveniently located for walking.

Useful Websites

San Francisco Travel (www.sanfrancisco.travel) Destination info, events calendar and accommodations bookings.

SF Station (www.sfstation.com) Nightlife, restaurants, shopping, events and the arts.

Lonely Planet (www.lonelyplanet.com/usa/san-francisco) Travel tips, travelers' forums, and hotel and hostel bookings.

Trips Through San Francisco: 1 2

Destination coverage: p84

Hollywood Blvd, Hollywood (p61)

LOS ANGELES

Loony LA is the land of starstruck dreams and Hollywood magic. You may think you know what to expect: celebrity worship, Botoxed blondes and endless traffic. But it's also California's most ethnically diverse city, with new immigrants arriving daily, infusing LA's ever-evolving arts, music and food scenes.

Getting Around

Freeway traffic jams are endless, but worst during extended morning and afternoon rush hours. LA's Metro operates slower buses and speedier subway and light-rail trains (fares $1.75), with limited night services. DASH minibuses (single ride 50¢) zip around downtown. Santa Monica's Big Blue Bus (fare $1.25) connects West LA. Taxis cost $2.70 per mile; meters start at $2.85.

Parking

Street parking is limited. Meters take coins, sometimes credit or debit cards; central pay stations accept coins or cards. Valet parking is ubiquitous, typically $5 to $10 plus tip. Overnight hotel parking averages $30 to $50.

Where to Eat

Food trucks and pop-up kitchens are a local obsession. Downtown LA cooks up a global mix, with Little Tokyo, Chinatown, Thai Town, Koreatown and Latin-flavored East LA nearby. Trendsetting eateries pop up in Hollywood, Santa Monica and Venice.

Where to Stay

For beach life, escape to Santa Monica or Venice. Long Beach is convenient to Disneyland and Orange County. Party people adore Hollywood and West Hollywood (WeHo). Culture vultures head to Downtown LA.

Useful Websites

LA Inc (www.discoverlos angeles.com) City's official tourism website for trip planning.

LA Weekly (www.laweekly. com) Arts, entertainment, dining and an events calendar.

Trips Through Los Angeles: 1

Destination coverage: p60

NEED TO KNOW

CURRENCY
US dollars ($)

LANGUAGE
English

VISAS
Generally not required for citizens of Visa Waiver Program (VWP) countries with ESTA approval (apply online at least 72 hours in advance).

FUEL
Gas stations are everywhere, except in national parks and sparsely populated areas. Expect to pay around $3 per US gallon.

RENTAL CARS
Car Rental Express (www.carrentalexpress.com)

Enterprise (www.enterprise.com)

Simply Rent-a-Car (www.simplyrac.com)

Super Cheap! Car Rental (www.supercheapcar.com)

IMPORTANT NUMBERS
American Automobile Association (AAA; ☎800-922-8228)

Emergencies (☎911)

Highway conditions (☎800-427-7623)

Climate

Arcata
GO Apr–Oct

San Francisco
GO Apr–Oct

Los Angeles
GO Apr–Oct

- Desert, dry climate
- Dry climate
- Warm to hot summers, mild winters
- Warm to hot summers, cold winters

When to Go

High Season (Jun–Aug)
» Accommodations prices up 50% to 100% on average.

» Major holidays are even busier and more expensive.

» Summer is low season in the desert, where temperatures exceed 100°F (38°C).

Shoulder (Apr–May & Sep–Oct)
» Crowds and prices drop, especially on the coast and in the mountains.

» Mild temperatures and sunny, cloudless days.

» Typically wetter in spring, drier in autumn.

Low Season (Nov–Mar)
» Accommodations rates lowest along the coast.

» Chilly temperatures, frequent rainstorms and heavy snow in the mountains.

» Winter is peak season in SoCal's desert regions.

Daily Costs

Budget: Less than $75
» Hostel dorm beds: $25–55
» Take-out meal: $6-12

Midrange: $75–200
» Two-star motel or hotel double room: $75–150
» Rental car per day, excluding insurance and gas: $30–75

Top End: Over $200
» Three-star hotel or beach resort room: $150–300
» Three-course meal in top restaurant: $75–100

Eating

Roadside diners & cafes
Cheap and simple.

Beach shacks Casual burgers, shakes and seafood.

National, state & theme parks Mostly so-so, overpriced cafeteria-style or deli picnic fare.

Eating price indicators represent the average cost of a main course at dinner:

$ less than $15
$$ $15 to $25
$$$ more than $25

Sleeping

Motels & hotels Ubiquitous along well-trafficked highways and in busy tourist areas.

Camping & cabins Ranges from rustic campsites to luxury 'glamping' resorts.

B&Bs Quaint, romantic inns in urban and rural areas.

Hostels Cheap and basic; almost exclusively in cities.

Sleeping price indicators represent the average cost of a double room with private bathroom during high season:

$ less than $100
$$ $100 to $250
$$$ more than $250

Arriving in California

Los Angeles International Airport (LAX) Taxis to most destinations ($30 to $50) take 30 minutes to one hour. Door-to-door shuttles ($16 to $27) operate 24 hours. FlyAway bus runs to Downtown LA ($9). Free airport shuttles to LAX City Bus Center & Metro Rail station.

San Francisco International Airport (SFO) Taxis into the city ($35 to $55) take 25 to 50 minutes. Door-to-door shuttles ($16 to $20) operate 24 hours. BART trains to downtown San Francisco ($8.95, 30 minutes) leave the airport between 5:30am and 11:45pm daily.

Cell Phones

The only foreign phones that will work in the USA are GSM multiband models. Network coverage is often spotty in remote and rural areas.

Internet Access

Wi-fi (free or fee-based) is available at most lodgings and coffee shops. Cybercafes ($6 to $12 per hour) are mostly in cities.

Money

ATMs are widely available. Credit cards are accepted almost universally and are usually required for reservations.

Tipping

Tipping is expected, not optional. Standard tipping is 18% to 20% in restaurants, 15% for taxi drivers, $1 minimum per drink in bars and $2 per bag for porters.

Opening Hours

Businesses, restaurants and shops may close earlier and on additional days during the off-season (usually winter, except summer in the deserts).

Bars 5pm-2am daily

Business hours (general) 9am-5pm Monday to Friday

Restaurants 7:30am-10:30am, 11:30am-2:30pm and 5pm-9pm daily, some later Friday and Saturday

Shops 10am-6pm Monday to Saturday, noon-5pm Sunday (malls open later)

Useful Websites

California Travel & Tourism Commission (www.visitcalifornia.com) Multilingual trip-planning guides.

Lonely Planet (www.lonelyplanet.com/usa/california) Destination info, hotel bookings, travelers' forums and more.

Sunset (www.sunset.com/travel/california) Insider travel tips.

For more, see California Driving Guide (p118).

Road Trips

Balboa Island (p38), Newport Beach
TRACEROUDA/GETTY IMAGES ©

Pacific Coast Highways

Our top pick for classic California dreamin'
snakes along the Pacific coast for more than
1000 miles. Uncover beaches, seafood shacks
and piers for catching sunsets over boundless
ocean horizons.

1

TRIP HIGHLIGHTS

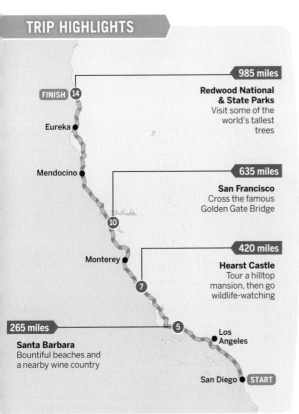

985 miles

Redwood National & State Parks
Visit some of the world's tallest trees

FINISH 14

Eureka

635 miles

San Francisco
Cross the famous Golden Gate Bridge

Mendocino

10

420 miles

Hearst Castle
Tour a hilltop mansion, then go wildlife-watching

Monterey

7

265 miles

Santa Barbara
Bountiful beaches and a nearby wine country

5

Los Angeles

San Diego START

7–10 DAYS
1030 MILES /
1660KM

GREAT FOR...

BEST TIME TO GO
Year-round, but July to October for the sunniest skies.

ESSENTIAL PHOTO
Golden Gate Bridge over San Francisco Bay.

BEST TWO DAYS
Santa Barbara north to Monterey via Big Sur.

Pacific Coast Highways

Make your escape from California's tangled, traffic-jammed freeways and cruise in the slow lane. Once you get rolling, it'll be almost painful to leave the ocean behind. Officially, only the short, sun-loving stretch of Hwy 1 through Orange and Los Angeles Counties can legally call itself Pacific Coast Hwy (PCH). But never mind those technicalities, because equally bewitching ribbons of Hwy 1 and Hwy 101 await all along this route.

❶ San Diego (p44)

Begin at the bottom of the state map, where the pretty peninsular beach town of **Coronado** is connected to the San Diego mainland by the white-sand beaches of the **Silver Strand**. If you've seen Marilyn Monroe cavort in *Some Like It Hot,* you'll recognize the **Hotel del Coronado** (☎619-435-6611; www.hoteldel.com; 1500 Orange Ave, Coronado; **P** 👪), which has hosted US presidents, celebrities and royalty, including the former Prince of Wales who gave up his throne to marry a Coronado divorcée. Wander the turreted palace's labyrinthine corridors, then

quaff tropical cocktails at ocean-view Babcock & Story Bar.

Be thrilled by driving over the 2.1-mile-long **San Diego–Coronado Bridge**. Detour inland to **Balboa Park**. Head west, then south to Point Loma's **Cabrillo National Monument** (☎619-557-5450; www.nps.gov/cabr; 1800 Cabrillo Memorial Dr; per car $10; ⏰9am-5pm; **P** 👪) for captivating bay panoramas from the 19th-century lighthouse and monument to the West Coast's first Spanish explorers. Roll north of **Mission Beach** and the old-fashioned amusement park at **Pacific Beach**, and suddenly you're in hoity-toity **La Jolla**,

beyond which lie North County's beach towns.

The Drive ›› It's a 70-mile trip from La Jolla north along coastal roads then the I-5 into Orange County (aka the 'OC'), passing Camp Pendleton Marine Corps Base and buxom-shaped San Onofre Nuclear Generating Station. Exit at San Clemente and follow Avenida del Mar downhill to the beach.

② San Clemente (p49)

Life behind the conservative 'Orange Curtain' is far different than in most other laid-back, liberal California beach towns. Apart from glamorous beaches where famous TV shows and movies have been filmed, you can still uncover the California beach culture of yesteryear here in off-the-beaten-path spots

LINK YOUR TRIP

3 Disneyland & Orange County Beaches (p35)

Soak up the SoCal sunshine in glam beach towns along PCH, then take the kids to Anaheim's world-famous theme parks.

2 Bay Area Culinary Tour (p27)

Hang out in California's cultural capital and follow rural roads along the coast and into wine country.

19

like San Clemente. Home to living surfing legends, top-notch surfboard companies and *Surfer* magazine, this may be the last place in the OC where you can authentically live the surf lifestyle. Ride your own board or swim at the city's main beach beside San Clemente Pier. A fast detour inland, the community's **Surfing Heritage & Culture Center** (📞949-388-0313; www.surfingheritage.org; 110 Calle Iglesia; suggested donation $5; ⏰11am-4pm Mon-Sat; P) exhibits surfboards ridden by the greats, from Duke Kahanamoku to Kelly Slater.

The Drive » Slingshot north on I-5, exiting onto Hwy 1 near Dana Point. Speed by

the wealthy artists' colony of Laguna Beach, wild Crystal Cove State Park, Newport Beach's yacht harbor and 'Surf City USA' Huntington Beach. Turn west off Hwy 1 near Naples toward Long Beach, about 45 miles from San Clemente.

- - - - - - - - - - - - - - - - - -

❸ Long Beach

In Long Beach, the biggest stars are the **Queen Mary** (📞877-342-0738; www.queenmary.com; 1126 Queens Hwy; tours adult/child from $27/17.50; ⏰tours 10am-6pm or later; P 🚹; 🚇Passport, 🚤AquaBus, AquaLink), a grand (and allegedly haunted) British ocean liner permanently moored here, and the giant **Aquarium of the Pacific** (📞tickets 562-590-3100; www.aquariumofpacific.org; 100 Aquarium Way; adult/senior/child $30/27/19; ⏰9am-6pm; P 🚹), a high-tech romp through an underwater world in which sharks dart and jellyfish float. Often overlooked, the **Long Beach Museum of Art** (📞562-439-2119; www.lbma.org; 2300 E Ocean Blvd; adult/student & senior/child $7/6/free, Fri free; ⏰11am-8pm Thu, to 5pm Fri-Sun; P) focuses on California modernism and contemporary mixed-media inside a 20th-century mansion by the ocean, while the urban **Museum of Latin American Art** (📞562-437-1689; www.molaa.org; 628 Alamitos Ave; adult/senior & student/child $10/7/free, Sun free; ⏰11am-5pm Wed, Thu, Sat & Sun, to 9pm Fri; P) shows off contemporary south-of-the-border art.

The Drive » Wind slowly around the ruggedly scenic Palos Verdes Peninsula. Follow Hwy 1 north past the South Bay's primetime beaches. Curving around LAX airport and Marina del Rey, Hwy 1 continues north to Venice, Santa Monica and all the way to Malibu, almost 60 miles from Long Beach.

- - - - - - - - - - - - - - - - - -

❹ Malibu (p65)

Leaving traffic-jammed LA behind, Hwy 1 breezes northwest of Santa Monica to Malibu. You'll feel like a movie star walking around on the public beaches, fronting gated compounds owned by Hollywood celebs. One mansion you can actually get a look inside is the

---

↱ DETOUR: CHANNEL ISLANDS NATIONAL PARK

Start: ❹ **Malibu**

Imagine hiking, kayaking, scuba diving, camping and whale-watching, and doing it all amid a raw, end-of-the-world landscape. Rich in unique flora and fauna, tide pools and kelp forests, the islands of this **national park** (📞805-658-5730; www.nps.gov/chis) are home to nearly 150 plant and animal species found nowhere else in the world, earning them the nickname 'California's Galapagos.' Anacapa and Santa Cruz, the most popular islands, are within an hour's boat ride of Ventura Harbor, off Hwy 101 almost 40 miles northwest of Malibu on the way to Santa Barbara. Reservations are essential for weekends, holidays and summer trips. Before you shove off from the mainland, stop by the park's **visitor center** (Robert J Lagomarsino Visitor Center; 📞805-658-5730; www.nps.gov/chis; 1901 Spinnaker Dr, Ventura; ⏰8:30am-5pm; 🚹) for educational natural history exhibits, a free 25-minute nature film and family-friendly activities.

Aquarium of the Pacific, Long Beach

Getty Villa (📞310-430-7300; www.getty.edu; 17985 Pacific Coast Hwy, Pacific Palisades; 🕙10am-5pm Wed-Mon; P 🚻; 🚃 line 534 to Coastline Dr), a hilltop showcase of Greek, Roman and Etruscan antiquities and manicured gardens. Next to **Malibu Lagoon State Beach** (Surfrider Beach; 📞310-305-9503, 310-457-8143; www.parks.ca.gov; 3999 Cross Creek Rd; per car $12; 🕙8am-sunset; P), west of the surfers by Malibu Pier, **Adamson House** (📞310-456-8432; www.adamsonhouse.org; 23200 Pacific Coast Hwy; adult/child $7/2; 🕙11am-3pm Thu-Sat; P) is a Spanish-Moorish villa lavishly decorated with locally made hand-painted tiles. Motoring further west along the coast, where the Santa Monica Mountains plunge into the sea, take time out for a frolic on Malibu's mega popular beaches like sandy Point Dume, Zuma or Leo Carrillo.

The Drive » Hwy 1 crosses into Ventura County, winding alongside the ocean and windy Point Mugu. In Oxnard join Hwy 101 northbound. Motor past Ventura, a jumping-off point for boat trips to Channel Islands National Park, to Santa Barbara, just over 90 miles from Malibu Pier.

⑤ Santa Barbara (p74)

Seaside Santa Barbara has almost perfect weather and a string of idyllic beaches, where surfers, kite flyers, dog walkers and surfers mingle. Get a close-up of the city's iconic Spanish Colonial Revival–style architecture along **State Street** downtown or from the county courthouse (p74), its tower rising above the red-tiled rooftops. Gaze south toward the busy harborfront and **Stearns Wharf** (Map p76; www.stearnswharf.org; ⊙ open daily, hours vary; P) or north to the historic Spanish Mission Santa Barbara (p74). Santa Barbara's balmy climate is also perfect for growing grapes. A 45-minute drive northwest along Hwy 154, visit Santa Barbara's **wine country**, made famous by the 2004 movie *Sideways*. Hit wine-tasting rooms in **Los Olivos**, then take Foxen Canyon Rd north past more wineries to rejoin Hwy 101.

The Drive » Keep following fast Hwy 101 northbound or detour west onto slow Hwy 1, which squiggles along the Pacific coastline past Guadalupe, gateway to North America's largest sand dunes. Both highways meet up again in Pismo Beach, 100 miles northwest of Santa Barbara.

⑥ Pismo Beach (p78)

A classic California beach town, Pismo Beach has a long, lazy stretch of sand for swimming, surfing and strolling out onto the pier at sunset. After digging into bowls of clam chowder and baskets of fried seafood at surf-casual cafes, check out the retro family fun at the bowling alley, billiards halls and bars uphill from the beach, or dash 10 miles up Hwy 101 to San Luis Obispo's vintage **Sunset Drive-In** (☎805-544-4475; www.facebook.com/sunsetdrivein; 255 Elks Lane; adult/child 5-11yr $9/4;), where you can put your feet up on the dash and munch on bottomless bags of popcorn while watching Hollywood blockbuster double-features.

The Drive » Follow Hwy 101 north past San Luis Obispo, exiting onto Hwy 1 west to landmark Morro Rock in Morro Bay. North of Cayucos, Hwy 1 rolls through bucolic pasture lands, only swinging back to the coast at Cambria. Ten miles further north stands Hearst Castle, about 60 miles from Pismo Beach.

⑦ Hearst Castle

Hilltop **Hearst Castle** (☎info 805-927-2020, reservations 800-444-4445; www.hearstcastle.org; 750 Hearst Castle Rd; tours adult/child 5-12yr from $25/12; ⊙ from 9am; P) is California's most famous monument to wealth and ambition. William Randolph Hearst, the early-20th-century newspaper magnate, entertained Hollywood stars and royalty at this fantasy estate furnished with European antiques, accented by shimmering pools and surrounded by flowering gardens. Try to make tour reservations in advance, especially for living-history evening programs during the Christmas holiday season and in spring.

About 4.5 miles further north along Hwy 1, park at the signposted vista point and amble the boardwalk to view the enormous **elephant seal colony** that breeds, molts, sleeps, plays and fights on the beach. Seals haul out year-round, but the winter birthing and mating season peaks on Valentine's Day. Nearby, **Piedras Blancas Light Station** (☎805-927-7361; www.piedrasblancas.gov; off Hwy 1; tours adult/child 6-17yr $10/5; ⊙ tours 9:45am Mon, Tue & Thu-Sat mid-Jun–Aug, 9:45am Tue, Thu & Sat Sep–mid-Jun) is an outstandingly scenic spot.

The Drive » Fill your car's gas tank before plunging north into the redwood forests of the remote Big Sur coast, where precipitous cliffs dominate the seascape, and tourist services are few and far between. Hwy 1 keeps curving north to the Monterey Peninsula, approximately a three-hour, 95-mile trip from Hearst Castle.

8 Monterey (p80)

As Big Sur loosens its condor's talons on the coastal highway, Hwy 1 rolls gently downhill toward Monterey Bay. The fishing community of Monterey is the heart of Nobel Prize–winning writer John Steinbeck's country, and although **Cannery Row** today is touristy claptrap, it's worth strolling down to step inside the mesmerizing **Monterey Bay Aquarium** (☑info 831-648-4800, tickets 866-963-9645; www.montereybayaquarium.org; 886 Cannery Row; adult/child 3-12yr/youth 13-17yr $50/30/40; ☺10am-6pm; 👶), inhabiting a converted sardine cannery on the shores of a national marine sanctuary. All kinds of aquatic denizens swim in giant tanks here, from sea stars to pot-bellied sea horses and comical sea otters.

The Drive ≫ It's a relatively quick 45-mile trip north to Santa Cruz. Hwy 1 traces the crescent shoreline of Monterey Bay, passing Elkhorn Slough wildlife refuge near Moss Landing boat harbor, Watsonville's strawberry and artichoke farms, and a string of tiny beach towns in Santa Cruz County.

9 Santa Cruz (p81)

Here, the flower power of the 1960s lives on, and bumper stickers on surfboard-laden woodies shout 'Keep Santa Cruz weird.' Next to the ocean,

Santa Cruz Beach Boardwalk (☑831-423-5590; www.beachboardwalk.com; 400 Beach St; per ride $4-7, all-day pass $37-82; ☺daily Apr-early Sep, seasonal hours vary; P 👶) has a glorious old-school Americana vibe and a 1911 Looff carousel. Its fun-for-all atmosphere is punctuated by squeals from nervous nellies on the stomach-turning Giant Dipper, a 1920s wooden roller coaster that's a national historic landmark, as seen in the vampire cult-classic movie *The Lost Boys*.

A kitschy, old-fashioned tourist trap, the **Mystery Spot** (☑831-423-8897; www.mysteryspot.com; 465 Mystery Spot Rd; $8; ☺10am-4pm Mon-Fri, to 5pm Sat & Sun Sep-May, 10am-6pm Mon-Fri, 9am-7pm Sat & Sun Jun-Aug; P 👶) makes compasses point crazily, while mysterious forces push you around and buildings lean at odd angles; call for directions, current opening hours and tour reservations.

The Drive ≫ It's a blissful 75-mile coastal run from Santa Cruz up to San Francisco past Pescadero, Half Moon Bay and

Pacifica, where Hwy 1 passes through the tunnels at Devil's Slide. Merge with heavy freeway traffic in Daly City, staying on Hwy 1 north through the city into Golden Gate Park.

TRIP HIGHLIGHT

10 San Francisco (p84)

Gridlock may shock your system after hundreds of lazy miles of wide-open, rolling coast. But don't despair. Hwy 1 runs straight through the city's biggest, most breathable green space: Golden Gate Park (p92). You could easily spend all day in the conservatory of flowers, arboretum and botanical gardens, or perusing the California Academy of Sciences (p92) and the fine arts de Young Museum (p92). Then follow Hwy 1 north over the **Golden Gate Bridge**. Guarding the entry to San Francisco Bay, this iconic bridge is named after the straits it spans, not for its 'International Orange' paint job. Park in the lots on the bridge's south or north side, then traipse

TROUBLE-FREE ROAD TRIPPING

In coastal areas, thick fog may impede driving – slow down, and if it's too soupy, get off the road. Along coastal cliffs, watch out for falling rocks and mudslides that could damage or disable your car if struck. For current highway conditions, including road closures (which aren't uncommon during the rainy winter season) and construction updates, call ☑800-427-7623 or visit www.dot.ca.gov.

out onto the pedestrian walkway for a photo.

The Drive » Past Sausalito, leave Hwy 101 in Marin City for slow-moving, wonderfully twisted Hwy 1 along the Marin County coast, passing nearby Point Reyes. Over the next 100 miles from Bodega Bay to Mendocino, revel in a remarkably uninterrupted stretch of coastal highway. More than halfway along, watch for the lighthouse road turnoff north of Point Arena town.

⑪ Around Point Arena (p110)

The fishing fleets of Bodega Bay and Jenner's harbor-seal colony are the last things you'll see before PCH dives into California's great rural northlands. Hwy 1 twists and turns past the Sonoma coast's state parks packed with hiking trails, sand dunes and beaches, as well as underwater marine reserves, rhododendron groves and a 19th-century Russian fur-trading fort. At **Sea Ranch**, don't let exclusive-looking vacation homes prevent you from following public-access trailhead signs and staircases down to empty beaches and across ocean bluffs. Further north, guarding an unbelievably windy point since 1908, **Point Arena Lighthouse** (☎707-882-2809; www.point arenalighthouse.com; 45500 Lighthouse Rd; adult/child $7.50/1; ⊙10am-3:30pm mid-Sep–mid-May, to 4:30pm mid-

May–mid-Sep; P) is the only lighthouse in California where you can actually climb to the top. Check in at the museum, then ascend the 115ft tower to inspect the Fresnel lens, and panoramas of the sea and the jagged San Andreas Fault below.

The Drive » It's an hour-long, 35-mile drive north along Hwy 1 from the Point Arena Lighthouse turnoff to Mendocino, crossing the Navarro, Little and Big Rivers. Feel free to stop and stretch at wind-tossed state beaches, parklands crisscrossed by hiking trails and tiny coastal towns along the way.

⑫ Mendocino (p111) & Fort Bragg (p113)

Looking more like Cape Cod than California, the quaint maritime town of **Mendocino** has white picket fences surrounding New England–style cottages with blooming gardens and redwood-built water towers. Its dramatic headlands jutting into the Pacific, this yesteryear timber town and shipping port was 'discovered' by artists and bohemians in the 1950s and has served as a scenic backdrop in over 50 movies. Once you've browsed the souvenir shops and art galleries selling everything from driftwood carvings to homemade fruit jams, escape north to workaday **Fort Bragg**, with its simple fishing harbor and brewpub, stopping first for a short hike on

the ecological staircase and pygmy forest trail at oceanfront **Jug Handle State Natural Reserve** (☎707-937-5804; www. parks.ca.gov; Hwy 1, Caspar; ⊙sunrise-sunset; P 🚹).

The Drive » About 25 miles north of Mendocino, Westport is the last hamlet along this rugged stretch of Hwy 1. Rejoin Hwy 101 northbound at Leggett for another 90 miles to Eureka, detouring along the Avenue of the Giants and, if you have more time to spare, to the Lost Coast.

⑬ Eureka (p114)

Hwy 101 trundles alongside **Humboldt Bay National Wildlife Refuge** (☎707-733-5406; www.fws. gov/refuge/humboldt_bay; 1020 Ranch Rd, Loleta; ⊙8am-5pm; P 🚹), a major stopover for migratory birds on the Pacific Flyway. Next comes the sleepy railroad town of Eureka. As you wander downtown, check out the ornate **Carson Mansion** (Ingomar Club; www.ingomar.org; 143 M St), built in the 1880s by a timber baron and adorned with dizzying Victorian turrets, towers, gables and gingerbread details. **Blue Ox Millworks & Historic Park** (☎707-444-3437; www.blueoxmill. com; 1 X St; adult/child 6-12yr $10/5; ⊙9am-5pm Mon-Fri year-round, plus 9am-4pm Sat Apr-Nov; 🚹) still creates Victorian detailing by hand using traditional carpentry and 19th-century equipment. Back by Eureka's harborfront,

Victorian house, Mendocino

climb aboard the blue-and-white 1910 **Madaket** (Madaket Cruises; ☏707-445-1910; www.humboldtbay maritimemuseum.com; 1st St; narrated cruises adult/child $22/18; ⊗1pm, 2:30pm & 4pm Wed-Sat, 1pm & 2:30pm Sun-Tue mid-May–mid-Oct; ▣), docked at the foot of C St. Sunset cocktail cruises serve from California's smallest licensed bar.

The Drive » Follow Hwy 101 north past the Rastafarian-hippie college town of Arcata and turnoffs for Trinidad State Beach and Patrick's Point State Park. Hwy 101 drops out of the trees beside marshy Humboldt Lagoons State Park, rolling north toward Orick, just over 40 miles from Eureka.

- - - - - - - - - - - - - - - - -

TRIP HIGHLIGHT

⑭ Redwood National & State Parks (p116)

At last, you'll reach Redwood National Park (p116). Get oriented to the tallest trees on earth at the coastal **Thomas H Kuchel Visitor Center** (☏707-465-7765; www.nps.gov/redw; Hwy 101, Orick; ⊗9am-5pm Apr-Oct, to 4pm Nov-Mar; ▣), just south of the tiny town of Orick. Then commune with the coastal giants on their own mossy turf inside **Lady Bird Johnson Grove** or the majestic **Tall Trees Grove** (free drive-and-hike permit required). For more untouched redwood forests, wind along the 8-mile Newton B Drury Scenic Parkway in **Prairie Creek Redwoods State Park** (☏707-488-2039; www.parks.ca.gov; Newton B Drury Scenic Pkwy; ⊗9am-5pm May-Sep, to 4pm Wed-Sun Oct-Apr; ▣), passing grassy meadows where Roosevelt elk roam, then follow Hwy 101 all the way north to **Crescent City**, the last pit stop before the Oregon border.

Bay Area Culinary Tour

Combining country and city, this drive is a deeply satisfying taste of California's good earth, ending at revolutionary chef Alice Waters' touchstone restaurant Chez Panisse.

2

TRIP HIGHLIGHTS

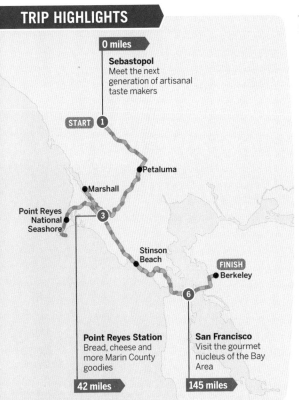

0 miles

Sebastopol
Meet the next generation of artisanal taste makers

START 1

●Petaluma

●Marshall

Point Reyes National Seashore ● 3

Stinson Beach

●Berkeley

6

Point Reyes Station
Bread, cheese and more Marin County goodies

42 miles

San Francisco
Visit the gourmet nucleus of the Bay Area

145 miles

2–3 DAYS
160 MILES / 255KM

GREAT FOR...

BEST TIME TO GO
Late summer or early fall, when farms deliver their tastiest bounty.

ESSENTIAL PHOTO
The lighthouse, bluffs and endless horizon at Point Reyes National Seashore.

✓ BEST PICNIC
Briny oysters, local bread and cheeses, and Heidrun sparkling mead at Hog Island Oyster Company.

Point Reyes National Seashore Point Reyes Lighthouse (p30)

27

2 Bay Area Culinary Tour

Making a delicious loop around the Bay Area, you'll wander through the aisles of celebrated farmers markets and drop in on artisanal food and drink producers, from Hog Island oyster farm to Cowgirl Creamery and more. Thankfully, a hike at Point Reyes National Seashore will work up a healthy appetite. You'll need it on this straight-from-the-source trip to foodie heaven.

TRIP HIGHLIGHT

❶ Sebastopol (p106)

This western Sonoma farm town was founded in the 19th century, when apples were its main cash crop. Swing by in April for the **Apple Blossom Festival** (www.appleblossom fest.com; ☺Apr) or in August for the **Gravenstein Apple Fair** (www.gravenstein applefair.com; ☺Aug), both lively weekend celebrations of local food, wines and brews, accompanied by live music and more.

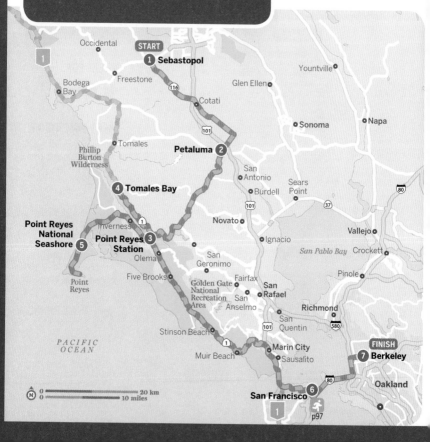

START ❶ Sebastopol
Occidental
Freestone
Bodega Bay
116
Cotati
Glen Ellen
Yountville
Tomales
Phillip Burton Wilderness
Petaluma ❷
101
Sonoma
Napa
❹ Tomales Bay
San Antonio
Burdell
Sears Point
37
80
Point Reyes National Seashore ❺
Inverness
Point Reyes Station ❸
Olema
Novato
Ignacio
Vallejo
San Pablo Bay
Crockett
Point Reyes
San Geronimo
Five Brooks
Fairfax
Golden Gate National Recreation Area
San Anselmo
San Rafael
Richmond
Pinole
80
580
San Quentin
PACIFIC OCEAN
Stinson Beach
Muir Beach
Marin City
Sausalito
FINISH ❼ Berkeley
0 ____ 20 km
0 ____ 10 miles
San Francisco ❻
p97
Oakland

In late summer and early autumn, you can pick your own apples at orchards on the outskirts of town along Sonoma County's **Farm Trails** (www.farmtrails.org).

But Sebastopol is about so much more than apples these days. Just look at the **Barlow** (☎707-824-5600; www. thebarlow.net; cnr Sebastopol & Morris Sts; ⊘hours vary; P), a former apple-processing plant that has been repurposed into a 12-acre village of food producers, artists, wine-makers, coffee roasters and spirits distillers who showcase West County's culinary and artistic diversity. Wander shed to shed, sample everything from microbrewed beer to nitrogen flash-frozen ice cream, and meet artisanal makers in their workshops.

The Drive » Follow Hwy 116 south out of town for 8 miles to Cotati. Keep going across Hwy 101 (the speedier but more boring route to Petaluma) and turn right onto Old Redwood Hwy. After 3 miles, go left on pastoral Old Adobe Rd for 6 miles, turning left

LINK YOUR TRIP

1 **Pacific Coast Highways (p17)**

Either north or south of the Bay Area, scenic Hwy 1 takes you along California's coast.

just past Petaluma Adobe State Historic Park.

---

2 Petaluma (p108)

Near the elegantly slouching Victorians of Petaluma is **Green String Farm** (☎707-778-7500; http://greenstringfarm. com; 3571 Old Adobe Rd; ⊘10am-6pm Wed-Sun). Bob Cannard has pioneered sustainable farming in the North Bay for 30 years, and you can taste the chemical-free fruits of his labors at the on-site farm store, which serves seasonal produce, local cheese and nuts. Instead of battling weeds with herbicides, Green String lets them coexist with cover vegetation and planted crops, creating a symbiotic ecosystem that yields a smaller crop but richer soil. The only weed eaters on hand are the fluffy sheep. Public tours are usually given on the first Saturday of the month, weather permitting.

Many farms around Petaluma are known for raising chickens and selling fresh eggs and dairy products. Across Hwy 101 and west of downtown, the **Petaluma Creamery** (☎707-762-9038; www.petalu macreamerycheeseshop.com; 711 Western Ave; items $3-7; ⊘7am-6pm Mon-Fri, 8am-6pm Sat & Sun) has been in business for more than a century. Stop by to sample organic cheeses or for a scoop of lavender

or Meyer lemon ice cream from the small specialty foods market and cafe.

The Drive » From downtown Petaluma, take D St southwest to Red Hill Rd and follow Point Reyes–Petaluma Rd toward the coast, turning left onto Hwy 1 for Point Reyes Station. It's a relaxing 19-mile country drive; stop en route for Camembert or Brie at the Marin French Cheese factory store.

TRIP HIGHLIGHT

3 Point Reyes Station (p108)

Surrounded by dairies and ranches, Point Reyes Station became a hub for artists in the 1960s. Today it offers a collection of art galleries, boutique shops and excellent food. The tour of the town's edibles begins by fighting your way through the spandex-clad crowd of weekend cyclists to grab a crusty loaf of fire-baked Brick-maiden Bread at **Bovine Bakery** (☎415-663-9420; www.bovinebakery ptreyes.com; 11315 Hwy 1; most items $2-6; ⊘6:30am-5pm Mon-Fri, 7am-5pm Sat, 7am-4pm Sun). Next, step down the block to the restored barn that houses one of California's most sought-after cheese makers, the **Cowgirl Creamery at Tomales Bay Foods** (☎415-663-9335; www.cow girlcreamery.com; 80 4th St; deli items $3-10; ⊘10am-6pm Wed-Sun). Reserve a spot in advance for the Friday-morning artisanal cheese-making demonstration and tasting ($5). In spring the must-buy is their St Pat's, a smooth, mellow round wrapped in wild nettle leaves. Otherwise, the Mt Tam (available year-round) is pretty damn good, and there's a gourmet deli for picking up picnic supplies. Heading north out of town, **Heidrun Meadery** (📞415-663-9122; www.heidrunmeadery.com; 11925 Hwy 1; tasting $15, incl tour $25; ⏱11am-4pm Mon & Wed-Fri, to 5pm Sat & Sun) pours tasting sips of sparkling mead, made from aromatic small-batch honey in the style of French champagne.

The Drive ⟫ Follow Hwy 1 north out of the tiny village of Point Reyes Station. Cruise for 9 miles along the east side of tranquil Tomales Bay, which flows many miles out into the Pacific. Just before the turnoff for rural Marshall–Petaluma Rd, look for the sign for bayfront Hog Island Oyster Company on your left.

❹ Tomales Bay

Only 10 minutes north of Point Reyes Station, you'll find the salty turnout for the **Hog Island Oyster Company** (📞415-663-9218; https://hogislandoysters.com; 20215 Hwy 1, Marshall; 12 oysters $13-16, picnic per person $5; ⏱shop 9am-5pm daily, picnic area from 10am, cafe 11am-5pm Fri-Mon). There's hardly much to see: just some picnic tables and BBQ grills, an outdoor cafe called Boat Oyster Bar and a small window vending the famously silky

oysters and a few other picnic provisions. While you can buy oysters to go (by the pound), for a fee you can nab a picnic table, borrow shucking tools and take a lesson on how to crack open and grill the oysters yourself. Lunch at the waterfront farm is unforgettable – and very popular, so reserve ahead for a picnic table or for a seat at the Boat Oyster Bar's communal tables.

The Drive ⟫ Backtrack 10 miles south on Hwy 1 through Point Reyes Station. Turn right onto Sir Francis Drake Blvd, following the signs for Point Reyes National Seashore, just on the other side of Tomales Bay.

❺ Point Reyes National Seashore (p109)

For another perfect picnic spot, look down the coast to **Point Reyes National Seashore** (📞415-654-5100; www.nps.gov/pore; 🅿 ♿). The windswept peninsula is rough-hewn beauty that lures marine mammals and migratory birds. The 110 sq miles of pristine ocean beaches also offer excellent hiking and camping opportunities. For an awe-inspiring view, follow Sir Francis Drake Blvd beside Tomales Bay all the way out toward the **Point Reyes Lighthouse** (📞415-669-1534; www.nps.gov/pore; end of Sir Francis Drake Blvd; ⏱10am-4:30pm Fri-Mon, lens room 2:30-4pm Fri-Mon; 🅿 ♿). Follow the

signs and turn left before the lighthouse to find the trailhead for the 1.6-mile round-trip hike to **Chimney Rock**, where wildflowers bloom in spring.

The Drive ⟫ Leaving the park, trace the eucalyptus-lined curves of Hwy 1 south toward Stinson Beach and past one stunning Pacific view after the next. If you don't stop, you'll be across the Golden Gate Bridge in about an hour and a half. From the bridge,

Ferry Building, San Francisco

follow Hwy 101 through the city to Broadway, then go east to the waterfront piers.

TRIP HIGHLIGHT

❻ San Francisco (p84)

From the center of the Golden Gate Bridge, it's possible to view the clock tower of the city's **Ferry Building** (Map p90; ☏415-983-8030; www.ferrybuilding marketplace.com; cnr Market St & the Embarcadero; ☺10am-7pm Mon-Fri, 8am-6pm Sat, 11am-5pm Sun; ♿; ☒2, 6, 9, 14, 21, 31, Ⓜ Embarcadero, ⒷEmbarcadero), a transit hub turned gourmet emporium, where foodies happily miss their ferries slurping Hog Island oysters and bubbly. Star chefs are frequently spotted at the thrice-weekly **Ferry Plaza Farmers Market** (Map p90; ☏415-291-3276; www.cuesa.org; cnr Market St & the Embarcadero; street food $3-12; ☺10am-2pm Tue & Thu, from 8am Sat; ♪♿; ☒2, 6, 9, 14, 21, 31, Ⓜ Embarcadero, ⒷEmbarcadero) that wraps around the building year-round. The largest market is on Saturday, when dozens of family farmers and artisanal food and flower vendors show up.

CHEZ PANISSE PROTÉGÉS

Operating a restaurant for 45 years, lauded chef Alice Waters has seen a whole lot of people come through the kitchen. Of her alumni in San Francisco, try Michael Tusk, who offers elegant, seasonally inspired Californian cuisine at **Quince** (Map p90; 📞415-775-8700; www.quincerestaurant.com; 470 Pacific Ave; 11-course tasting menu $250, 9-course menu Mon-Thu $210; ⏱5:30-9:30pm Mon-Thu, from 5pm Fri & Sat; 🚇3, 10) and more rustic Italian fare at **Cotogna** (Map p90; 📞415-775-8508; www.cotognasf.com; 490 Pacific Ave; mains $19-35; ⏱11:30am-10:30pm Mon-Thu, to 11pm Fri & Sat, 5-9:30pm Sun; 🚇; 🚇10, 12), or Gayle Pirie, who operates **Foreign Cinema** (Map p90; 📞415-648-7600; www.foreigncinema.com; 2534 Mission St; mains $22-33; ⏱5:30-10pm Sun-Wed, to 11pm Thu-Sat, brunch 11am-2:30pm Sat & Sun; 🚇12, 14, 33, 48, 49, 🅱24th St Mission), a gourmet movie house in the Mission District.

More casual eateries by other Waters' protégés are found across the Bay in Oakland. Charlie Hallowell turns out immaculate wood-fired pizzas at a pair of neighborhood restaurants, **Pizzaiolo** and **Boot & Shoe Service** (Map p90; 📞510-763-2668; www.bootandshoeservice.com; 3308 Grand Ave; pizzas $14-22; ⏱7am-noon & 5:30-10pm Tue-Thu, 7am-noon & 5-10:30pm Fri, 10am-2pm & 5-10:30pm Sat, 10am-2pm & 5-10pm Sun; 🚇; 🚇AC Transit 12); you can tuck into earthy Californian dishes cooked over an open fire at Russell Moore's **Camino** (Map p90; 📞510-547-5035; www.caminorestaurant.com; 3917 Grand Ave; dinner mains $32-42; ⏱5:30-9:30pm Mon, Wed & Thu, to 10pm Fri, 10am-2pm & 5:30-10pm Sat, to 9:30pm Sun; 🚇; 🚇AC Transit 12); and Alison Barakat serves what may be the Bay Area's best fried-chicken sandwich at **Bakesale Betty** (Map p90; 📞510-985-1213; www.bakesalebetty.com; 5098 Telegraph Ave; sandwiches $9; ⏱11am-2pm Tue-Sat; 🚇AC Transit 6).

From dry-farmed tomatoes to organic kimchi, the bounty may seem like an embarrassment of riches. If your trip doesn't coincide with a market day, never fear: dozens of local purveyors await indoors at the **Ferry Building Marketplace**. Take a taste of McEvoy Ranch and Stonehouse olive oils, Boccalone Salumeria sausages, fresh-baked loaves from Acme Bread Company and Humphry Slocombe ice cream.

The Drive » It is a straight shot over the San Francisco–Oakland Bay Bridge and into Berkeley via I-80 eastbound. Exit at University Ave and follow it east to Shattuck Ave, then go north of downtown Berkeley to the 'Gourmet Ghetto.'

❼ Berkeley (p102)

San Francisco might host a handful of banner dining rooms, but California's food revolution got started across the Bay, in Berkeley. You may spot the inventor of California cuisine, famed chef Alice Waters, in her element and in raptures at the **North Berkeley Farmers Market** (Map p90; 📞510-548-3333; www.ecologycenter.org; Shattuck Ave, at Rose St; ⏱3-7pm Thu; 🚇🚲; 🚇AC Transit 79), run by the Ecology Center. It's in the so-called 'Gourmet Ghetto' – a neighborhood that marries the progressive 1960s ideals of Berkeley with haute-dining

sensibility. The neighborhood's anchor, and an appropriate final stop, is **Chez Panisse** (🚇cafe 510-548-5049, restaurant 510-548-5525; www.chezpanisse.com; 1517 Shattuck Ave; cafe dinner mains $22-35, restaurant prix-fixe dinner $75-125; ⏱cafe 11:30am-2:45pm & 5-10:30pm Mon-Thu, 11:30am-3pm & 5-11:30pm Fri & Sat, restaurant seatings 5:30pm & 8pm Mon-Sat; 🚇; 🚇AC Transit 7), Alice Waters' influential restaurant. It's unpretentious, and every mind-altering, soul-sanctifying bite of the food is emblematic of the chef's revolutionary food principles. The kitchen is even open so diners can peek behind the scenes.

Chez Panisse, Berkeley

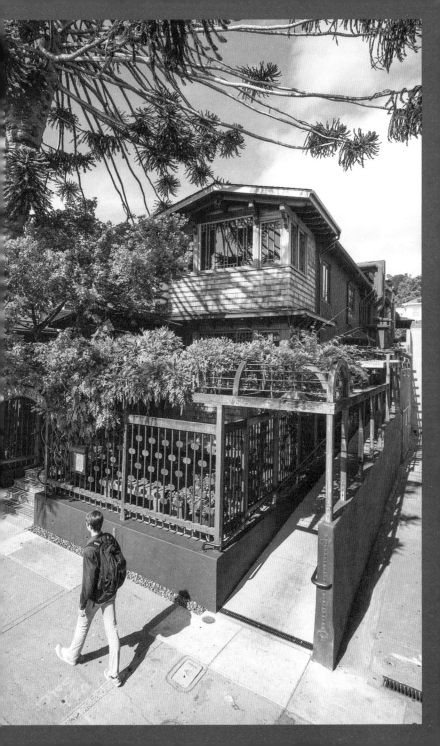

Disneyland & Orange County Beaches

3

On this fun coastal getaway, let the kids loose at the 'Happiest Place on Earth,' then strike out for sunny SoCal beaches – as seen on TV and the silver screen.

TRIP HIGHLIGHTS

0 miles

Disneyland
Party with Mickey Mouse and the Pixar gang

START **1**

Seal Beach

Sunset Beach

30 miles

Huntington Beach
Laze on the golden sands of Surf City USA

3

40 miles

4

Newport Beach
Beaches, historic architecture and retro-cool amusements

Crystal Cove State Park

7

FINISH
Dana Point

Laguna Beach
An artist's dreamy seascape

55 miles

2–4 DAYS
65 MILES / 105KM

GREAT FOR...

BEST TIME TO GO
June to September for summer beach season.

ESSENTIAL PHOTO
Surfers at Huntington Beach Pier.

BEST FOR VIEWS
Corona del Mar's Lookout Point.

Huntington Beach Huntington Beach Pier (p38)

Disneyland & Orange County Beaches

3

It's true you'll find gorgeous sunsets, prime surfing breaks and just-off-the-boat seafood when road tripping down the OC's sun-kissed coastal Hwy 1. Yet it's the unexpected and serendipitous discoveries you'll remember long after you've left this blissful 42 miles of surf and sand behind. Start it all off with a day or two at Disneyland's theme parks and let's call it a wrap for the perfect SoCal family vacation.

TRIP HIGHLIGHT

❶ Disneyland (p54)

No SoCal theme park welcomes more millions of visitors every year than Disneyland (p55). From the ghostly skeletons of Pirates of the Caribbean to the screeching monkeys of the Indiana Jones Adventure, there's magical detail everywhere. Retro-futuristic Tomorrowland is the home of the Finding Nemo Submarine Voyage and the

Star Wars–themed Star Tours and Jedi Training: Trials of the Temple. Use the FASTPASS system and you'll be hurtling through Space Mountain – still the park's best adrenaline pumper – in no time. After dark, watch fireworks explode over Sleeping Beauty Castle.

Any fear of heights? Then ditch the Twilight Zone Tower of Terror at Disney California Adventure (p57), Disneyland's younger neighbor. DCA's lightheartedly themed areas highlight the best of the Golden State, while plenty of adventures like Route 66–themed Cars Land don't involve losing your lunch. An exception is rockin' California Screamin' at Paradise Pier: this whip-fast coaster looks like an old-school carnival ride, but from the moment it blasts forward with a cannon-shot whoosh, this monster never lets go. Catch the

LINK YOUR TRIP

1 Pacific Coast Highways (p17)

Orange County is California's official section of the Pacific Coast Hwy (PCH), running along Hwy 1 between Seal Beach and Dana Point.

DETOUR: KNOTT'S BERRY FARM

Start: ❶ Disneyland

Hear the screams? Got teens? Hello, **Knott's Berry Farm** (☎714-220-5200; www.knotts.com; 8039 Beach Blvd, Buena Park; adult/child 3-11yr $75/42; ⏰from 10am, closing hours vary 5-11pm; 🅿🚻), America's first theme park, which opened in 1940. Today high-scream coasters lure fast-track fanatics. Look up as you enter to see the bare feet of riders who've removed their flip-flops for the Silver Bullet, the suspended coaster careening past overhead, famed for its corkscrew, double spiral and outside loop. In October, Knott's hosts SoCal's scariest after-dark Halloween party. Year-round, the *Peanuts* gang keeps moppets happy in Camp Snoopy, while the next-door water park **Knott's Soak City** (☎714-220-5200; www.soakcityoc.com; 8039 Beach Blvd, Buena Park; adult/child 3-11yr $43/38; ⏰10am-5pm, 6pm or 7pm mid-May–mid-Sep; 🅿🚻) keeps you cool on blazing-hot summer days. Knott's is a 20-minute drive from Disneyland via I-5 north to Hwy 91 west to Beach Blvd south.

---

enthusiasm of the Pixar Play Parade by day and World of Color special-effects show at night.

Just outside the parks, **Downtown Disney** pedestrian mall is packed with souvenir shops, family restaurants, after-dark bars and entertainment venues.

The Drive ❯❯ Follow I-5 south, then take Hwy 22 west through inland Orange County, merging onto the I-405 north. After another mile or so, exit onto Seal Beach Blvd, which crawls 3 miles toward the coast. Turn right onto Hwy 1, also known as the Pacific Coast Hwy (PCH) throughout Orange County, then take a left onto Main St in Seal Beach.

❷ Seal Beach

In the SoCal beauty pageant for pint-sized beach towns, Seal Beach is the winner of the crown. It's a refreshingly unhurried alternative to the more crowded Orange County coast further south. Its three-block **Main Street** is a stoplight-free zone that bustles with mom-and-pop restaurants and indie shops that are low on 'tude and high on nostalgia. Follow barefoot surfers trotting toward the beach where Main St ends, then walk out onto **Seal Beach Pier**. The 1906 original first fell victim to winter storms in the

1930s, and since then it has been rebuilt three times with a splintery, wooden boardwalk. Down on the beach, you'll find families spread out on blankets, building sandcastles and playing in the water – all of them ignoring that hideous oil derrick offshore. The gentle waves make Seal Beach a great place to learn to surf. **M&M Surfing School** (714-846-7873; www.surfingschool.com; 802 Ocean Ave; 1/3hr group lesson $77/85; lessons 8am-noon early Sep–mid-Jun and Sat & Sun year-round, to 2pm Mon-Fri mid-Jun–early Sep;) parks its van in the lot just north of the pier, off Ocean Ave at 8th St.

The Drive » Past a short bridge south along Hwy 1, drivers drop onto a mile-long spit of land known as Sunset Beach, with its biker bars and harborside kayak and stand-up paddle boarding (SUP) rental shops. Keep cruising Hwy 1 south another 6 miles past Bolsa Chica State Beach and Ecological Reserve to Huntington Beach Pier.

TRIP HIGHLIGHT

3 Huntington Beach (p52)

In 'Surf City USA,' SoCal's obsession with wave riding hits its frenzied peak. There's a statue of Hawaiian surfer Duke Kahanamoku at the intersection of Main St and PCH, and if you look down, you'll see names of legendary surfers in the sidewalk **Surfers' Hall of Fame** (www.hsssurf.com/shof; 300 Pacific Coast Hwy). A few blocks east, the **International Surfing Museum** (714-960-3483; www.surfingmuseum.org; 411 Olive Ave; adult/child $2/1; noon-5pm Tue-Sun) honors those same legends. Join the crowds on the **Huntington Beach Pier**, where you can catch up-close views of dare-devils barreling through tubes. The surf here may not be the ideal place to test your newbie skills, however – locals can be territorial. In summer, the US Open of Surfing draws more than 600 world-class surfers and 500,000 spectators with a mini-village of concerts and more. As for **Huntington City Beach** itself, it's wide and flat – a perfect place to snooze on the sand on a giant beach towel. Snag a fire pit just south of the pier to build an evening bonfire with friends.

The Drive » From the Huntington Beach Pier at the intersection of Main St, drive south on Hwy 1 alongside the ocean for another 4 miles to Newport Beach. Turn right onto W Balboa Blvd, leading onto the Balboa Peninsula, squeezed between the ocean and Balboa Island, off Newport Harbor.

TRIP HIGHLIGHT

4 Newport Beach (p51)

As seen on Bravo's *Real Housewives of Orange County* and Fox's *The OC* and *Arrested Development,* in glitzy Newport Beach wealthy socialites, glamorous teens and gorgeous beaches all share the spotlight. Bikini vixens strut down the sandy beach stretching between the peninsula's twin piers, while boogie boarders brave human-eating waves at the Wedge (p51) and the ballet of yachts in the harbor makes you dream of being rich and famous. From the harbor, hop aboard a ferry over to old-fashioned **Balboa Island** (http://explorebalboaisland.com; P) or climb aboard the Ferris wheel at the pint-sized **Balboa Fun Zone** (www.thebalboafun

Balboa Pavilion, Newport Beach

zone.com; 600 E Bay Ave; Ferris wheel $4; ⊘Ferris wheel 11am-6pm Sun-Thu, to 9pm Fri, to 10pm Sat; 🚻), near the landmark 1906 **Balboa Pavilion** (www.balboapavil ion.com; 400 Main St). Just inland, visit the cutting-edge contemporary **Orange County Museum of Art** (☎949-759-1122; www. ocma.net; 850 San Clemente Dr; adult/student & senior/ child under 12yr $10/7.50/free; ⊘11am-5pm Wed-Sun, to 8pm Fri; P 🚻) to escape SoCal's vainglorious pop culture.

The Drive >> South of Newport Beach, prime-time ocean views are just a short detour off Hwy 1. First drive south across the bridge over Newport Channel,

then after 3 miles turn right onto Marguerite Ave in Corona del Mar. Once you reach the coast, take another right onto Ocean Blvd.

- - - - - - - - - - - - - - - - - - - -

5 Corona del Mar

Savor some of SoCal's most celebrated ocean views from the bluffs of Corona del Mar, a chichi bedroom community south of Newport Channel. Several postcard beaches, rocky coves and child-friendly tide pools beckon along this idyllic stretch of coast. One of the best viewpoints is at breezy **Lookout Point** on Ocean Blvd near

Heliotrope Ave. Below the rocky cliffs to the east is half-mile-long **Main Beach** (Corona del Mar State Beach; ☎949-644-3151; www.newportbeachca.gov; off E Shore Ave; ⊘6am-10pm; P 🚻), with fire rings and volleyball courts (arrive early on weekends to get a parking spot). Stairs lead down to **Pirates Cove**, which has a great, waveless pocket beach for families – scenes from the classic TV show *Gilligan's Island* were shot here. Head east on Ocean Blvd to **Inspiration Point**, near the corner of Orchid Ave, for more vistas of surf, sand and sea.

DETOUR: PACIFIC MARINE MAMMAL CENTER

Start: ❼ Laguna Beach

About 3 miles inland from Laguna Beach is the heart-warming **Pacific Marine Mammal Center** (☎949-494-3050; www.pacificmmc.org; 20612 Laguna Canyon Rd; donations welcome; ⏱10am-4pm; P ♿), dedicated to rescuing and rehabilitating injured or ill marine mammals. This nonprofit center has a small staff and many volunteers who help nurse rescued pinnipeds (mostly sea lions and seals) back to health before releasing them into the wild. Stop by and take a self-guided facility tour to learn more about these marine mammals and to visit the 'patients' out back.

The Drive » Follow Orchid Ave back north to Hwy 1, then turn right and drive southbound. Traffic thins out as ocean views become more wild and uncluttered by housing developments that head up into the hills on your left. It's just a couple of miles to the entrance of Crystal Cove State Park.

❻ Crystal Cove State Park (p50)

With more than 3 miles of open beach and 2400 acres of undeveloped woodland, **Crystal Cove State Park** (☎949-494-3539; www.parks.ca.gov; 8471 N Coast Hwy; per car $15; ⏱6am-sunset; P ♿) lets you almost forget that you're in a crowded metro area. That is, once you get past the parking lot and stake out a place on the sand. Many visitors don't know it, but it's also an underwater park where scuba enthusiasts

can check out the wreck of a Navy Corsair fighter plane that went down in 1949. Or just go tide pooling, fishing, kayaking and surfing along Crystal Cove's exhilaratingly wild, windy shoreline. On the inland side of Hwy 1, miles of hiking and mountain-biking trails wait for landlubbers.

The Drive » Drive south on Hwy 1 for another 4 miles or so. As shops, restaurants, art galleries, motels and hotels start to crowd the highway once again, you've arrived in Laguna Beach. Downtown is a maze of one-way streets just east of the Laguna Canyon Rd (Hwy 133) intersection.

TRIP HIGHLIGHT

❼ Laguna Beach (p49)

This early-20th-century artist colony's secluded coves, romantic-looking cliffs and arts-and-

crafts bungalows come as a relief after miles of suburban beige-box architecture. With joie de vivre, Laguna celebrates its bohemian roots with summer arts festivals, dozens of galleries and the acclaimed **Laguna Art Museum** (☎949-494-8971; www.lagunaartmuseum.org; 307 Cliff Dr; adult/student & senior/child under 13yr $7/5/free, 5-9pm 1st Thu of month free; ⏱11am-5pm Fri-Tue, to 9pm Thu). In downtown's village, it's easy to while away an afternoon browsing the chic boutiques. Down on the shore, **Main Beach** is crowded with volleyball players and sunbathers. Just north atop the bluffs, **Heisler Park** winds past public art, palm trees, picnic tables and grand views of rocky shores and tide pools. Drop down to **Divers Cove**, a deep, protected inlet. Heading south, dozens of public beaches sprawl along just a few miles of coastline. Keep a sharp eye out for 'beach access' signs off Hwy 1, or pull into locals' favorite Aliso Beach County Park (p49).

The Drive » Keep driving south of downtown Laguna Beach on Hwy 1 (PCH) for about 3 miles to Aliso Beach County Park, then another 4 miles into the town of Dana Point. Turn right onto Green Lantern St, then left onto Cove Rd, which winds past the state beach and Ocean Institute onto Dana Point Harbor Dr.

Heisler Park, Laguna Beach

8 Dana Point

Marina-flanked Dana Point is the namesake of 19th-century adventurer Richard Dana, who famously thought it was the only romantic place on the coast. These days it's more about family fun and sportfishing boats at **Dana Point Harbor**.

Designed for kids, the **Ocean Institute** (☎949-496-2274; www.ocean-institute.org; 24200 Dana Pt Harbor Dr; adult/child 2-12yr $10/7.50; ⏰10am-4pm Mon-Fri, 10am-3pm Sat & Sun, last entry 2:15pm; P ♿) owns replicas of historic tall ships, maritime-related exhibits and a floating research lab. East of the harbor,

Doheny State Beach (☎949-496-6171; www.dohenystatebeach.org; 25300 Dana Point Harbor Dr; per car $15; ⏰park 6am-10pm, visitor center 10am-4pm Wed-Sun; P ♿) is where you'll find picnic tables, volleyball courts, an oceanfront bike path and a sandy beach for swimming, surfing and tide pooling.

Destinations

San Diego, Orange County & Los Angeles (p44)
Warm winter sun and coastal drives, modernist homes and Hollywood lore, martinis and wildflowers in the desert.

Santa Barbara & the Central Coast (p74)
This fairy-tale stretch of California coast is packed with wild beaches, misty redwood forests where hot springs hide, and rolling golden hills of fertile vineyards and farm fields.

San Francisco & the Bay Area (p84)
If there's a skateboard move yet to be busted, a technology still unimagined, a poem left unspoken or a green scheme untested, chances are it's about to happen here.

North Coast & Redwoods (p110)
Spectral fog and an outsider spirit have fostered the world's tallest trees, most potent weed and a string of idiosyncratic two-stoplight towns.

Hollywood Blvd, Los Angeles (p60)
SEAN PAVONE/SHUTTERSTOCK ©

San Diego, Orange County & Los Angeles

This diverse area is home to deep pockets of individuality, beauty and different ways of thinking.

SAN DIEGO

POP 1,394,928

New York has its cabbie, Chicago its bluesman and Seattle its coffee-drinking boho. San Diego has its surfer dude, with his tousled hair, great tan and gentle enthusiasm; he looks like he's on a perennial vacation, and when he wishes you welcome, he really means it.

San Diego calls itself 'America's Finest City' and its breezy confidence and sunny countenance filter down even to folks you encounter every day on the street. It feels like a collection of villages each with their own personality, but it's the nation's eighth-largest city and we're hard-pressed to think of a place of any size that's more laid-back.

◉ Sights

★ **New Children's Museum** MUSEUM
(☑ 619-233-8792; www.thinkplaycreate.org; 200 W Island Ave; $13; ⊙ 10am-4pm Mon, Wed, Thu & Sat, 9:30am-4pm Fri, noon-4pm Sun; 🚼) This children's museum offers interactive art meant for kids. Installations are designed by artists, so tykes can learn principles of movement and physics while simultaneously being exposed to art and working out the ants in their pants. Exhibits change every 18 months or so, so there's always something new.

★ **San Diego Zoo** ZOO
(☑ 619-231-1515; http://zoo.sandiego.org; 2920 Zoo Dr; 1-day pass adult/child from $52/42, 2-visit pass to zoo &/or safari park adult/child $83.25/73.25; ⊙ 9am-9pm mid-Jun–early Sep, to 5pm or 6pm early Sep–mid-Jun; ℗🚼) 🌱 This justifiably famous zoo is one of SoCal's biggest attractions, showing more than 3000 animals representing more than 650 species in a beautifully landscaped setting, typically in enclosures that replicate their natural habitats. Its sister park is **San Diego Zoo Safari Park** (☑ 760-747-8702; www.sdzsafaripark.org; 15500 San Pasqual Valley Rd, Escondido; 1-day pass adult/child $52/42, 2-visit pass to zoo &/or safari park adult/child $83.25/73.25; ⊙ 8am-6pm, to 7pm late Jun–mid-Aug; ℗🚼) in northern San Diego County. Arrive early, as many of the animals are most active in the morning – though many perk up again in the afternoon. Pick up a map at the zoo entrance to find your favorite exhibits.

Maritime Museum MUSEUM
(☑ 619-234-9153; www.sdmaritime.org; 1492 N Harbor Dr; adult/child $16/8; ⊙ 9am-9pm late May-early Sep, to 8pm early Sep-late May; 🚼) This museum is easy to find: look for the 100ft-high masts of the iron-hulled square-rigger *Star of India*. Built on the Isle of Man and launched in 1863, the tall ship plied the England–India

trade route, carried immigrants to New Zealand, became a trading ship based in Hawaii and, finally, ferried cargo in Alaska. It's a handsome vessel, but don't expect anything romantic or glamorous on board.

Old Town San Diego
State Historic Park   HISTORIC SITE
(☑ 619-220-5422; www.parks.ca.gov; 4002 Wallace St; ⊙ visitor center & museums 10am-5pm; P ⛟) **FREE** This park has an excellent history museum in the Robinson-Rose House at the southern end of the plaza. You'll also find a diorama depicting the original pueblo at the park's visitor center, where you can pick up a copy of the *Old Town San Diego State Historic Park Tour Guide & Brief History* ($3), or a presentation tour (free) at 11am and 2pm daily. Personal tours cost $10 and depart at 11:30am and 1pm.

Mingei International Museum   MUSEUM
(☑ 619-239-0003; www.mingei.org; 1439 El Prado; adult/youth/child $10/7/free; ⊙ 10am-5pm Tue-Sun; ⛟) With a diverse collection of folk art, costumes, toys, jewelry, utensils and other handmade objects of traditional cultures from around the world, plus changing exhibitions covering beads to surfboards. Check the website to find out what's on.

🏃 Activities

Boating
San Diego offers rental of powerboats (from $130 per hour), sailboats (from $30 per hour), and kayaks (from $18 per hour) and canoes on Mission Bay from Mission Bay Sportcenter (☑ 858-488-1004; www.missionbaysportcenter.com; 1010 Santa Clara Pl; rentals $3-230). Ocean kayaking is a good way to see sea life, and explore cliffs and caves inaccessible from land.

Surfing
A good number of residents moved to San Diego just for the surfing, and boy, is it good. Even beginners will understand why it's so popular.

Fall brings strong swells and offshore Santa Ana winds. In summer swells come from the south and southwest, and in winter from the west and northwest. Spring brings more frequent onshore winds, but the surfing can still be good. For the latest beach, weather and surf reports, call San Diego County Lifeguard Services (☑ 619-221-8824).

Beginners should head to Mission or Pacific Beach, for beach breaks (soft-sand bottomed). North of Crystal Pier, Tourmaline Surfing Park is a crowded, but good,

improvers' spot for those comfortable surfing reef. Rental rates vary depending on the quality of the equipment, but figure on soft boards from around $15/45 per hour/full day; wet suits cost $7/28. Packages are available.

Whale-Watching
Gray whales pass San Diego from mid-December to late February on their way south to Baja California, and again in mid-March on their way back up to Alaskan waters. Their 12,000-mile round-trip journey is the longest migration of any mammal on earth.

Cabrillo National Monument (p18) is the best place to see the whales from land, where you'll also find exhibits, whale-related ranger programs and a shelter from which to watch the whales breach (bring binoculars).

Half-day whale-watching boat trips are offered by most of the companies that run daily fishing trips, like Seaforth Sportfishing (☑ 619-224-3383; www.seaforthlanding.com; 1717 Quivira Rd, Mission Bay; trips $24-300). The trips generally cost $24 per adult excursion, sometimes with a guaranteed sighting or a free ticket. Look for coupons and special offers at tourist kiosks and online.

🛏 Sleeping

For camping try Campland on the Bay (☑ 858-581-4260, 800-422-9386; www.campland. com; 2211 Pacific Beach Dr, Mission Bay; RV & tent sites $55-432, beachfront from $225; P 🌐 🏊) or KOA (☑ 800-562-9877, 619-427-3601; www.sand iegokoa.com; 111 N 2nd Ave, Chula Vista; tent sites from $55, RV sites with hookups from $66, cabins from $95, deluxe cabins from $210; P @ 🌐 🏊 🐾), about 8 miles south, with good camping facilities for families like a pool, bike rental, Jacuzzi and off-leash dog park; deluxe cabins include linens, private bathrooms, and pots and pans.

USA Hostels San Diego   HOSTEL $
(☑ 619-232-3100, 800-438-8622; www.usahostels. com; 726 5th Ave; dm/r with shared bath from $32/80; ✳ @ 🌐) Lots of charm and color at this convivial hostel in a former Victorian-era hotel. Look for cheerful rooms, a full kitchen, and a communal lounge for chilling. Rates include linens, lockers and bagels for breakfast. Surrounded by bars, it's smack-bang in the middle of Gaslamp's nightlife scene, so bring earplugs if you're a light sleeper.

La Pensione Hotel   BOUTIQUE HOTEL $$
(☑ 619-236-8000, 800-232-4683; www.lapensione hotel.com; 606 W Date St; r $145-200; P ✳ 🌐) Despite the name, Little Italy's La Pensione isn't

Downtown San Diego

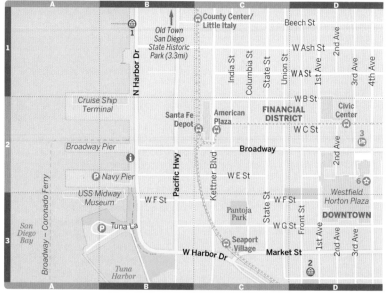

a pension but an intimate, friendly, recently renovated hotel of 67 rooms with queen-size beds and private bathrooms. It's set around a frescoed courtyard and is just steps to the neighborhood's dining, cafes and galleries, and walking distance to most Downtown attractions. There's an attractive cafe downstairs, and a recently introduced spa. Parking is $20.

US Grant Hotel　　　　LUXURY HOTEL **$$$**
(☑ 800-237-5029, 619-232-3121; www.starwood. com; 326 Broadway; r from $211; 🅿 ❇ @ 🛜) This 11-stories-high 1910 hotel was built as the fancy city counterpart to the Hotel del

Coronado and hosted everyone from Albert Einstein to Harry Truman. Today's quietly flashy lobby combines chocolate-brown and ocean-blue accents, and rooms boast original artwork on the headboards. It's owned by members of the Sycuan tribe of Native Americans. Parking costs $48.

★ Hotel del Coronado　　　LUXURY HOTEL **$$$**
(☑ 800-468-3533, 619-435-6611; www.hoteldel. com; 1500 Orange Ave; r from $297; 🅿 ❂ ❇ @ 🛜 ☷ ✦) San Diego's iconic hotel provides the essential Coronado experience: over a century of history (p18), a pool, full-service spa, shops, restaurants, manicured grounds, a white-sand beach and an ice-skating rink during Christmas season. Even the basic rooms have luxurious marbled bathrooms. Note: half the accommodations are not in the main Victorian-era hotel (368 rooms) but in an adjacent seven-story building constructed in the 1970s. For a sense of place, book a room in the original hotel. Self-parking is $39.

✕ Eating

Carnitas' Snack Shack　　　MEXICAN **$**
(☑ 619-294-7665; http://carnitassnackshack.com; 2632 University Ave; mains $8-13; ⊙ 11am-midnight; 🖐) Eat honestly priced, pork-inspired slow food in a cute outdoor patio with natural

Map showing area with streets including Beech St, Ash St, A St, B St, C St, Broadway, E St, F St, G St, Market St, Island Ave, Park Blvd, EAST VILLAGE, San Diego City College, City College, Balboa Park, Mingei International Museum (1.1mi); San Diego Zoo (1.5mi)

Hash House a Go Go
AMERICAN $$

(☎ 619-298-4646; www.hashhouseagogo.com; 3628 5th Ave, Hillcrest; breakfast $10-22, dinner mains $15-29; ⊙ 7:30am-2:30pm Mon, 7:30am-2pm & 5:30-9pm Tue-Thu, to 2:30pm and 9:30pm Fri-Sun; ♿) This buzzing bungalow makes biscuits and gravy straight outta Indiana, towering Benedicts, large-as-your-head pancakes and – wait for it – hash seven different ways. Eat your whole breakfast, and you won't need to eat the rest of the day. It's worth coming back for the equally massive burgers, sage-fried chicken and award-winning meatloaf sandwich. No wonder it's called 'twisted farm food.'

Old Town Mexican Café
MEXICAN $$

(☎ 619-297-4330; www.oldtownmexcafe.com; 2489 San Diego Ave; mains $5-17; ⊙ 7-11pm weekdays, to midnight weekends; ♿) Other restaurants come and go, but this place has been in this busy adobe with hardwood booths since the 1970s. While you wait to be seated, watch the staff turn out tortillas. Then enjoy *machacas, carnitas* (slow-roasted pork) and Mexican ribs. For breakfast: *chilaquiles* (tortilla chips with salsa or mole, broiled or grilled with cheese).

★ Juniper & Ivy
CALIFORNIAN $$$

(☎ 619-269-9036; www.juniperandivy.com; 2228 Kettner Blvd; small plates $10-23, mains $19-45; ⊙ 5-10pm Sun-Thu, to 11pm Fri & Sat) The menu changes daily at chef Richard Blais' highly rated San Diego restaurant, opened in 2014. The molecular gastronomy includes dishes in the vein of lobster congee, Hawaiian snapper with Valencia Pride mango and ahi (yellowfin tuna) with creamed black trumpets. It's in a rockin' refurbished warehouse.

🍷 Drinking

Bang Bang
BAR

(☎ 619-677-2264; www.bangbangsd.com; 526 Market St; cocktails $14-26; ⊙ 5-10:30pm Wed-Thu, to 2am Fri & Sat) Beneath lantern light, the Gaslamp's hottest new spot brings in local and world-renowned DJs and serves sushi and Asian small plates like dumplings and *panko*-crusted shrimp to accompany the imaginative cocktails (some in giant goblets meant for sharing with your posse). Plus, the bathrooms are shrines to Ryan Gosling and Hello Kitty: in a word, awesome.

Coin-Op Game Room
BAR

(☎ 619-255-8523; www.coinopsd.com; 3926 30th St, North Park; ⊙ 4pm-1am Mon-Fri, noon-1am Sat & Sun) Dozens of classic arcade games – pinball to Mortal Kombat, Pac-Man and Big

---

wooden features. Wash dishes like the triple-threat pork sandwich (with schnitzel, bacon, pepperoncini, pickle relish, shack aioli and an Amish bun) down with local craft ales. Happy hour runs from 3pm to 6pm Monday to Friday with $5 tacos, $5 drafts and $6 wines.

Clayton's Coffee Shop
DINER $

(☎ 619-435-5425; www.facebook.com/claytonscoffee shop; 979 Orange Ave; mains $7-13; ⊙ 6am-10pm; ♿) Some diners only look old-fashioned. This one is the real deal from the 1940s, with red leatherette swivel stools and booths with mini jukeboxes. It does famous all-American breakfasts and some Mexican specialties like *machaca* (shredded pork with onions and peppers) with eggs and cheese, and it's not above panini and croque monsieur sandwiches. For dessert: mile-high pie from the counter.

Hodad's
BURGERS $

(☎ 619-224-4623; www.hodadies.com; 5010 Newport Ave; dishes $4-15; ⊙ 11am-10pm) Since the flower-power days of 1969, OB's legendary burger joint has served great shakes, massive baskets of onion rings and succulent hamburgers wrapped in paper. The walls are covered in license plates, grunge/surf rock plays (loud!) and your bearded, tattooed server might sidle into your booth to take your order. No shirt, no shoes, no problem, dude.

San Onofre State Beach, San Clemente

Buck Safari to Master Beer Bong – line the walls of this hipster bar in North Park. All the better to quaff craft beers and cocktails like the Dorothy Mantooth (gin, Giffard Violette, lime, cucumber, champagne) and chow on truffle-parm tots, fried-chicken sandwiches or fried Oreos.

Polite Provisions COCKTAIL BAR
(☑ 619-677-3784; www.politeprovisions.com; 4696 30th St, North Park; ☺ 3pm-2am Mon-Thu, 11:30am-2am Fri-Sun) Attracted by its French-bistro feel and old-world charm, Polite Provisions' hip clientele sip cocktails at the marble bar, under a glass ceiling, and in a beautifully designed space, complete with vintage cash register, wood-paneled walls and tiled floors. Many cocktail ingredients, syrups, sodas and infusions are homemade and displayed in apothecary-esque bottles.

☆ Entertainment

Check out the San Diego *City Beat* or *UT San Diego* for the latest movies, theater, galleries and music gigs around town. **Arts Tix** (☑ 858-437-9850; www.sdartstix.com; 28 Horton Plaza, next to Balboa Theatre; ☺ 10am-4pm Tue-Thu, to 6pm Fri & Sat, to 2pm Sun) has half-price tickets for same-day evening or next-day matinee performances and offers discounted tickets to other events. **Ticketmaster** (☑ 800-653-8000; www.ticketmaster.com) and **House of Blues** (☑ 619-299-2583; www.houseofblues.com/sandiego; 1055 5th Ave; ☺ 4-11pm) sell tickets to other gigs around the city.

ℹ Information

International Visitor Information Center (☑ 619-236-1242; www.sandiego.org; 1140 N Harbor Dr; ☺ 9am-5pm Jun-Sep, to 4pm Oct-May) Across from the B St Cruise Ship Terminal, helpful staff offer very detailed neighborhood maps, sell discounted tickets to attractions and maintain a hotel-reservation hotline.

Coronado Visitors Center (☑ 619-437-8788, 866-599-7242; www.coronadovisitorcenter.com; 1100 Orange Ave; ☺ 9am-5pm Mon-Fri, 10am-5pm Sat & Sun)

ORANGE COUNTY

It's true you'll find gorgeous sunsets, prime surfing and just-off-the-boat seafood when traveling the OC's blissful 42 miles of surf and sand. But it's also the unexpected, serendipitous discoveries you'll remember: learning to surf the waves in Seal Beach, playing Frisbee with your pooch at Huntington Dog Beach, piloting your own boat around Newport Harbor, wandering around eclectic art displays in Laguna Beach, or spotting whales on a cruise from Dana Point.

Your mission is to find out which beach town suits you best. Seal Beach is the OC's northernmost beach town. From there, crawl along Route 1, aka Pacific Coast Hwy (PCH), south along the ocean for more than 40 miles, passing through Sunset Beach, Huntington Beach, Newport Beach, Laguna Beach and San Clemente. The drive takes at least an hour (much more with bumper-to-bumper beach-front traffic on summer weekends). Don't worry: it's almost always worth it.

San Clemente

📞 949 / POP 65,326

Just before reaching San Diego County, PCH slows down and rolls past the laid-back surf town of San Clemente. Home to surfing legends, top-notch surfboard companies, the Surfing Heritage & Culture Center (p20) and the dearly departed *Surfing* magazine (1964–2017), this unpretentious enclave may be one of the last spots in the OC where you can authentically live the surf lifestyle. Right on, brah.

The city center is also one of SoCal's most picturesque as the sun glimmers off the ocean. Head south off PCH and follow Avenida del Mar as it winds south through San Clemente's retro downtown district, where antiques and vintage shops, eclectic boutiques, cafes, restaurants and bars line the main drag. Keep curving downhill toward the ocean.

Further south along the coast, at the foot of Trafalgar St, T-Street is a popular surf break, as is Trestles Beach in San Onofre State Beach (📞949-492-4872; www.parks.ca.gov; parking per day $15; 🅿).

There's lovely lodging right across from the pier, and worthwhile campgrounds at San Onofre State Beach (📞949-361-2531, reservations 800-444-7275; www.reserveamerica.com; San Mateo Campground, 830 Cristianitos Rd, San Onofre State Beach; San Mateo sites $40-65, bluff sites $40; 🅿). There are also chain motels further inland, closer to the 5 Fwy.

Laguna Beach

📞 949 / POP 23,341

It's easy to love Laguna: secluded coves, romantic cliffs, azure waves and waterfront parks imbue the city with a Riviera-like feel. But nature isn't the only draw. From public sculptures and art festivals to free summer shuttles, the city has taken thoughtful steps to promote tourism while discreetly maintaining its moneyed quality of life (MTV's reality show *Laguna Beach* being one drunken, shameless exception).

One of the earliest incorporated cities in California, Laguna has a strong tradition in the arts, starting with the *plein air* impressionists who lived and worked here in the early 1900s. Today it's the home of renowned arts festivals, galleries, a well-known museum and exquisitely preserved arts-and-crafts cottages and bungalows. It's also the OC's most prominent gay enclave (even if the gay nightlife scene is a shadow of its former self).

👁 Sights

Laguna Art Museum   MUSEUM
See p40.

Heisler Park   VIEWPOINT
(375 Cliff Dr) The grassy, bluff-top Heisler Park offers vistas of craggy coves and deep-blue sea. Bring your camera – with its palm trees and bougainvillea-dotted bluffs, the scene is definitely one for posterity.

Main Beach   BEACH
Near downtown's village, Main Beach has volleyball and basketball courts, a playground and restrooms. It's the first beach you see as you come down Laguna Canyon Blvd from the 405 Fwy, and it's Laguna's best beach for swimming.

Picnic Beach   BEACH
Just north of Main Beach, Picnic Beach is too rocky to surf but has excellent tide pooling.

Aliso Beach County Park   BEACH
(📞949-923-2280; http://ocparks.com/beaches/aliso; 31131 S Pacific Coast Hwy; parking per hr $1; ⏰6am-10pm; 🅿🚻) South of downtown Laguna Beach, the locals' favorite Aliso Beach County Park is popular with surfers, boogie boarders and skimboarders. With picnic tables, fire pits and a play area, it's also good for families. Pay-and-display parking costs $1 per hour. Or drive south and park on PCH for free.

Thousand Steps Beach   BEACH
(off 9th Ave) Jealously guarded by locals, Thousand Steps Beach is about 1 mile south of Aliso Beach, hidden off Hwy 1 just south of Mission Hospital (📞949-499-1311; www.mission forhealth.com; 31872 Coast Hwy; ⏰24hr). At the south end of 9th St, more than 200 steps (way less than 1000) lead down to the sand. Though rocky, the beach is great for sunbathing, surfing and bodysurfing.

West Street Beach   BEACH
(West St) South of central Laguna, this beach has long been a hangout for Laguna's (and the OC's) LGBT community (with an emphasis on the G). The eye candy can be considerable.

🛏 Sleeping & Eating

Art Hotel   MOTEL $$

(☑ 949-494-6464, 877-363-7229; www.arthotellaguna beach.com; 1404 N Coast Hwy; r $184-214; 🅿 ➘ ❋ @ 🤍 ≋ ⛱) A mile northwest of the village, this easygoing, better-than-average shingled motel charges bargain rates, at least for Laguna. In keeping with the theme, colorful murals adorn the public spaces – like the fantastic bas-relief of old Laguna around the pool deck – and works of a different artist hang in each of the 28 rooms. Take the shuttle downtown.

★Montage   RESORT $$$

(☑ 949-715-6000; www.montagelagunabeach.com; 30801 S Coast Hwy; r from $595; 🅿 @ 🤍 ≋) You'll find nowhere more indulgent on the OC's coast than this over-the-top luxury waterside resort, especially if you hide away with your lover in a secluded bungalow. Even the most basic of its 248 rooms are plush and generous, offering California craftsman style, marble bathrooms, lemon verbena bath products and unobstructed ocean views.

Orange Inn   DINER $

(☑ 949-494-6085; www.orangeinncafe.com; 703 S Coast Hwy, Suite 200; mains $7-13; ☺ 5:30am-5:30pm) Birthplace of the smoothie (in the *Guinness World Records*), this little shop from 1931 continues to pack in surfers fueling up before hitting the waves. It also serves date shakes, big omelets and breakfast burritos, homemade muffins and deli sandwiches on whole-wheat or sourdough bread.

Big Fish Tavern   SEAFOOD $$

(☑ 949-715-4500; www.bigfishtavernlaguna.com; 540 S Coast Hwy; mains $12-27; ☺ 11:30am Mon-Sat, 11am Sun through dinner, closing hours vary) Sustainably raised Hawaii-style *poke* (marinated raw fish), Baja-style fish tacos, coconut shrimp and the fresh catch o' the day are about all you need. That, and views

across rooftops to the ocean. And there are dozens of beers including about one-third from California. Make reservations.

★Driftwood Kitchen   AMERICAN $$$

(☑ 949-715-7700; www.driftwoodkitchen.com; 619 Sleepy Hollow Lane; mains lunch $15-36, dinner $24-39; ☺ 9am-2:30pm Sat & Sun, 9-10:30am & 11am-2:30pm Mon-Fri, 5-9:30pm Sun-Thu, to 10:30pm Fri & Sat) Ocean views and ridonkulous sunsets alone ought to be enough to bring folks in, but gourmet Driftwood steps up the food with seasonal menus centered around fresh, sustainable seafood, plus options for land-lubbers. Inside it's all beachy casual, white-washed and pale woods. And the cocktails are smart and creative.

🛍 Shopping

Hobie Surf Shop   SPORTS & OUTDOORS

(☑ 949-497-3304; www.hobiesurfshop.com; 294 Forest Ave; ☺ 9am-7pm) Hobart 'Hobie' Alter started his internationally known surf line in his parents' Laguna Beach garage in 1950. Today, this is one of only a handful of logo retail shops where you can stock up on surfboards and beachwear (love those flip-flops in rainbow colors!) for both babes and dudes.

Laguna Beach Books   BOOKS

(☑ 949-494-4779; www.lagunabeachbooks.com; Old Pottery Place, 1200 S Coast Hwy, Suite 105; ☺ 10am-8pm) Friendly indie bookshop stocks everything, including surf culture and SoCal local-interest titles.

ℹ Information

Visit Laguna Beach Visitors Center (☑ 949-497-9229; www.lagunabeachinfo.com; 381 Forest Ave; ☺ 10am-5pm; 🤍) Helpful staff, bus schedules, restaurant menus and free brochures on everything from hiking trails to self-guided walking tours.

The **Visit Laguna Beach app** (www.visitlaguna beach.com/app) puts tons of information in the palm of your hand, from sights and restaurants to the next bus arrival times.

Crystal Cove State Park

Explore the open beach and 2400 acres of undeveloped woodland at this state park (p40). Overnight guests (reserve well in advance) can stay in the dozens of vintage 1930s to '50s cottages (☑ reservations 800-444-7275; www.crystalcovealliance.org; 35 Crystal Cove, Crystal Cove State Park Historic District; r with shared bath $35-140, cottages $171-249; ☺ check-in 4-9pm; 🅿) or at

the campground (📞800-444-7275; www.reserve
america.com; 8471 N Coast Hwy, Laguna Beach; tent
& RV sites $25-75; 🅿). And anyone can stop for
a meal or cocktails at the landmark **Beach-
comber Café** (📞949-376-6900; www.thebeach
combercafe.com; 15 Crystal Cove; mains breakfast
$9-19, lunch $14-21, dinner $20-47; ⊙7am-9:30pm).

Newport Beach

📞949 / POP 87,266

There are really three Newport Beaches:
paradise for wealthy Bentley- and Porsche-
driving yachtsmen and their trophy wives;
perfect waves and beachside dives for surfers
and stoners; and glorious sunsets and seafood
for the rest of the folk, trying to live the day-
to-day. Somehow, these diverse communities
all seem to live – mostly – harmoniously.

For visitors, the pleasures are many: just-
off-the-boat seafood, boogie-boarding the
waves at the Wedge, and the ballet of yachts
in the harbor. Just inland, more lifestyles of
the rich and famous revolve around **Fashion
Island** (📞949-721-2000, 855-658-8527; www.
shopfashionisland.com; 401 Newport Center Dr;
⊙10am-9pm Mon-Fri, to 7pm Sat, 11am-6pm Sun),
a posh outdoor mall and one of the OC's biggest shopping centers.

⊙ Sights & Activities

Orange County Museum of Art   MUSEUM
See p39.

Balboa Island   ISLAND
See p38.

Balboa Fun Zone   AMUSEMENT PARK
See p38.

Balboa Peninsula   AREA
Four miles long but less than a half-mile
wide, the Balboa Peninsula has a white-sand
beach on its ocean side and countless stylish homes, including the 1926 **Lovell Beach
House** (1242 W Ocean Front). It's just inland
from the paved beachfront recreational
path, across from a small playground. Hotels, restaurants and bars cluster around the
peninsula's two famous piers: **Newport Pier**
near the western end and **Balboa Pier** at the
eastern end. The 2-mile oceanfront strip between them teems with beachgoers; people-
watching is great.

The Wedge   BEACH
At the end of the Balboa Peninsula, the Wedge
is famous for its perfectly hollow waves that
can swell up to 30ft high. The waves are

shore-breakers that crest on the sand, not
out to sea, so you can easily slam your head.
There's usually a small crowd watching the action. This is not a good place for learning how
to handle the currents; try a few blocks west.

Davey's Locker   BOATING
(📞949-673-1434; www.daveyslocker.com; 400
Main St; per adult/child 3-12yr & senior 2½hr
whale-watching cruise from $32/26, half-day sport-
fishing $41.50/34) At Balboa Pavilion; offers
whale-watching and sportfishing trips.

Duffy Electric Boat Rentals   BOATING
(📞949-645-6812; www.duffyofnewportbeach.com;
2001 W Coast Hwy; first 2hr $199; ⊙10am-8pm)
These heated electric boats with canopies
are a Newport tradition. Bring tunes, food
and drinks for a fun evening toodling around
the harbor like a local. No boating experience
required; maps provided.

15th Street Surf & Supply   SURFING
(📞949-751-7867; https://15thstsurfsupply.com;
103 15th St; boogie boards per hour/day $7/15, surf-
boards $15/40; ⊙9am-7pm) Rent a full com-
pliment of boogie boards, surfboards and
accessories from wet suits to umbrellas, at
this easygoing shop in business since 1961.
Prices may fluctuate and shop hours are var-
iable, so call ahead to check.

🛏 Sleeping & Eating

**Newport Dunes
Waterfront Resort**   CABIN, CAMPGROUND **$**
(📞949-729-3863; www.newportdunes.com; 1131
Back Bay Dr; campsite from $64, cottage/1-bedroom
cottage from $90/165; 🅿@🛜🛝🐾) RVs and
tents aren't required for a stay at this upscale campground: two dozen tiny, well-kept
A-frames and picket-fenced one-bedroom
cottages are available, all within view of Newport Bay. A fitness center and walking trails,
kayak rentals, board games, family bingo, ice-
cream socials, horseshoe and volleyball tour-
naments, an outdoor pool and playground,
and summertime movies on the beach await.

⭐**Newport Beach Hotel**   BOUTIQUE HOTEL **$$**
(📞949-673-7030; www.thenewportbeachhotel.
com; 2306 W Oceanfront; r/ste from $235/425;
🅿♿❄🛜) There's charm to spare in this in-
timate, 20-room beachfront inn, built in 1904
and updated with beach-chic style. Relax over
tea, fruit and cookies in the ocean-view lob-
by with rattan chairs and white wainscoting,
then head upstairs where rooms of different
sizes are done up with clean whites and pastel
blues, some with spa tubs and ocean views.

51

Doryman's Oceanfront Inn
B&B **$$$**

(☑949-675-7300; www.dorymansinn.com; 2102 W Oceanfront; r $299-399; P🐾❄🛜) This 2nd-floor oceanfront B&B was built in 1891 and retains that Victorian country style. Each of the 11 rooms is unique, and some boast ocean views and fireplaces. It has a great location by Newport Pier (view it from the roof deck), although it can get loud in summer with the 24-hour activities. Parking and breakfast (quiche, bagels, fruit and more) included.

★ Bear Flag Fish Company
SEAFOOD **$**

(☑949-673-3474; www.bearflagfishco.com; 3421 Via Lido; mains $10-16; ⊘11am-9pm Tue-Sat, to 8pm Sun & Mon; 🍴) This is *the* place for generously sized, grilled and *panko*-breaded fish tacos, ahi burritos, spankin' fresh ceviche and oysters. Pick out what you want from the ice-cold display cases, then grab a picnic-table seat. About the only way this seafood could be any fresher is if you caught and hauled it off the boat yourself!

Dory Deli
DELI **$**

(☑949-220-7886; www.dorydeli.com; 2108 W Oceanfront; mains $7-12; ⊘6am-8pm Sun-Thu, to 9pm Fri & Sat) This hip new beachfront storefront does hot and cold sandwiches like the Rubinstein, Lifeguard Club and the steak-filled Rocky Balboa, plus fresh-caught fish-and-chips. For breakfast, you could be good and get the Yoga Pants burrito, or sin a little with chicken and waffles. Full bar too!

Eat Chow
CALIFORNIAN **$$**

(☑949-423-7080; www.eatchownow.com; 211 62nd St; mains $9-18; ⊘8am-9pm Mon-Thu, to 10pm Fri, 7am-10pm Sat, 7am-9pm Sun) Hidden a block behind W Coast Hwy, Eat Chow's caters to a crowd that's equal parts tatted hipsters and ladies who lunch, which makes it very Newport indeed. They all queue happily for rib-eye Thai beef salads, grilled-salmon tacos with curry slaw, and bodacious burgers like the Chow BBQ burger with homemade barbecue sauce, smoked Gouda, crispy onions and more. Groovy indie-rock soundtrack.

🍷 Drinking & Entertainment

Alta Coffee Warehouse
COFFEE

(www.altacoffeeshop.com; 506 31st St; ⊘6am-10pm Mon-Fri, from 7am Sat & Sun) Hidden on a side street, this cozy coffeehouse in a beach bungalow with a covered patio lures locals with live music and poetry readings, art on the brick walls and honest baristas who dish the lowdown on the day's soups, savories,

popular comfort food and baked goods like carrot cake and cheesecake.

It's the kind of place that keeps a shelf of mugs for frequent customers, of whom there are many. The kitchen closes at 9:30pm.

Muldoon's
BAR

(☑949-640-4110; www.muldoonspub.com; 202 Newport Center Dr; ⊘from 11:30am Mon-Sat, 10am Sun, closing hours vary) At upscale, upbeat, much-admired Muldoon's, choose from indoor, outdoor (under a leafy tree) and bar seating and enjoy decent, if pricey, Irish pub grub, 10 beers on tap and live acoustic sounds Thursday through Saturday nights and many Sunday afternoons. Our only complaint: it's a drive from the beach, in an office park by Fashion Island (p51).

Regency Lido
CINEMA

(☑949-673-8350; www.regencymovies.com; 3459 Via Lido; tickets $9-11.50) Showing movies since 1938, the Lido screens mostly mainstream Hollywood fare but some indie flicks too. Fully restored, it has a red-velvet waterfall curtain and Italian tile work.

ⓘ Information

Visit Newport Beach (www.visitnewportbeach. com; 401 Newport Center Dr, Fashion Island, Atrium Court, 2nd fl; ⊘10am-9pm Mon-Fri, to 7pm Sat, to 6pm Sun) The city's official visitor center hands out free brochures and maps.

Huntington Beach

☑714, 949, 562 / POP 200,809

'No worries' is the phrase you'll hear over and over in Huntington Beach, the town that goes by the trademarked nickname 'Surf City USA.' In 1910 real-estate developer and railroad magnate Henry Huntington hired Hawaiian-Irish surfing star George Freeth to give demonstrations. When legendary surfer Duke Kahanamoku moved here in 1925, that solidified its status as a surf destination. Buyers for major retailers come here to see what surfers are wearing, then market the look.

◉ Sights & Activities

Huntington is a one-stop shop for outdoor pleasures by OC beaches. If you forgot to pack beach gear, you can rent umbrellas, beach chairs, volleyballs and other essentials from **Zack's** (☑714-536-0215; www.zackssurfcity. com; 405 Pacific Coast Hwy; group lessons $85, surfboard rentals per hour/day $12/35, wet suits $5/15), just north of the pier. Just south of the pier on the Strand, friendly Dwight's Beach Concession (714-536-8083; www.dwightsbeachconcession.com; 201 Pacific Coast Hwy; surfboard rentals per hour/day $10/40, bicycle rentals from $10/30; 9am-5pm Mon-Fri, to 6pm Sat & Sun), around since 1932, rents bikes, boogie boards, umbrellas and chairs. Huntington Surf & Sport (www.hsssurf.com; 300 Pacific Coast Hwy; 8am-9pm Sun-Thu, to 10pm Fri & Sat) also rents boards and wet suits.

International Surfing Museum   MUSEUM
See p38.

Surfers' Hall of Fame   LANDMARK
See p38.

Huntington City Beach   BEACH
(www.huntingtonbeachca.gov; 5am-10pm; P) One of SoCal's best beaches, the sand surrounding the pier at the foot of Main St gets packed on summer weekends with surfers, volleyball players, swimmers and families. Bathrooms and showers are located north of the pier at the back of the snack-bar complex. In the evening volleyball games give way to beach bonfires.

Bolsa Chica Ecological Reserve   NATURE RESERVE
(714-846-1114; http://bolsachica.org; 18000 Pacific Coast Hwy; sunrise-sunset; P) You'd be forgiven for overlooking Bolsa Chica, at least on first glance. Against a backdrop of nodding oil derricks, this flat expanse of wetlands doesn't exactly promise the unspoiled splendors of nature. However, more than 200 bird species aren't so aesthetically prejudiced, either making the wetlands their home throughout the year, or dropping by mid-migration. Simply put, the restored salt marsh is an environmental success story.

Bolsa Chica State Beach   BEACH
(www.parks.ca.gov; Pacific Coast Hwy, btwn Seapoint & Warner Aves; parking $15; 6am-10pm; P) A 3-mile-long strip of sand favored by surfers, volleyball players and fishers, Bolsa Chica State Beach stretches alongside Pacific Coast Hwy between Huntington Dog Beach (www.dogbeach.org; 100 Goldenwest Street; 5am-10pm; P) to the south and Sunset Beach to the north. Even though it faces a monstrous offshore oil rig, Bolsa Chica (meaning 'Little Pocket' in Spanish) gets mobbed on summer weekends. You'll find picnic tables, fire rings and beach showers, plus a bike path running north to Anderson Ave in Sunset Beach and south to Huntington State Beach.

Common yellowthroat, Bolsa Chica Ecological Reserve
SUSANGARYPHOTOGRAPHY/GETTY IMAGES ©

Huntington Beach Disc Golf Course   OUTDOORS
(714-931-4559; www.huntingtonbeachca.gov; Huntington Central Park, 18381 Goldenwest St; admission $2-3; 9am-dusk Mon-Fri, from 8am Sat & Sun) While of course you could throw a disc back and forth for hours on the beach, this scenic, inland, 18-hole disc golf course lets you test your skills. It's the only one in the OC, downhill from the sports complex. Newbies and seasoned players welcome. The on-site pro shop sells and rents discs and equipment.

🛏 Sleeping

There aren't many budget options in HB, especially near the water, and *especially* especially during summer vacation season. Off-season, you may be able to score a deal. Otherwise, head inland along mind-numbing Hwy 39 toward the I-405 (San Diego Fwy) to find cheaper cookie-cutter motels and hotels.

Huntington Surf Inn   MOTEL $$
(714-536-2444; www.huntingtonsurfinn.com; 720 Pacific Coast Hwy; r $119-209; P) You're paying for location at this two-story 1960s-era motel just north of Main St and across from the beach. Smallish rooms are individually decorated with surf and skateboard art – cool, brah – with firm mattresses and fridges, and microwaves on request. There's a small common deck area with a beach view.

Shorebreak Hotel   BOUTIQUE HOTEL $$$
(714-861-4470; www.shorebreakhotel.com; 500 Pacific Coast Hwy; r from $269; P)

Stow your surfboard (lockers provided) as you head inside HB's hippest hotel, a stone's throw from the pier. The Shorebreak has 'surf ambassadors,' a wet suit mural in the lobby, pseudo-steampunk fitness center with climbing wall, and hardwood furniture and surfboard headboards in geometric-patterned rooms. Minibars stock temporary tattoos and surfboard wax, in case you, you know, forgot yours.

★ **Paséa** RESORT $$$
(☑888-674-3634; http://meritagecollection.com/paseahotel; 21080 Pacific Coast Hwy; r from $359; P♿❄@✿⛱) This hotel is slick and serene, with tons of light and air. Floors are themed for shades of blue from denim to sky, and each of its 250 shimmery, minimalist, high-ceilinged rooms has an ocean-view balcony. As if the stunning pool, gym and Balinese-inspired spa weren't enough, it connects to **Pacific City** (www.gopacificcity.com; 21010 Pacific Coast Hwy; ⊘hours vary) mall.

✗ Eating

★ **Lot 579** FOOD HALL $
(www.gopacificcity.com/lot-579; Pacific City, 21010 Pacific Coast Hwy; ⊘hours vary; P✿🐾) The food court at HB's stunning new ocean-view mall offers some unique and fun restaurants for pressed sandwiches (Burnt Crumbs – the spaghetti grilled cheese is so Instagramma-ble), Aussie meat pies (Pie Not), coffee (Portola) and ice cream (Han's). For best views, take your takeout to the deck, or eat at American Dream (brewpub) or Bear Flag Fish Company.

Sancho's Tacos MEXICAN $
(☑714-536-8226; www.sanchostacos.com; 602 Pacific Coast Hwy; mains $3-10; ⊘8am-9pm Mon-Sat, to 8pm Sun; P) There's no shortage of taco stands in HB, but locals are fiercely dedicated to Sancho's, across from the beach. This two-room shack with patio grills flounder, shrimp and tri-tip to order. Trippy Mexican-meets-skater art. Eat at red leatherette booths or on the outdoor patio across from the ocean.

Cucina Alessá ITALIAN $$
(☑714-969-2148; http://cucinaalessarestaurants.com; 520 Main St; mains lunch $9-13, dinner $12-25; ⊘11am-10pm) Every beach town needs its favorite go-to Italian kitchen. Alessa wins hearts and stomachs with classics like Neapolitan lasagna, butternut-squash ravioli and chicken marsala. Lunch brings out panini, pizzas and pastas, plus breakfasts including frittata and 'famous' French toast. Get sidewalk seating, or sit behind big glass windows.

🍷 Drinking & Nightlife

It's easy to find a bar in HB: just walk up Main St. There's everything from breweries to Irish pubs and meat markets, sometimes one and the same. And in Pacific City are a few new hot spots.

★ **Bungalow** CLUB
(☑714-374-0399; www.thebungalow.com/hb; Pacific City, 21058 Pacific Coast Hwy, Suite 240; ⊘5pm-2am Mon-Fri, noon-2am Sat, noon-10pm Sun) This Santa Monica landmark of cool has opened a second location here in Pacific City, and with its combination of lounge spaces, outdoor patio, cozy, rustic-vintage design, specialty cocktails, DJs who know how to get the crowd going and – let's not forget – ocean views, it's already setting new standards for the OC. The food menu's pretty great too.

Main Street Wine Company WINE BAR
(www.mainstreetwinecompany.com; 301 Main St, Suite 105; ⊘4-9pm Mon, noon-10pm Tue-Thu, noon-11pm Fri, 1-11pm Sat, 1-9pm Sun) Boutique California-wine shop with a sleek bar, generous pours and meet-your-(wine)maker nights.

Disneyland & Anaheim
☑714

When Walt Disney opened Disneyland on July 17, 1955, he declared it the 'Happiest Place on Earth.' More than six decades years later, it's hard to argue. During the 1990s, Anaheim undertook a staggering $4.2 billion revamp and expansion, cleaning up rundown stretches and establishing the first tourist police force in the US. In 2001 a second theme park, Disney California Adventure (DCA), was added, designed to salute the state's most famous natural landmarks and cultural history. More recently added was Downtown Disney, an outdoor pedestrian mall. The ensemble is called Disneyland Resort.

Meanwhile, Anaheim continues to fill in with malls like Anaheim GardenWalk (p59), and shopping and entertainment areas like the **Packing District** (www.anaheimpackingdistrict.com; S Anaheim Bl) and **Center Street** (www.centerstreetanaheim.com; W Center St), plus improved roads and transit.

⊙ Sights

Disneyland is open 365 days a year; hours vary seasonally and sometimes daily, but generally you can count on at least 10am to 8pm. Check the current schedule (www.disneyland.com) in advance when timing your visit. Don't

ℹ FASTPASS

Disneyland and Disney California Adventure's FastPass system can significantly cut your wait times.

➤ Walk up to a FastPass ticket machine – located near the entrance to select theme-park rides – and insert your park entrance ticket or annual passport. You'll receive a slip of paper showing the 'return time' for boarding (it's always at least 40 minutes later).

➤ Show up within the window of time on the ticket and join the ride's FastPass line. There'll still be a wait, but it's shorter (typically 15 minutes or less). Hang on to your FastPass ticket until you board the ride.

➤ If you're running late and miss the time window printed on your FastPass ticket, you can still try joining the FastPass line, although showing up before your FastPass time window is a no-no.

You're thinking, what's the catch, right? When you get a FastPass, you will have to wait at least two hours before getting another one (check the 'next available' time printed at the bottom of your ticket).

So, make it count. Before getting a FastPass, check the display above the machine, which will tell you what the 'return time' for boarding is. If it's much later in the day, or doesn't fit your schedule, a FastPass may not be worth it. Ditto if the ride's current wait time is just 15 to 30 minutes.

worry about getting stuck waiting for a ride or attraction at closing time. Parks stay open until the last guest in line has had their fun.

There is a multitude of ticket options. Single-day ticket prices vary daily but on low-traffic days (typically Monday to Wednesday in the off- or shoulder season) one-day tickets start at adult/child $97/91 for either Disneyland or Disney California Adventure, and a variety of multiday and 'park-hopper' passes are available. Children's tickets apply to kids aged three to nine.

◉ Disneyland Park

It's hard to deny the change in atmosphere as you're whisked by tram from the parking lot into the heart of **Disneyland** (🖉 714-781-4636; www.disneyland.com; 1313 Harbor Blvd; adult/child 3-9yr 1-day pass from $97/91, 2-day park-hopper pass $244/232; ⊙ open daily, seasonal hours vary). Wide-eyed children lean forward with anticipation while stressed-out parents sit back, finally relaxing. Uncle Walt's in charge, and he's taken care of every possible detail.

Main Street USA   AREA
Fashioned after Walt's hometown of Marceline, Missouri, bustling Main Street USA resembles the classic turn-of-the-20th-century, all-American town. It's an idyllic, relentlessly upbeat representation, complete with barbershop quartet, penny arcades, ice-cream shops and a steam train. The music playing in the background is from American musicals,

and there's a flag-retreat ceremony every afternoon.

Great Moments with Mr Lincoln, a 15-minute audio-animatronic presentation on Honest Abe, sits inside the fascinating **Disneyland Story** exhibit. Nearby, kids love seeing old-school Disney cartoons like *Steamboat Willie* inside **Main Street Cinema**.

Main Street ends in the **Central Plaza**. Lording over the plaza is **Sleeping Beauty Castle**, the castle featured on the Disney logo. Inside the iconic structure (fashioned after a real 19th-century Bavarian castle), dolls and big books tell the story of Sleeping Beauty. As if you didn't know it already.

Tomorrowland   AREA
How did 1950s imagineers envision the future? As a galaxy-minded community filled with monorails, rockets and Googie-style architecture, apparently. In 1998 this 'land' was revamped to honor three timeless futurists: Jules Verne, HG Wells and Leonardo da Vinci. These days, though, the *Star Wars* franchise gets top billing. **Hyperspace Mountain**, Tomorrowland's signature attraction and one of the USA's best roller coasters, hurtles you into complete darkness at frightening speed, and **Star Wars Launch Bay** shows movie props and memorabilia.

Meanwhile, **Star Tours** clamps you into a Starspeeder shuttle for a wild and bumpy 3-D ride through the desert canyons of Tatooine on a space mission. If it's retro high-tech you're after, the **monorail** glides to a

DISNEYLAND TO-DO LIST

➡ Make area hotel reservations or book a Disneyland vacation package.

➡ Sign up for online resources including blogs, e-newsletters and resort updates, such as Disney Fans Insider.

➡ Check the parks' opening hours, live show and entertainment schedules online.

➡ Make dining reservations for sit-down restaurants or special meals with Disney characters.

➡ Buy print-at-home tickets and passes online.

➡ Recheck the next day's opening hours and Anaheim Resort Transportation (p60) or hotel shuttle schedules.

➡ Pack a small day pack with sunscreen, hat, sunglasses, swimwear, change of clothes, jacket or hoodie, lightweight plastic rain poncho, and extra batteries and memory cards for digital and video cameras.

➡ Fully charge your electronic devices, including cameras and phones.

➡ Download the Disneyland app to your smartphone.

stop in Tomorrowland, its rubber tires traveling a 13-minute, 2.5-mile round-trip route to Downtown Disney. Just outside Tomorrowland station, kiddies will want to shoot laser beams on Buzz Lightyear Astro Blaster and drive their own miniature cars in the classic Autopia ride. Then jump aboard the Finding Nemo Submarine Voyage to look for the world's most famous clownfish from within a refurbished submarine and rumble through an underwater volcanic eruption.

Fantasyland   AREA

Fantasyland is filled with the characters of classic children's stories. If you only see one attraction here, visit It's a Small World, a boat ride past hundreds of audio-animatronic children from different cultures all singing an earworm of a theme song.

Another classic, the Matterhorn Bobsleds is a steel-frame roller coaster that mimics a bobsled ride down a mountain. Fans of old-school attractions will also get a kick out of *The Wind in the Willows*–inspired Mr Toad's Wild Ride, a loopy jaunt in an open-air jalopy through London.

Younger kids love whirling around the Mad Tea Party teacup ride and King Arthur Carrousel, then cavorting with characters in nearby Mickey's Toontown, a topsy-turvy minimetropolis where kiddos can traipse through Mickey and Minnie's houses and dozens of storefronts.

Frontierland   AREA

This Disney 'land' is a salute to old Americana: the Mississippi-style paddle-wheel Mark

Twain Riverboat, the 18th-century replica Sailing Ship Columbia, a rip-roarin' Old West town with a shooting gallery and the Big Thunder Mountain Railroad, a mining-themed roller coaster. The former Tom Sawyer Island – the only attraction in the park personally designed by Uncle Walt – has been reimagined in the wake of the *Pirates of the Caribbean* movies and renamed the Pirate's Lair on Tom Sawyer Island.

Adventureland   AREA

Loosely deriving its jungle theme from Southeast Asia and Africa, Adventureland has a number of attractions, but the hands-down highlight is the safari-style Indiana Jones Adventure. Nearby, little ones love climbing the stairways of Tarzan's Treehouse. Cool down on the Jungle Cruise, viewing exotic audio-animatronic animals from rivers of South America, India, Africa and Southeast Asia. And the classic Enchanted Tiki Room features carvings of Hawaiian gods and goddesses, and a show of singing, dancing audio-animatronic birds and flowers.

Pirates of the Caribbean   RIDE

Pirates of the Caribbean is the longest ride in Disneyland (17 minutes) and one of the longest running, opened in 1967. That's half a century of folks hearing audio-animatronic pirates singing 'Yo ho, yo ho, a pirate's life for me' as they cruise by on a boat. You'll float through the subterranean haunts of tawdry pirates, where dead buccaneers perch atop their mounds of booty and Jack Sparrow pops up occasionally.

Critter Country
AREA

Critter Country's main attraction is **Splash Mountain**, a flume ride through the story of Brer Rabbit and Brer Bear, based on the controversial 1946 film *Song of the South*. Just past Splash Mountain, hop in a mobile beehive on the **Many Adventures of Winnie the Pooh**. Nearby on the Rivers of America, you can paddle **Davy Crockett's Explorer Canoes** on summer weekends.

◉ Disney California Adventure

Across the plaza from Disneyland's monument to fantasy and make-believe is **Disney California Adventure** (DCA; ☑ 714-781-4565; https://disneyland.disney.go.com; 1313 Harbor Blvd, Anaheim; single-day ticket prices vary daily, 2-day pass adult/child from $199/187; P ♿), an ode to California's geography, history and culture – or at least a sanitized G-rated version. DCA, which opened in 2001, covers more acres than Disneyland and feels less crowded, and it has more modern rides and attractions inspired by coastal amusement parks, the inland mountains and redwood forests, the magic of Hollywood, and car culture by way of the movie *Cars*.

Cars Land
AREA

This land gets kudos for its incredibly detailed design based on the popular Disney Pixar *Cars* movies. Top billing goes to the wacky **Radiator Springs Racers**, a race-car ride that bumps and jumps around a track painstakingly decked out like the Great American West.

Grizzly Peak
AREA

Grizzly Peak is broken into sections highlighting California's natural and human achievements. Its main attraction, **Soarin' Around the World**, is a virtual hang-gliding ride using Omnimax technology that 'flies' you over famous landmarks. Enjoy the light breeze as you soar, keeping your nostrils open for aromas blowing in the wind. **Grizzly River Run** takes you 'rafting' down a faux Sierra Nevada river – be warned, you will get wet.

Paradise Pier
AREA

If you like carnival rides, you'll love Paradise Pier, designed to look like a combination of all the beachside amusement piers in California. The state-of-the-art **California Screamin'** roller coaster resembles an old wooden coaster, but it's got a smooth-as-silk steel track: it feels like you're being shot out of a cannon. Just as popular is **Toy Story**

Midway Mania! – a 4-D ride where you earn points by shooting at targets while your carnival car swivels and careens through an oversize, old-fashioned game arcade.

Hollywood Land
AREA

California's biggest factory of dreams is presented here in miniature, with soundstages, movable props and – of course – a studio store. A *Guardians of the Galaxy*–themed ride was in the works as we went to press, but for now one of the top attractions is a one-hour live stage version of *Frozen*, at the **Hyperion Theater** (https://disneyland.disney. go.com/entertainment/disney-california-adventure/ frozen-live-at-hyperion).

🎿 Activities

Redwood Creek Challenge Trail
CLIMBING

(Grizzly Peak) At this attraction in Disney California Adventure, more-active kids of all ages can tackle the Redwood Creek Challenge Trail, climbing rock faces, sliding down a rock slide and walking through the 35ft 'Big Sir' redwood stump. Flat-hatted faux park rangers look on.

🛏 Sleeping

🛏 Disneyland Resort

For the full-on Disney experience, there are three different hotels within Disneyland Resort, though there are less-expensive options just beyond the Disney gates in Anaheim. If you want a theme-park hotel for less money, try **Knott's Berry Farm** (☑ 714-995-1111, 866-752-2444; www.knottshotel.com; 7675 Crescent Ave, Buena Park; r $79-169; P @ 🛜 🏊).

★ Disney's Grand Californian Hotel & Spa
RESORT $$$

(☑ info 714-635-2300, reservations 714-956-6425; https://disneyland.disney.go.com/grand-californian-hotel; 1600 S Disneyland Dr, Anaheim; d from $360; P ✳ @ 🛜 🏊) Soaring timber beams rise above the cathedral-like lobby of the six-story Grand Californian, Disney's homage to the arts-and-crafts architectural movement. Cushy rooms have triple-sheeted beds, down pillows, bathrobes and all-custom furnishings. Outside there's a faux-redwood waterslide into the pool. At night, kids wind down with bedtime stories by the lobby's giant stone hearth.

Disneyland Hotel
HOTEL $$$

(☑ 714-778-6600; www.disneyland.com; 1150 Magic Way, Anaheim; r $210-395; P @ 🛜 🏊) Built in

1955, the year Disneyland opened, the park's original hotel has been rejuvenated with a dash of bibbidi-bobbidi-boo. There are three towers with themed lobbies (adventure, fantasy and frontier), and the 972 good-sized rooms now boast Mickey-hand wall sconces in bathrooms and headboards lit like the fireworks over Sleeping Beauty Castle (p55).

Paradise Pier Hotel
HOTEL $$$

(📋info 714-999-0990, reservations 714-956-6425; http://disneyland.disney.go.com/paradise-pier-hotel; 1717 S Disneyland Dr, Anaheim; d from $240; P ❄ @ 🐾 🏊 ✈) Sunbursts, surfboards and a giant superslide are all on deck at the Paradise Pier Hotel, the smallest (472 rooms), cheapest and maybe the most fun of the Disney hotel trio. Kids will love the beachy decor and game arcade, not to mention the pool and the tiny-tot video room.

🛏 Anaheim

While the Disney resorts have their own hotels, there are a number of worthwhile hotels just off-site or a few miles away, and every stripe of chain hotel you can imagine. Generally Anaheim's hotels are good value relative to those in the OC beach towns.

Ayres Hotel Anaheim
HOTEL $$

(📋714-634-2106; www.ayreshotels.com/anaheim; 2550 E Katella Ave; r $139-219; P ➡ ❄ @ 🐾 ✈) This well-run minichain of business hotels delivers solid-gold value. The 133 recently renovated rooms have microwaves, mini-fridges, safes, wet bar, pillow-top mattresses and design inspired by the Californian arts-and-crafts movement. Fourth-floor rooms have extra-high ceilings. Rates include a full breakfast and evening social hours Monday to Thursday with beer, wine and snacks.

Residence Inn Anaheim Resort/ Convention Center
HOTEL $$

(📋714-782-7500; www.marriott.com; 640 W Katella Ave; r from $179; P ➡ ❄ @ 🐾 ✈ 🐕) This new hotel near the convention center shines with sleek linens, marble tables and glass walls within in-room kitchens, big windows and a sweet rooftop pool deck with Jacuzzi and a splash zone for kids. Rates include full breakfast, and there's also a gym and laundry machines.

Hotel Indigo Anaheim
BOUTIQUE HOTEL $$

(📋714-772-7755; www.ihg.com; 435 W Katella Ave; r from $170; P ➡ @ 🐾 ✈ 🐕) This friendly, professional 104-room hotel has a clean,

mid-century modernist look with hardwood floor and pops of color, fitness center, pool and guest laundry. Mosaic murals are modeled after the walnut trees that once bloomed here. It's about 15 minutes' walk or a quick drive to Disneyland and steps from shops and restaurants at Anaheim GardenWalk.

🍴 Eating

From stroll-and-eat Mickey-shaped pretzels ($4) and jumbo turkey legs ($10) to deluxe, gourmet dinners (sky's the limit), there's no shortage of eating options, though mostly pretty expensive and targeted to mainstream tastes. Phone **Disney Dining** (📋714-781-3463; http://disneyland.disney.go.com/dining) to make reservations up to 60 days in advance. Restaurant hours vary seasonally, sometimes daily. Check the Disneyland app or Disney Dining website for same-day hours. Driving just a couple miles into Anaheim will expand the offerings and price points considerably.

🍴 Disneyland Park

Jolly Holiday Bakery Cafe
BAKERY $

(https://disneyland.disney.go.com/dining/disneyland/jolly-holiday-bakery-cafe; Main Street USA; mains $8.50-11; ⏰breakfast, lunch & dinner; 🍴) At this Mary Poppins–themed restaurant, the Jolly Holiday combo (grilled cheese and tomato basil soup for $9) is a decent deal and very satisfying. The cafe does other sandwiches on the sophisticated side, like the mozzarella caprese or turkey on ciabatta. Great people-watching from outdoor seating.

Blue Bayou
SOUTHERN US $$$

(📋714-781-3463; https://disneyland.disney.go.com/dining/disneyland/blue-bayou-restaurant; New Orleans Sq; mains lunch $28-41, dinner $30-48; ⏰lunch & dinner; 🍴) Surrounded by the 'bayou' inside the Pirates of the Caribbean (p56) attraction, this is the top choice for sit-down dining in Disneyland Park and is famous for its Creole and Cajun specialties at dinner. Order fresh-baked pecan pie topped by a piratey souvenir for dessert (*ahh*, then *argh!*).

🍴 Downtown Disney & Hotels

⭐Napa Rose
CALIFORNIAN $$$

(📋714-300-7170; https://disneyland.disney.go.com/dining; Disney's Grand Californian Hotel & Spa; mains $38-48, 4-course prix-fixe dinner from $100; ⏰5:30-10pm; 🍴) High-back arts-and-crafts-style chairs, leaded-glass windows and towering ceilings befit Disneyland Resort's top-drawer restaurant. On the plate, seasonal 'California Wine Country' (read: NorCal) cuisine is as impeccably crafted as Sleeping Beauty Castle. Kids' menu available. Reservations essential. Enter the hotel from Disney California Adventure or Downtown Disney.

Steakhouse 55   AMERICAN $$$
(🖉 714-781-3463; 1150 Magic Way, Disneyland Hotel; mains breakfast $14-25, dinner $31-57; ⊙ 7am-11pm & 5-10:30pm) Nothing at Disneyland is exactly a secret, but this clubby, grown-up hideaway comes pretty darn close. Dry-rubbed, bone-in rib eye, Australian lobster tail, heirloom potatoes and green beans with applewood-smoked bacon uphold a respectable chophouse menu. There's also a full bar, good wine list and (we hope well-behaved) kids' menu.

✖ Disney California Adventure

Pacific Wharf Cafe   FOOD HALL $
(https://disneyland.disney.go.com/dining/disney-california-adventure/pacific-wharf-cafe; mains $10-11.50; ⊙ breakfast, lunch & dinner) This counter-service collection of restaurants shows off some of California's ethnic cuisines (Chinese, Mexican etc) as well as hearty soups in sourdough bread bowls, farmers-market salads and deli sandwiches. We like to eat at umbrella-covered tables by the water.

Wine Country Trattoria   ITALIAN $$
(https://disneyland.disney.go.com/dining/disney-california-adventure/wine-country-trattoria; Pacific Wharf; mains lunch $15-21, dinner $17-23; ⊙ lunch & dinner; 🗐) If you can't quite swing the Napa Rose or Carthay Circle, this sunny Cal-Italian terrace restaurant is a fine backup. Fork into Italian pastas, salads or veggie paninis, washed down with Napa Valley wines.

★ Carthay Circle   AMERICAN $$$
(https://disneyland.disney.go.com/dining/disney-california-adventure/carthay-circle-restaurant; Buena Vista St; mains lunch $24-34, dinner $32-45; ⊙ lunch & dinner; 🗐) Decked out like a Hollywood country club, new Carthay Circle is the best dining in either park, with seasonal steaks, seafood, pasta, smart service and a good wine list. Your table needs at least one order of fried biscuits, stuffed with white cheddar, bacon and jalapeño, and served with apricot honey butter.

✖ Anaheim

Most restaurants on the streets surrounding Disneyland are chains, though **Anaheim**

GardenWalk (www.anaheimgardenwalk.com; 400 W Disney Way; ⊙ 11am-9pm; 🗐) has some upscale ones. It's about a 10-minute walk from Disneyland's main gate.

Olive Tree   MIDDLE EASTERN $$
(🖉 714-535-2878; 512 S Brookhurst St; mains $8-16; ⊙ 10am-9pm Mon-Sat, to 8pm Sun) In Little Arabia, this simple restaurant in a nondescript strip mall ringed by flags of Arab nations has earned accolades from local papers to *Saveur* magazine. You *could* get standards like falafel and kebabs, but daily specials are where it's at; Saturday's *kabseh* is righteous, fall-off-the-bone lamb shank over spiced rice with currants and onions.

Umami Burger   BURGERS $$
(🖉 714-991-8626; www.umamiburger.com; 338 S Anaheim Blvd; mains $11-15; ⊙ 11am-11pm Sun-Thu, to midnight Fri & Sat) The Anaheim outpost of this LA-based mini-chain sets the right tone for the Packing District (p54). Burgers span classic to truffled. Try the Hatch burger with roasted green chilies or the Manly with beer cheddar and bacon lardons. Get 'em with deep-fried 'smushed' potatoes with house-made ketchup, and top it off with a salted chocolate ice-cream sandwich. Full bar.

🍷 Drinking

You can't buy alcohol in Disneyland, but you can at Disney California Adventure, Downtown Disney and Disney's trio of resort hotels. Downtown Disney offers bars, live music, a 12-screen cinema and more. Some restaurants and bars stay open as late as midnight on Fridays and Saturdays.

Golden Vine Winery   BAR
(Pacific Wharf, Disney California Adventure) This centrally located terrace is a great place for relaxing and regrouping in Disney California Adventure.

ℹ Information

Before you arrive, visit **Disneyland Resort** (🖉 live assistance 714-781-7290, recorded info 714-781-4565; www.disneyland.com) for more information. You can also download the Disneyland Explorer app for your mobile device.

LOCKERS
Self-service lockers with in-and-out privileges cost $7 to $15 per day. You'll find them on **Main Street USA** (Disneyland), in **Sunshine Plaza** (Disney California Adventure) and at the **picnic area** just outside the theme park's main entrance, near Downtown Disney.

MEDICAL SERVICES

You'll find first-aid facilities at Disneyland (Main Street USA), Disney California Adventure (Pacific Wharf) and Downtown Disney (next to Ralph Brennan's Jazz Kitchen).

Anaheim Urgent Care (☑714-533-2273; 831 S State College Blvd, Anaheim; ⊘8am-8pm Mon-Fri, 9am-5pm Sat & Sun) Walk-in non-emergency medical clinic.

Anaheim Global Medical Center (☑657-230-0265; www.anaheim-gmc.com; 1025 S Anaheim Blvd, Anaheim; ⊘24hr) Hospital emergency room.

TOURIST INFORMATION

For information or help inside the parks, just ask any cast member or visit Disneyland's **City Hall** (☑714-781-4565; Main Street USA) or Disney California Adventure's guest relations lobby.

Visit Anaheim (☑855-405-5020; http:// visitanaheim.org; 800 W Katella Ave, Anaheim Convention Center) The city's official tourism bureau has information on lodging, dining and transportation, during events at the Convention Center.

ⓘ Getting There & Away

CAR & MOTORCYCLE

Disneyland Resort is just off I-5 (Santa Ana Fwy), about 30 miles southeast of Downtown LA. Take the Disneyland Dr exit if you're coming from the north, or the Katella Ave/Disney Way exit from the south.

Arriving at Disneyland Resort is like arriving at an airport. Giant, easy-to-read overhead signs indicate which ramps you need to take for the theme parks, hotels or Anaheim's streets.

SHUTTLE

Anaheim Resort Transportation (ART; ☑888-364-2787; www.rideart.org; adult/child fare $3/1, day pass $5.50/2, multiple-day passes available) operates some 20 shuttle routes between Disneyland and area hotels, convention centers, malls, stadiums and the transit center, saving traffic jams and parking headaches. Shuttles typically start running an hour before Disneyland opens, operating from 7am to midnight daily during summer. Departures are typically two to three times per hour, depending on the route. Purchase single or multiday ART passes at kiosks near ART shuttle stops or via the ART Ticketing app (www.rideart.org/ fares-and-passes).

Many hotels and motels offer their own free shuttles to Disneyland and other area attractions; ask when booking.

ⓘ Getting Around

CAR & MOTORCYCLE

All-day parking at Disneyland Resort costs $20 ($25 for oversize vehicles). Enter the 'Mickey & Friends' parking structure from southbound Disneyland Dr, off Ball Rd. Walk outside and follow the signs to board the free tram to Downtown Disney and the theme parks. The parking garage opens one hour before the parks do.

TRAIN & MONORAIL

With an admission ticket to Disneyland, you can ride the monorail between Tomorrowland and the far end of Downtown Disney, near the Disneyland Hotel. It sure beats walking both ways along crowded Downtown Disney.

LOS ANGELES

POP 10.1 MILLION

LA runs deeper than her blond beaches, bosomy hills and ubiquitous beemers would have you believe. She's a myth. A beacon for countless small-town dreamers, rockers and risk-takers, an open-minded angel who encourages her people to live and let live without judgment or shame. She has given us Quentin Tarantino, Jim Morrison and Serena and Venus Williams, spawned skateboarding and gangsta rap, popularized implants, electrolysis and spandex, and has nurtured not just great writers, performers and directors, but also the ground-breaking yogis who first brought Eastern wisdom to the Western world.

LA is best defined by those simple life-affirming moments. A cracked-ice, jazz-age cocktail on Beverly Blvd, a hike high into the Hollywood Hills sagebrush, a pink-washed sunset over a thundering Venice Beach drum circle, the perfect taco. And her night music. There is always night music.

⊙ Sights & Activities

⊙ Downtown Los Angeles & Boyle Heights

Downtown Los Angeles is historical, multi-layered and fascinating. It's a city within a city, alive with young professionals, designers and artists who have snapped up stylish lofts in rehabbed art-deco buildings. The growing gallery district along Main and Spring Sts draws thousands to its monthly art walks.

★ Walt Disney Concert Hall   NOTABLE BUILDING

(Map p64; ☎ 323-850-2000; www.laphil.org; 111 S Grand Ave; ☺guided tours usually noon & 1:15pm Thu-Sat, 10am & 11am Sun; P; M Red/Purple Lines to Civic Center/Grand Park) FREE A molten blend of steel, music and psychedelic architecture, this iconic concert venue is the home base of the Los Angeles Philharmonic, but has also hosted contemporary bands such as Phoenix and classic jazz men such as Sonny Rollins. Frank Gehry pulled out all the stops: the building is a gravity-defying sculpture of heaving and billowing stainless steel.

MOCA Grand   MUSEUM

(Museum of Contemporary Art; Map p64; ☎ 213-626-6222; www.moca.org; 250 S Grand Ave; adult/child $15/free, 5-8pm Thu free; ☺11am-6pm Mon, Wed & Fri, to 8pm Thu, to 5pm Sat & Sun) MOCA's superlative art collection focuses mainly on works created from the 1940s to the present. There's no shortage of luminaries, among them Mark Rothko, Dan Flavin, Willem de Kooning, Joseph Cornell and David Hockney, their creations housed in a postmodern building by award-winning Japanese architect Arata Isozaki. Galleries are below ground, yet sky-lit bright.

Grammy Museum   MUSEUM

(Map p64; ☎ 213-765-6800; www.grammymuseum. org; 800 W Olympic Blvd; adult/child $13/11; ☺10:30am-6:30pm Mon-Fri, from 10am Sat & Sun; P ♿) It's the highlight of LA Live (Map p64; ☎ 866-548-3452, 213-763-5483; www.lalive.com; 800 W Olympic Blvd; P ♿). Music lovers will get lost in interactive exhibits, which define, differentiate and link musical genres. Spanning three levels, the museum's rotating exhibitions might include threads worn by the likes of Michael Jackson, Whitney Houston and Beyoncé, scribbled words from the hands of Count Basie and Taylor Swift, and instruments once used by world-renowned rock deities. Inspired? Interactive sound chambers allow you to try your own hand at singing, mixing and remixing.

Union Station   NOTABLE BUILDING

(Map p64; www.amtrak.com; 800 N Alameda St; P) Built on the site of LA's original Chinatown, Union Station opened in 1939 as America's last grand rail station. It's a glamorous exercise in Mission Revival style with art deco and Native American accents. The marble-floored main hall, with cathedral ceilings, original leather chairs and 3000-pound chandeliers, is breathtaking. The station's Traxx Bar was once the

Grauman's Chinese Theatre
SEAN PAVONE/SHUTTERSTOCK ©

telephone room, complete with operator to place customers' calls. The LA Conservancy runs 2½-hour walking tours of the station on Saturdays at 10am (book online at www.lacon servancy.org).

⊙ Hollywood

No other corner of LA is steeped in as much mythology as Hollywood. It's here that you'll find the Hollywood Walk of Fame, the Capitol Records Tower and Grauman's Chinese Theatre, where the hand- and footprints of entertainment deities are immortalized in concrete. Look beyond the tourist-swamped landmarks of Hollywood Blvd and you'll discover a nuanced, multifaceted neighborhood where industrial streets are punctuated by edgy galleries and boutiques, where strip malls hide swinging French bistros and where steep, sleepy streets harbor the homes of long-gone silver-screen stars.

Grauman's Chinese Theatre   LANDMARK

(TCL Chinese Theatres; Map p64; ☎ 323-461-3331; www.tclchinesetheatres.com; 6925 Hollywood Blvd; guided tour adult/senior/child $16/13.50/8; ♿; M Red Line to Hollywood/Highland) Ever wondered what it's like to be in George Clooney's shoes? Just find his footprints in the forecourt of this world-famous movie palace. The exotic pagoda theater – complete with temple bells and stone heaven dogs from China – has shown movies since 1927 when Cecil B DeMille's *The King of Kings* first flickered across the screen.

Griffith Observatory
CHECUBUS/SHUTTERSTOCK ©

awards and the Daytime Emmy Awards. The venue is home to the annual PaleyFest, the country's premier TV festival, held in March. Guided tours of the theater will have you sniffing around the auditorium, admiring a VIP room and nosing up to an Oscar statuette.

Hollywood Forever Cemetery　CEMETERY
(Map p64; ☑ 323-469-1181; www.hollywoodforever. com; 6000 Santa Monica Blvd; ⊙ usually 8:30am-5pm, flower shop 9am-5pm Mon-Fri, to 4pm Sat & Sun; ℗) Paradisiacal landscaping, vainglorious tombstones and epic mausoleums set an appropriate resting place for some of Hollywood's most iconic dearly departed. Residents include Cecil B DeMille, Mickey Rooney, Jayne Mansfield, punk rockers Johnny and Dee Dee Ramone, and *Golden Girls* star Estelle Getty. Valentino lies in the Cathedral Mausoleum (open from 10am to 2pm), while Judy Garland rests in the Abbey of the Psalms. For a full list of residents, purchase a map ($5) at the flower shop.

Hollywood Museum　MUSEUM
(Map p64; ☑ 323-464-7776; www.thehollywoodmuseum.com; 1660 N Highland Ave; adult/child $15/5; ⊙ 10am-5pm Wed-Sun; Ⓜ Red Line to Hollywood/Highland) For a taste of Old Hollywood, do not miss this musty temple to the stars, its four floors crammed with movie and TV costumes and props. The museum is housed inside the Max Factor Building, built in 1914 and relaunched as a glamorous beauty salon in 1935. At the helm was Polish-Jewish businessman Max Factor, Hollywood's leading authority on cosmetics. And it was right here that he worked his magic on Hollywood's most famous screen queens.

Hollywood Walk of Fame　LANDMARK
(Map p64; www.walkoffame.com; Hollywood Blvd; Ⓜ Red Line to Hollywood/Highland) Big Bird, Bob Hope, Marilyn Monroe and Aretha Franklin are among the stars being sought out, worshipped, photographed and stepped on along the Hollywood Walk of Fame. Since 1960 more than 2600 performers – from legends to bit-part players – have been honored with a pink-marble sidewalk star.

Dolby Theatre　THEATER
(Map p64; ☑ 323-308-6300; www.dolbytheatre. com; 6801 Hollywood Blvd; tours adult/child, student & senior $23/18; ⊙ 10:30am-4pm; ℗; Ⓜ Red Line to Hollywood/Highland) The Academy Awards are handed out at the Dolby Theatre, which has also hosted the *American Idol* finale, the Excellence in Sports Performance Yearly (ESPY)

Runyon Canyon　HIKING
(Map p64; www.runyoncanyonhike.com; 2000 N Fuller Ave; ⊙ dawn-dusk) A chaparral-draped cut in the Hollywood Hills, this 130-acre public park is as famous for its buff runners and exercising celebrities as it is for the panoramic views from the upper ridge. Follow the wide, partially paved fire road up then take the smaller track down to the canyon, where you'll pass the remains of the Runyon estate.

⊙ Los Feliz & Griffith Park

Five times the size of New York's Central Park, Griffith Park is home to the world-famous Griffith Observatory, the oft-overlooked Autry Museum of the American West and the take-it-or-leave-it city **zoo** (Map p64; ☑ 323-644-4200; www.lazoo.org; 5333 Zoo Dr, Griffith Park; adult/senior/child $20/17/15; ⊙ 10am-5pm, closed Christmas Day; ℗ ⼤). Rising above the southern edge of Los Feliz, Barnsdall Art Park is crowned by architect Frank Lloyd Wright's Californian debut, **Hollyhock House** (Map p64; ☑ 323-913-4031; www.barnsdall.org/hollyhock-house/about; Barnsdall Art Park, 4800 Hollywood Blvd, Los Feliz; adult/student/child $7/3/free; ⊙ tours 11am-4pm Thu-Sun; ℗; Ⓜ Red Line to Vermont/Sunset).

Griffith Park　PARK
(Map p64; ☑ 323-644-2050; www.laparks.org; 4730 Crystal Springs Dr; ⊙ 5am-10pm, trails sunrise-sunset; ℗ ⼤) FREE A gift to the city in 1896 by mining mogul Griffith J Griffith,

Griffith Park is one of the country's largest urban green spaces. It contains a major outdoor theater, the city zoo, an observatory, two museums, golf courses, playgrounds, 53 miles of hiking trails, Batman's caves and the Hollywood sign.

★ Griffith Observatory   MUSEUM
(Map p64; ☑ 213-473-0890; www.griffithobserva tory.org; 2800 E Observatory Rd; admission free, planetarium shows adult/child $7/3; ☉noon-10pm Tue-Fri, from 10am Sat & Sun; P ♿; ☐DASH Observatory) **FREE** LA's landmark 1935 observatory opens a window onto the universe from its perch on the southern slopes of Mt Hollywood. Its planetarium claims the world's most advanced star projector, while its astronomical touch displays explore some mind-bending topics, from the evolution of the telescope and the ultraviolet x-rays used to map our solar system to the cosmos itself. Then, of course, there are the views, which (on clear days) take in the entire LA basin, surrounding mountains and Pacific Ocean.

◉ Silver Lake & Echo Park

Pimped with stencil art, inked skin and skinny jeans, Silver Lake and Echo Park are the epicenter of LA hipsterdom. Echo Park, one of LA's oldest neighborhoods, offers a contrasting jumble of rickety homes, Mexican *panderías* (bakeries), indie rock bars, vintage stores, design-literate coffee shops and the serenity of its namesake lake, featured in Polanski's *Chinatown*. These areas are more about the vibe than ticking off sights. Consider starting your explorations at Silver Lake Junction (the intersection of Sunset and Santa Monica Blvds), grabbing coffee and exploring the well-curated stores that dot Sunset Blvd. The Echo Park stretch of Sunset Blvd is home to its own booty of small galleries and cool shops.

◉ West Hollywood & Mid-City

Welcome to West Hollywood (WeHo), an independent city with way more personality (some might say, frivolity) than its 1.9-sq-mile frame might suggest. Upscale and low-rent (but rising), gay fabulous and Russian-ghetto chic, this is a bastion of LA's fashionista best and home to some of the trashiest shops you'll ever see. Mid-City, to the south and east, encompasses the Miracle Mile (home to some of the best museums in the west), the Orthodox-Jewish-meets-hipster Fairfax district and the legendary rock, punk and vintage shopping strip of Melrose Ave.

Original Farmers Market   MARKET
(Map p64; ☑ 323-933-9211; www.farmersmarketla. com; 6333 W 3rd St, Fairfax District; ☉9am-9pm Mon-Fri, to 8pm Sat, 10am-7pm Sun; P ♿) Long before the city was flooded with farmers markets, there was *the* farmers market. Fresh produce, roasted nuts, doughnuts, cheeses, blini – you'll find them all at this 1934 landmark. Casual and kid friendly, it's a fun place for a browse, snack or for people-watching.

★ Los Angeles County Museum of Art   MUSEUM
(LACMA; Map p64; ☑ 323-857-6000; www.lacma. org; 5905 Wilshire Blvd, Mid-City; adult/child $15/ free, 2nd Tue of month free; ☉11am-5pm Mon, Tue & Thu, to 8pm Fri, 10am-7pm Sat & Sun; P ; ☐Metro lines 20, 217, 720, 780 to Wilshire & Fairfax) The depth and wealth of the collection at the largest museum in the western US is stunning. LACMA holds all the major players – Rembrandt, Cézanne, Magritte, Mary Cassat, Ansel Adams – plus millennia worth of Chinese, Japanese, pre-Columbian and ancient Greek, Roman and Egyptian sculpture. Recent acquisitions include massive outdoor installations such as Chris Burden's *Urban Light* (a surreal selfie backdrop of hundreds of vintage LA streetlamps) and Michael Heizer's *Levitated Mass,* a surprisingly inspirational 340-ton boulder perched over a walkway.

Petersen Automotive Museum   MUSEUM
(Map p64; ☑ 323-930-2277; www.petersen.org; 6060 Wilshire Blvd, Mid-City; adult/student & senior/child $15/12/7; ☉10am-6pm; P ♿; ☐Metro lines 20, 217, 720, 780 to Wilshire & Fairfax) A four-story ode to the auto, the Petersen Automotive Museum is a treat even for those who can't tell a piston from a carburetor. A headlights-to-brakelights futuristic makeover (by Kohn Pederson Fox) in late 2015 left it fairly gleaming from the outside; the exterior is undulating bands of stainless steel on a hot-rod-red background.

La Brea Tar Pits & Museum   MUSEUM
(Map p64; www.tarpits.org; 5801 Wilshire Blvd, Mid-City; adult/student & senior/child $12/9/5, 1st Tue of month Sep-Jun free; ☉9:30am-5pm; P ♿) Mammoths, saber-toothed cats and dire wolves used to roam LA's savannah in prehistoric times. We know this because of an archaeological trove of skulls and bones unearthed here at the La Brea Tar Pits, one of the world's most fecund and famous fossil sites. A museum has been built here, where generations of young dino-hunters have come to seek out fossils and learn about paleontology from docents and demonstrations in on-site labs.

Hollywood

Hollywood

◉ Beverly Hills, Bel Air, Brentwood & Westwood

A triptych of megamansions, luxury wheels and tweaked cheekbones, Beverly Hills, Bel Air and Brentwood encapsulate the LA of international fantasies.

★ **Getty Center**   MUSEUM
(Map p64; ☑ 310-440-7300; www.getty.edu; 1200 Getty Center Dr, off I-405 Fwy; ⊙10am-5:30pm Tue-Fri & Sun, to 9pm Sat; ᴘ⍈; ⌨734, 234) FREE In its billion-dollar, in-the-clouds perch, high above the city grit and grime, the Getty Center presents triple delights: a stellar art collection (everything from medieval triptychs

to baroque sculpture and impressionist brushstrokes), Richard Meier's cutting-edge architecture, and the visual splendor of seasonally changing gardens. Admission is free, but parking is $15 ($10 after 3pm).

Museum of Tolerance   MUSEUM
(Map p64; ☑ reservations 310-772-2505; www.museumoftolerance.com; 9786 W Pico Blvd; adult/senior/student $15.50/12.50/11.50, Anne Frank Exhibit adult/senior/student $15.50/13.50/12.50; ⊙10am-5pm Sun-Wed & Fri, to 9:30pm Thu, to 3:30pm Fri Nov-Mar; ᴘ) Run by the Simon Wiesenthal Center, this powerful, deeply moving museum uses interactive technology to engage visitors in discussion and contemplation around racism and bigotry. Particular focus is given to the Holocaust, with a major basement exhibition that examines the social, political and economic conditions that led to the genocide as well as the experience of the millions persecuted. On the museum's 2nd floor, another major exhibition offers an intimate look into the life and legacy of Anne Frank.

Westwood Village
Memorial Park Cemetery   CEMETERY
(Map p64; ☑ 310-474-1579; 1218 Glendon Ave, Westwood; ⊙8am-6pm; ᴘ) You'll be spending quiet time with entertainment heavyweights at this compact cemetery, hidden behind Wilshire Blvd's wall of high-rise towers. The northeast mausoleum houses Marilyn Monroe's simple crypt, while just south of it, the Sanctuary of Love harbors Dean Martin's crypt. Beneath the central lawn lie a number of iconic names, including actress Natalie Wood, pin-up Bettie Page and crooner Roy Orbison (the latter lies in an unmarked grave

to the left of a marker labeled 'Grandma Martha Monroe').

Malibu & Pacific Palisades

Malibu enjoys near-mythical status thanks to its large celebrity population (it's been celebrity central since the 1930s) and the incredible beauty of its 27 miles of coastal mountains, pristine coves, wide sweeps of golden sand and epic waves. Despite its wealth and star quotient, the best way to appreciate Malibu is through its natural assets, so grab your sunscreen and a towel and head to the beach.

★ Getty Villa
See p21.

Malibu Lagoon State Beach
See p21.

Adamson House
See p21.

El Matador State Beach   BEACH
(☑ 818-880-0363; 32215 Pacific Coast Hwy, Malibu; ℙ) Arguably Malibu's most stunning beach, where you park on the bluffs and stroll down a trail to sandstone rock towers that rise from emerald coves. Topless sunbathers stroll through the tides, and dolphins breech the surface beyond the waves. It's been impacted by coastal erosion, but you can still find a sliver of dry sand tucked against the bluffs.

Zuma Beach   BEACH
(30000 Pacific Coast Hwy, Malibu; ℙ; ⊟ MTA 534) Zuma is easy to find, and thanks to the wide sweep of blonde sand that has been attracting valley kids to the shore since the 1970s, it gets busy on weekends and summer afternoons. Pass around Point Dume to **Westward Beach** (6800 Westward Rd, Malibu; ℙ; ⊟ MTA 534).

Will Rogers
State Historic Park   MONUMENT, PARK
(Map p64; ☑ 310-454-8212; www.parks.ca.gov; 1501 Will Rogers State Park Rd, Pacific Palisades; parking $12; ⊙ 8am-sunset, ranch house tours hourly 11am-3pm Thu & Fri, 10am-4pm Sat & Sun; ℙ; ⊟ MTA lines 2 & 302) This park sprawls across ranch land once owned by Will Rogers (1875–1935), an Oklahoma-born cowboy turned humorist, radio-show host and movie star (in the early 1930s he was the highest-paid actor in Hollywood). In the late '20s, he traded his Beverly Hills manse for a 31-room **ranch house** (Map p64; ☑ tours 310-454-8212 ext 103; www.parks. ca.gov/?page_id=26257; 1501 Will Rogers State Park Rd, Pacific Palisades, Will Rogers State Historic Park;

⊙ tours hourly 11am-3pm Thu & Fri, 10am-4pm Sat & Sun) and lived here until his tragic 1935 death in a plane crash.

Topanga Canyon   SCENIC DRIVE
(Topanga Canyon Rd) Take this sinuous road from the sea and climb into a primordial canyon cut deep in the Santa Monica Mountains. The drive lays bare naked boulders and reveals jagged chaparral-covered peaks from every hairpin turn. The road is shadowed by lazy oaks and glimmering sycamores, and the whole thing smells of wind-blown black sage and 'cowboy cologne' (artemisia).

Santa Monica

Santa Monica is LA's cute, alluring, hippie-chic little sister, its karmic counterbalance and, to many, its salvation. Surrounded by LA on three sides and the Pacific on the fourth, SaMo is a place where real-life Lebowskis sip White Russians next to martini-swilling Hollywood producers, celebrity chefs dine at family-owned taquerias, and soccer moms and career bachelors shop at abundant farmers markets. All the while, kids, out-of-towners and those who love them flock to wide beaches and the pier, where the landmark Ferris wheel and roller coaster welcome one and all.

Once the very end of the mythical Route 66, and still a tourist love affair, the **Santa Monica Pier** (Map p64; ☑ 310-458-8901; www. santamonicapier.org; ♿) dates back to 1908, is stocked with rides and arcade games and blessed with spectacular views, and is the city's most compelling landmark. After a stroll on the pier, hit the **beach** (Map p64; ☑ 310-458-8411; www.smgov.net/portals/beach; ⊟ Big Blue Bus 1). We like the stretch just north of Ocean Park Blvd. Or rent a bike or some skates from **Perry's Café** (Map p64; ☑ 310-939-0000; www.perryscafe.com; Ocean Front Walk; bikes per hour/day from $10/30, boogie boards $7/20; ⊙ 9am-7:30pm Mon-Fri, from 8:30am Sat & Sun) and explore the 22-mile **South Bay Bicycle Trail** (Map p64; ⊙ sunrise-sunset; ♿).

Venice

If you were born too late, and have always been a little jealous of the hippie heyday, come down to the Boardwalk and inhale a (not just) incense-scented whiff of Venice, a boho beach town and longtime haven for artists, new agers, road-weary tramps, freaks and free spirits. This is where Jim Morrison and the Doors lit their fire, where Arnold Schwarzenegger pumped himself to stardom, and the place the late Dennis Hopper once called home. These days, even as tech titans move in, the Old Venice spirit endures.

★ Venice Boardwalk   WATERFRONT
(Ocean Front Walk; Map p64; Venice Pier to Rose Ave) Life in Venice moves to a different rhythm and nowhere more so than on the famous Venice Boardwalk, officially known as Ocean Front Walk. It's a freak show, a human zoo and a wacky carnival alive with Hula-hoop magicians, old-timey jazz combos, solo distorted garage rockers and artists (good and bad) – as far as LA experiences go, it's a must.

Abbot Kinney Boulevard   AREA
(Map p64; ☐Big Blue Bus line 18) Abbot Kinney, who founded Venice in the early 1900s, would probably be delighted to find that one of Venice's best-loved streets bears his name. Sort of a seaside Melrose with a Venetian flavor, the mile-long stretch of Abbot Kinney Blvd between Venice Blvd and Main St is full of upscale boutiques, galleries, lofts and sensational restaurants. A few years back, GQ named it America's coolest street, and that cachet has only grown since.

Venice Skatepark   SKATEBOARDING
(Map p64; www.veniceskatepark.com; 1500 Ocean Front Walk; ⊗dawn-dusk) Long the destination of local skate punks, the concrete at this skate park has now been molded and steel-fringed into 17,000 sq ft of vert, tranny and street terrain with unbroken ocean views. The old-school-style skate run and the world-class pool are most popular for high flyers

and gawking spectators. Great photo opps, especially as the sun sets.

Muscle Beach   GYM
(Map p64; ☑310-399-2775; www.musclebeach.net; 1800 Ocean Front Walk; per day $10; ⊗8am-7pm Mon-Sat, 10am-4pm Sun Apr-Sep, shorter hours rest of year) Gym rats with an exhibitionist streak can get a tan and a workout at this famous outdoor gym right on the Venice Boardwalk, where Arnold Schwarzenegger and Franco Columbo once bulked up.

Venice Boardwalk Bike Rental   CYCLING
(Map p64; ☑310-396-2453; 517 Ocean Front Walk; 1hr/2hr/day bikes $7/12/20, surfboards $10/20/30, skates $7/12/20) Located in the Gingerbread Court complex, which was built by Charlie Chaplin, are a few shops, a cafe, some apartments above and this reliable Venice outfitter.

◉ Long Beach
Along LA County's southern shore and adjacent to Orange County, the twin ports of Long Beach and San Pedro provide attractions from ship to hip. Ramble around the art-deco ocean liner *Queen Mary* (p20), visit the Long Beach Museum of Art (p20) or immerse yourself in the Aquarium of the Pacific (p20). Then go for retro shopping and coastal cliff views.

⌒ Tours

Paramount Pictures   TOURS
(Map p64; ☑323-956-1777; www.paramountstudio tour.com; 5555 Melrose Ave, Hollywood; tours from $55; ⊗tours 9:30am-5pm, last tour 3pm) *Star Trek, Indiana Jones* and *Shrek* are among the

---

UNIVERSAL STUDIOS HOLLYWOOD

Although **Universal** (Map p64; ☑800-864-8377; www.universalstudioshollywood.com; 100 Universal City Plaza, Universal City; admission from $99, child under 3yr free; ⊗daily, hours vary; P ♿; Ⓜ Red Line to Universal City) is one of the world's oldest continuously operating movie studios, the chances of seeing any filming action here, let alone a star, are slim to none. But never mind. This theme park on the studio's back lot presents an entertaining mix of thrill rides, live-action shows and a tram tour.

First-timers should head straight for the 45-minute narrated **Studio Tour** aboard a multicar tram that drives around the soundstages in the front lot then heads to the back lot past the crash site from *War of the Worlds*, vehicles from *Jurassic Park* and the spooky Bates Motel from *Psycho*. Also prepare to brave a flash flood, survive a shark attack, a spitting dino and an 8.3-magnitude earthquake, before facing down King Kong in a new 3-D exhibit created by Peter Jackson. It's a bit hokey, but fun.

Newly opened, the phenomenally popular **Wizarding World of Harry Potter** is the park's biggest attraction. Climb aboard the Flight of the Hippogriff roller coaster and the 3-D ride Harry Potter and the Forbidden Journey.

blockbusters that originated at Paramount, the country's second-oldest movie studio and the only one still in Hollywood proper. Two-hour tours of the studio complex are offered year-round, taking in the back lots and soundstages. Guides are usually passionate and knowledgeable, offering fascinating insight into the studio's history and the movie-making process in general.

Esotouric
BUS

(☏213-915-8687; www.esotouric.com; tours $58) Discover LA's lurid and fascinating underbelly on these offbeat, insightful and entertaining walking and bus tours themed around famous crime sites (Black Dahlia, anyone?), literary lions (Chandler to Bukowski) and more.

Los Angeles Conservancy
WALKING

(☏213-623-2489; www.laconservancy.org; adult/child $15/10) Downtown LA's intriguing historical and architectural gems – from an art-deco penthouse to a beaux-arts ballroom and a dazzling silent-movie theater – are revealed on this nonprofit group's 2½-hour walking tours. To see some of LA's grand historic movie theaters from the inside, the conservancy also offers the Last Remaining Seats film series, screening classic movies in gilded theaters.

🛌 Sleeping

From rock-and-roll Downtown digs to fabled Hollywood hideaways, LA serves up a dizzying array of slumber options. The key is to plan well ahead. Do your research and find out which neighborhood is most convenient for your plans and best appeals to your style and interests. Trawl the internet for deals, and consider visiting between January and April, when room rates and occupancy are usually at their lowest (Oscars week aside).

HI Los Angeles-Santa Monica
HOSTEL $

(Map p64; ☏310-393-9913; www.hilosangeles.org; 1436 2nd St; dm low season $27-45, May-Oct $40-55, r with shared bath $109-140, with private bath $160-230; ➡✳@🛜; Ⓜ Expo Line to Downtown Santa Monica) Near the beach and Promenade, this hostel has an enviable location and recently modernized facilities that rival properties charging many times more. Its approximately 275 beds in single-sex dorms are clean and safe, private rooms are decorated with hipster chic, and public spaces (courtyard, library, TV room, dining room, communal kitchen) let you lounge and surf.

Samesun
HOSTEL $

(Map p64; ☏310-399-7649, reservations 888-718-8287; www.samesun.com; 25 Windward Ave, Venice; dm $39-60, r with shared/private bath from $110/150; ➡✳🛜) This hostel in a refurbished 1904 building has spectacular rooftop views of Venice Beach, bright, beachy swatches of color and four- to eight-person dorms, as well as some private rooms with either en suite or shared bathrooms. Breakfast is included and it's steps from the beach, restaurants and nightlife. All guests must present a passport.

Bissell House B&B
B&B $$

(Map p64; ☏626-441-3535; www.bissellhouse.com; 201 S Orange Grove Ave, South Pasadena; r from $159; P🛜✳) Antiques, hardwood floors and a crackling fireplace make this secluded Victorian (1887) B&B on 'Millionaire's Row' a bastion of warmth and romance. The hedge-framed garden feels like a sanctuary, and there's a pool for cooling off on hot summer days. The Prince Albert room has gorgeous wallpaper and a claw-foot tub. All seven rooms have private baths.

Mama Shelter
BOUTIQUE HOTEL $$

(Map p64; ☏323-785-6666; www.mamashelter.com; 6500 Selma Ave, Hollywood; r from $179; ✳@🛜; Ⓜ Red Line to Hollywood/Vine) Hip, affordable Mama Shelter keeps things playful with its lobby gumball machines, foosball table and live streaming of guests' selfies and videos. Standard rooms are small but cool, with quality beds and linen and subway-tiled bathrooms with decent-sized showers. Quirky in-room touches include movie scripts, masks and Apple TVs with free Netflix. The rooftop bar is one of LA's best.

Palihouse
BOUTIQUE HOTEL $$$

(Map p64; ☏310-394-1279; www.palihousesantamonica.com; 1001 3rd St, Santa Monica; r/studios from $315/350; P✳@🛜) LA's grooviest hotel brand (not named Ace) occupies the 38 rooms, studios and one-bedroom apartments of the 1927 Spanish-Colonial Embassy Hotel, with antique-meets-hipster-chic style. Each comfy room is slightly different, but look for picnic-table-style desks, and wallpaper with intricate sketches of animals. Most rooms have full kitchens (and we love the coffee mugs with lifelike drawings of fish).

Petit Ermitage
BOUTIQUE HOTEL $$$

(Map p64; ☏310-854-1114; www.petitermitage.com; 8822 Cynthia St, West Hollywood; ste from

🏃 City Walk
Downtown Revealed

START VERVE
END GRAND CENTRAL MARKET
LENGTH 2.5 MILES; 2½ TO THREE HOURS

Grab a coffee at **①Verve** then head one block northwest along 9th St to Broadway. Dominating the intersection is the turquoise-and-gold **②Eastern Columbia Building**, an art-deco beauty with a spectacular entrance. Head north on Broadway through the old theater district. Take note of the **③State Theatre**, **④Palace Theatre** and **⑤Los Angeles Theatre**. The Palace made a cameo in Michael Jackson's *Thriller* music video.

Turn left at 6th St and continue along for two blocks, passing **⑥Pershing Square** on your way to the historic **⑦Millennium Biltmore Hotel**; its cameos include *Ghostbusters*, *Fight Club* and *Mad Men*. Step inside for a look at its opulent interiors and ask for directions to the Historical Corridor to scan the fascinating photograph of the 1937 Academy Awards, held on this very site. Head right into Grand Ave, which will lead you to one of

Downtown's most extraordinary contemporary buildings: modern-art museum **⑧ Broad**. The flanking courtyard – planted with century-old olive trees – is home to hot-spot restaurant Otium. The restaurant's exterior features a fishy mural by British artist Damian Hirst. On the other side of the Broad is Frank Gehry's showstopping **⑨Walt Disney Concert Hall** (p61), home to the LA Philharmonic. Beside it is the LA Phil's former home, '60s throwback **⑩Dorothy Chandler Pavilion**. Across the street is **⑪Grand Park**, a good spot to catch your breath and post those pics using the free wi-fi.

Soaring at the end of the park is **⑫City Hall**. Head up its tower for stunning (and free) views of the city and take in the building's breathtaking rotunda on level three. Done, head south along Main St, turning right into 1st St and passing the art-deco headquarters of the **⑬Los Angeles Times**. Turn left onto Broadway, eyeing up the beautiful atrium inside the **⑭Bradbury Building** before a well-earned lunch at the appetite-whetting **⑮Grand Central Market**.

$315; Ⓟ✳@🛜✉) Bohemian-chic environs with Turkish rugs, old-world antiques, rooftop bars and fine booze set apart this intimate, one-of-a-kind hotel. No two of its 79 suites are the same, but all feature Venetian-style plaster walls, fireplaces, fun minibar snacks, and some have wet bar and kitchenette. Guests have exclusive access to an impressive art collection lining the halls, lots of chill spaces, and the rooftop bar/butterfly sanctuary.

✕ Eating

✕ Downtown Los Angeles & Boyle Heights

★ Mariscos 4 Vientos   MEXICAN $
(Map p64; ☑323-266-4045; www.facebook.com/Mariscos4Vientos; 3000 E Olympic Blvd; dishes $2.25-14; ◷9am-5:30pm Mon-Thu, to 6pm Fri-Sun) You'll find the greatest shrimp taco of your life at no-frills Mariscos 4 Vientos. Order from the truck (if you're in a hurry) or grab a table inside the bustling dining room. Either way, surrender to corn tortillas folded and stuffed with fresh shrimp, then fried and smothered in *pico de gallo* (fresh salsa).

Maccheroni Republic   ITALIAN $$
(Map p64; ☑213-346-9725; www.maccheronirepublic.com; 332 S Broadway; mains $11-18; ◷11:30am-2:30pm & 5:30-10pm Mon-Thu, 11:30am-2:30pm & 5:30-10:30pm Fri, 11:30am-10:30pm Sat, 11:30am-9pm Sun) Tucked away on a still-ungentrified corner is this gem with a leafy heated patio and tremendous Italian slow-cooked food. Don't miss the *polpettine di gamberi* (flattened ground shrimp cakes fried in olive oil), and its range of delicious housemade pastas. Perfectly al dente, the pasta is made using organic semolina flour and served with gorgeous crusty bread to mop up the sauce.

★ Bestia   ITALIAN $$$
(Map p64; ☑213-514-5724; www.bestiala.com; 2121 7th Pl; pizzas $16-19, pasta $19-29, mains $28-120; ◷5-11pm Sun-Thu, to midnight Fri & Sat; Ⓟ) Years on, this loud, buzzing, industrial dining space remains the most sought-after reservation in town (book at least a week ahead). The draw remains its clever, produce-driven takes on Italian flavors, from charred pizzas topped with housemade 'nduja (a spicy Calabrian paste), to a sultry stinging-nettle raviolo with egg, mixed mushrooms, hazelnut and ricotta. The wine list celebrates the boutique and obscure.

Otium   MODERN AMERICAN $$$
(Map p64; ☑213-935-8500; http://otiumla.com; 222 S Hope St; dishes $15-45; ◷11:30am-2:30pm & 5:30-10pm Tue-Thu, 11:30am-2:30pm & 5:30-11pm Fri, 11am-2:30pm & 5:30-11pm Sat, 11am-2:30pm & 5:30-10pm Sun; 🛜) In a modernist pavilion beside the Broad is this fun, of-the-moment hot spot helmed by chef Timothy Hollingsworth. Prime ingredients conspire in unexpected ways, from the crunch of wild rice and amaranth in an eye-candy salad of avocado, beets and pomegranate, to a twist of lime and sake in flawlessly al dente whole-wheat bucatini with Dungeness crab.

✕ Hollywood

Salt's Cure   MODERN AMERICAN $$
(Map p64; ☑323-465-7258; http://saltscure.com; 1155 N Highland Ave; mains $17-34; ◷11am-11pm Mon-Thu, to midnight Fri, 10am-midnight Sat, 10am-11pm Sun) Wood-paneled, concrete-floored Salt's Cure is an out, proud locavore. From the in-season vegetables to the house-butchered and cured meats, the menu celebrates all things Californian. Expect sophisticated takes on rustic comfort grub, whether it's *capicollo* (pork cold cut) with chili paste or tender duck breast paired with impressively light oatmeal griddle cakes and blackberry compote.

Musso & Frank Grill   STEAK $$
(Map p64; ☑323-467-7788; www.mussoandfrank.com; 6667 Hollywood Blvd; mains $15-52; ◷11am-11pm Tue-Sat, 4-9pm Sun; Ⓟ; Ⓜ Red Line to Hollywood/Highland) Hollywood history hangs in the thick air at Musso & Frank Grill, Tinseltown's oldest eatery (since 1919). Charlie Chaplin used to knock back vodka gimlets, Raymond Chandler penned scripts in the high-backed booths, and movie deals were made on the old phone at the back (the booth closest to the phone is favored by Jack Nicholson and Johnny Depp).

★ Providence   MODERN AMERICAN $$$
(Map p64; ☑323-460-4170; www.providencela.com; 5955 Melrose Ave; lunch mains $40-45, tasting menus $120-250; ◷noon-2pm & 6-10pm Mon-Fri, 5:30-10pm Sat, 5:30-9pm Sun; Ⓟ) The top restaurant pick by preeminent LA food critic Jonathan Gold for four years running, this two-starred Michelin darling turns superlative seafood into arresting, nuanced dishes that might see abalone paired with eggplant, turnip and nori, or spiny lobster conspire decadently with macadamia nut and earthy black truffle. À la carte options are available at lunch only.

Santa Monica & Venice

Santa Monica & Venice

✗ West Hollywood & Mid-City

Night + Market THAI **$**

(Map p64; ☑ 310-275-9724; www.nightmarketla.
com; 9043 W Sunset Blvd, West Hollywood; dishes $8-
15; ☉ 11:30am-2:30pm Tue-Thu, 5-10:30pm Tue-Sun)
Set behind Talésai, a long-running Thai joint,
this related kitchen pumps out outstanding
Thai street food and Thai-inspired hybrids
such as catfish tamales. Pique the appetite
with *larb lanna* (chopped pork salad), push
the envelope with rich pork *toro* (grilled pork
collar) then move onto winners like *chien-
grei* herb sausage and a pad Thai that makes
standard LA versions seem overly sweet.

Gracias Madre VEGAN, MEXICAN **$$**

(Map p64; ☑ 323-978-2170; www.graciasmadreweho.
com; 8905 Melrose Ave, West Hollywood; mains lunch
$10-13, dinner $12-18; ☉ 11am-11pm Mon-Fri, from
10am Sat & Sun; ☑) Gracias Madre shows just
how tasty – and chichi – organic, plant-based
Mexican cooking can be. Sit on the gracious
patio or in the cozy interior and feel good as
you eat healthy: sweet-potato flautas, coconut
'bacon,' plantain 'quesadillas,' plus salads and
bowls. We're consistently surprised at innova-
tions like cashew 'cheese,' mushroom 'chorizo'
and heart-of-palm 'crab cakes.'

Ray's MODERN AMERICAN **$$$**

(Map p64; ☑ 323-857-6180; www.raysandstarkbar.
com; 5905 Wilshire Blvd, Los Angeles County Museum of Art, Mid-City; mains $17-36; ☉ 11:30am-8pm

Map labels
Pacific Palisades (1.6mi);
Malibu (17mi)
Washington Ave
California Ave Milo & Olive (1.4mi);
Brentwood (2.6mi)
Wilshire Blvd
SANTA MONICA
Palisades Beach Rd
Ocean Ave
3rd St
4th St
Santa Monica Blvd
7th St
Lincoln Blvd
Broadway
Colorado Ave
Santa Monica Fwy
South Bay Bicycle Trail
Pico Blvd
Bay St
Neilson Way
2nd St
4th St
6th St
Ocean Park Blvd
Santa Monica Bay
Hill St
Ashland Ave
Barnard Way
Santa Monica State Beach
Marine St
3rd St
Ocean Front Walk
Rose Ave
Speedway
2nd St
Sunset Ave
Pacific Ave
Main St
Broadway St
Venice Beach
Abbot Kinney Blvd
San Juan Ave
Market St
Windward Ave
Grand Blvd
VENICE
Ocean Front Walk
Speedway
N Venice Blvd
S Venice Blvd
Canal Park

Mon-Tue & Thu, to 10pm Fri, 10am-8pm Sat & Sun; [P]; [⊡] MTA 20) Seldom does a restaurant blessed with as golden a location as this one – on the plaza of LACMA (p63) – live up to the address. Ray's does. Menus change seasonally and often daily with farm-to-table fresh ingredients – some grown in the restaurant's own garden. You can expect some form of burrata, kale salad and pizzas to be on the menu.

✖ Beverly Hills

⭐ Joss Cuisine   CHINESE $$
(Map p64; [✍] 310-277-3888; www.josscuisine.com; 9919 S Santa Monica Blvd; dishes $15-30; ⊙ noon-3pm Mon-Fri, 5:30-10pm daily) With fans including Barbra Streisand, Gwyenth Paltrow and Jackie Chan, this warm, intimate nosh spot serves up superlative, MSG-free Chinese cuisine at noncelebrity prices. Premium produce drives a menu of exceptional dishes, from flawless dim sum and ginger fish broth, to crispy mustard prawns and one of the finest Peking ducks you'll encounter this side of East Asia. Reservations recommended.

✖ Santa Monica

⭐ Santa Monica
Farmers Markets   MARKET $
(Map p64; www.smgov.net/portals/farmersmarket; Arizona Ave, btwn 2nd & 3rd Sts; ⊙ Arizona Ave 8:30am-1:30pm Wed, 8am-1pm Sat, Main St 8:30am-1:30pm Sun; [♿]) ✦ You haven't really experienced Santa Monica until you've explored one of its weekly outdoor farmers markets stocked with organic fruits, vegetables, flowers, baked goods and freshly shucked oysters. The highlight is the Wednesday market, around the intersection of 3rd and Arizona – it's the biggest and arguably the best for fresh produce, and often patrolled by local chefs.

Milo & Olive   ITALIAN $$
(Map p64; [✍] 310-453-6776; www.miloandolive.com; 2723 Wilshire Blvd; dishes $7-20; ⊙ 7am-11pm) We love this place for its small-batch wines, incredible pizzas, terrific breakfasts (creamy polenta and poached eggs, anyone?), breads and pastries, all of which you may enjoy at the marble bar or shoulder to shoulder with new friends at one of two common tables. It's a cozy neighborhood joint so it doesn't take reservations.

Cassia   SOUTHEAST ASIAN $$$
(Map p64; [✍] 310-393-6699; 1314 7th St; appetizers $12-24, mains $18-77; ⊙ 5-10pm Sun-Thu, to 11pm Fri & Sat; [P]) Ever since it opened in 2015, open,

airy Cassia has made about every local and national 'best' list of LA restaurants. Chef Bryant Ng draws on his Chinese-Singaporean heritage in dishes such as *kaya* toast (with coconut jam, butter and a slow-cooked egg), 'sunbathing' prawns, and the encompassing Vietnamese *pot au feu:* short-rib stew, veggies, bone marrow and delectable accompaniments.

✖ Venice

Butcher's Daughter   VEGETARIAN, CAFE $$
(Map p64; [✍] 310-981-3004; www.thebutchersdaughter.com; 1205 Abbot Kinney Blvd; dishes $10-22; ⊙ 8am-10pm) Find yourself a seat around the central counter or facing busy Abbot Kinney to tuck in to stone-oven pizzas, hand-made pastas and veggie faves such as whole roasted cauliflower and butternut-squash risotto. It's Aussie-owned, meaning great coffee. Light, airy and fun. Welcome to California!

Gjelina   AMERICAN $$$
(Map p64; [✍] 310-450-1429; www.gjelina.com; 1429 Abbot Kinney Blvd; veggies, salads & pizzas $10-18, large plates $15-45; ⊙ 8am-midnight; [♿]; [⊡] Big Blue Bus line 18) If one restaurant defines the new Venice, it's this. Carve out a slip on the communal table between the hipsters and yuppies, or get your own slab of wood on the elegant stone terrace, and dine on imaginative small plates (raw yellowtail spiced with chili and mint and drenched in olive oil and blood orange) and sensational thin-crust, wood-fired pizza.

🍸 Drinking

🍸 Downtown Los Angeles & Boyle Heights

Everson Royce Bar   COCKTAIL BAR
(Map p64; [✍] 213-335-6166; www.erbla.com; 1936 E 7th St; ⊙ 5pm-2am) Don't be fooled by the unceremonious gray exterior. Behind that wall lies a hopping Arts District hangout, with a buzzy, bulb-strung outdoor patio. The barkeeps here are some of the city's best, using craft liquor to concoct drinks such as the prickly-pear Mateo Street Margarita. Bar bites are equally scrumptious, including the roasted pork-belly steamed buns.

Clifton's Republic   COCKTAIL BAR
(Map p64; [✍] 213-627-1673; www.cliftonsla.com; 648 S Broadway; ⊙ 11am-midnight Tue-Thu, to 2am Fri, 10am-2:30am Sat, 10am-midnight Sun; [☎]; [Ⓜ] Red/

Purple Lines to Pershing Sq) Opened in 1935 and back after a $10-million renovation, multi-level, mixed-crowd Clifton's defies description. You can chow retro-cafeteria classics (meals around $14.75) by a forest waterfall, order drinks from a Gothic church altar, watch burlesque performers shimmy in the shadow of a 40ft faux redwood, or slip through a glass-paneled door to a luxe tiki paradise where DJs spin in a repurposed speedboat.

Upstairs at the Ace Hotel   BAR

(Map p64; www.acehotel.com/losangeles; 929 S Broadway; ⊙11am-2am) What's not to love about a rooftop bar with knockout Downtown views, powerful cocktails and a luxe, safari-inspired fit out? Perched on the 14th floor of the Ace Hotel, this chilled, sophisticated space has on-point DJs and specially commissioned artworks that include an installation made using Skid Row blankets.

🍷 Hollywood

Sassafras Saloon   BAR

(Map p64; ☑323-467-2800; www.sassafrashollywood.com; 1233 N Vine St; ⊙5pm-2am) You'll be pining for the bayou at the hospitable Sassafras Saloon, where hanging moss and life-size facades evoke sultry Savannah. Cocktails include a barrel-aged Sazerac, while themed nights include live jazz on Sunday and Monday, brass bands and acrobatics on Tuesday, burlesque and blues on Wednesday, karaoke on Thursday, and DJ-spun tunes on Friday and Saturday.

Sayers Club   CLUB

(Map p64; ☑323-871-8233; www.facebook.com/TheSayersClub; 1645 Wilcox Ave; cover varies; ⊙9pm-2am Tue & Thu-Sat; Ⓜ Red Line to Hollywood/Vine)

When established stars such as the Black Keys, and even movie stars such as Joseph Gordon-Levitt, decide to play secret shows in intimate environs, they come to the back room at this brick-house Hollywood nightspot, where the booths are leather, the lighting is moody and the music always satisfying.

No Vacancy   BAR

(Map p64; ☑323-465-1902; www.novacancyla.com; 1727 N Hudson Ave; ⊙8pm-2am; Ⓜ Red Line to Hollywood/Vine) If you prefer your cocktail sessions with plenty of wow factor, make a reservation online, style up (no sportswear, shorts or logos) and head to this old shingled Victorian. A vintage scene of dark timber panels and elegant banquettes, it has bars in nearly every corner, tended by clever barkeeps while burlesque dancers and a tightrope walker entertain the droves of party people.

🍷 West Hollywood & Mid-City

★ **Abbey**   GAY & LESBIAN

(Map p64; ☑310-289-8410; www.theabbeyweho.com; 692 N Robertson Blvd, West Hollywood; ⊙11am-2am Mon-Thu, from 10am Fri, from 9am Sat & Sun) It's been called the best gay bar in the world, and who are we to argue? Once a humble coffeehouse, the Abbey has expanded into WeHo's bar/club/restaurant of record. Always a party, it has so many different flavored martinis and mojitos that you'd think they were invented here, plus a full menu of upscale pub food (mains $14 to $21).

Bar Marmont   BAR

(Map p64; ☑323-650-0575; www.chateaumarmont.com; 8171 Sunset Blvd, West Hollywood;

LA'S BEST ENTERTAINMENT VENUES

Walt Disney Concert Hall (p61) Sublime acoustics, striking architecture and the world-class LA Philharmonic.

Hollywood Bowl (Map p64; ☑323-850-2000; www.hollywoodbowl.com; 2301 N Highland Ave; ⊙Jun-Sep) LA's most famous outdoor concert venue, with everything from classical to jazz.

Mark Taper Forum (Map p64; ☑213-628-2772; www.centertheatregroup.org; 135 N Grand Ave) Part of the multivenue Music Center and home to award-winning theater.

Ahmanson Theatre (Map p64; ☑213-628-2772; www.centertheatregroup.org; 135 N Grand Ave) Known for its buzz-inducing musicals on their way to or from Broadway.

Pantages Theatre (Map p64; ☑323-468-1770; http://hollywoodpantages.com; 6233 Hollywood Blvd) 'It' status Broadway musicals in a historic Hollywood venue.

Geffen Playhouse (Map p64; ☑310-208-5454; www.geffenplayhouse.com; 10886 Le Conte Ave, Westwood) A well-regarded center for classic American theater and fresh new works.

LA'S TOP SHOPS

Melrose Ave & Robertson Blvd (Map p64) Two uber-fashionable strips with hip, unique retailers luring trendsetting celebs.

Abbot Kinney Blvd (p66) An eclectic, artful mix of unique and indie boutiques by the beach in Venice.

Last Bookstore in Los Angeles (Map p64; ☑ 213-488-0599; www.lastbookstorela.com; 453 S Spring St; ☺ 10am-10pm Mon-Thu, to 11pm Fri & Sat, to 9pm Sun) A sprawling Downtown wonder, with new and used titles and vinyl to boot.

Amoeba Music (Map p64; ☑ 323-245-6400; www.amoeba.com; 6400 W Sunset Blvd; ☺ 10:30am-11pm Mon-Sat, 11am-10pm Sun) An oversized Valhalla for music lovers in Hollywood.

Rose Bowl Flea Market (Map p64; www.rgcshows.com; 1001 Rose Bowl Dr, Pasadena; admission from $9; ☺ 9am-4:30pm 2nd Sun each month, last entry 3pm, early admission from 5am) The granddaddy of all flea markets awaits in Pasadena.

☺ 6pm-2am) Elegant, but not stuck up; been around, yet still cherished. With high ceilings, molded walls and terrific martinis, the famous and the wish-they-weres still flock here. If you time it right you might see celebs – the Marmont doesn't share who (or else they'd stop coming – get it?). Come midweek. Weekends are for amateurs.

ℹ️ Information

TOURIST INFORMATION

Beverly Hills Visitors Center (Map p64; ☑ 310-248-1015; www.lovebeverlyhills.com; 9400 S Santa Monica Blvd, Beverly Hills; ☺ 9am-5pm Mon-Fri, from 10am Sat & Sun; 🛜) Sightseeing, activities, dining and accommodations information focused on the Beverly Hills area.

Downtown LA Visitor Center (Map p64; www.discoverlosangeles.com; Union Station, 800 N Alameda St; ☺ 9am-5pm; Ⓜ Red/Purple/Gold Lines to Union Station) Maps and general tourist information in the lobby of Union Station.

Visit West Hollywood (Map p64; www.visitwesthollywood.com; Pacific Design Center Blue Bldg, 8687 Melrose Ave, Suite M60, West Hollywood; ☺ 9am-5pm Mon-Fri; 🛜) Information on attractions, accommodations, tours and more in the West Hollywood area.

GETTING AROUND

Bicycle

Most buses have bike racks, and bikes ride for free, although you must securely load and unload them yourself. Bicycles are also allowed on Metro Rail trains at all times.

LA has a number of bike-sharing programs. The following are especially useful for visitors:

Metro Bike Share (https://bikeshare.metro.net) Has more than 60 self-serve bike kiosks in the Downtown area, including Chinatown, Little Tokyo and the Arts District. Pay using your debit

or credit card ($3.50 per 30 minutes) or TAP card, though you will first need to register it on the Metro Bike Share website. The smartphone app offers real-time bike and rack availability.

Breeze Bike Share (www.santamonicabikeshare.com; per hour $7, monthly/annually $25/99) Runs self-serve kiosks all over Santa Monica, Venice and Marina del Rey.

Car & Motorcycle

Unless time is no factor – or money is extremely tight – you're going to want to spend some time behind the wheel, although this means contending with some of the worst traffic in the country.

Parking at motels and cheaper hotels is usually free, while fancier ones charge anywhere from $8 to around $45 for the privilege.

The usual international car-rental agencies have branches at LAX and throughout LA. For Harley rentals, go to **Route 66** (www.rt66mc.com). Rates start from $149 per six hours, or $185 for one day. Discounts are available for longer rentals.

Public Transportation

Most public transportation is handled by **Metro** (☑ 323-466-3876; www.metro.net), which offers maps, schedules and trip-planning help through its website.

To ride Metro trains and buses, buy a reusable TAP card. Available from TAP vending machines at Metro stations with a $1 surcharge, the cards allow you to add a preset cash value or day passes. The regular base fare is $1.75 per boarding, or $7 for a day pass with unlimited rides. Both single-trip tickets and TAP cards loaded with a day pass are available on Metro buses (ensure you have the exact change). When using a TAP card, tap the card against the sensor at station entrances and aboard buses.

TAP cards are accepted on DASH and municipal bus services and can be reloaded at vending machines or online on the TAP website (www.taptogo.net).

Santa Barbara & the Central Coast

Coastal Hwy 1 pulls out all the stops, scenery wise. Flower-power Santa Cruz and the historic port town of Monterey are gateways to the rugged wilderness of the coast.

SANTA BARBARA

📞 805 / POP 91,842

Perfect weather, beautiful buildings, excellent bars and restaurants, and activities for all tastes and budgets make Santa Barbara a great place to live (as the locals will proudly tell you) and a must-see place for visitors to Southern California. Check out the Spanish mission church first, then just see where the day takes you.

👁 Sights & Activities

Stearns Wharf
See p22.

★**Santa Barbara County Courthouse**   HISTORIC BUILDING
(📞805-962-6464; http://sbcourthouse.org; 1100 Anacapa St; ⊘8am-5pm Mon-Fri, 10am-5pm Sat & Sun) FREE Built in Spanish-Moorish Revival style in 1929, the courthouse features hand-painted ceilings, wrought-iron chandeliers, and tiles from Tunisia and Spain. On the 2nd floor, step inside the hushed mural room depicting Spanish-colonial history, then head up to El Mirador, the 85ft clock tower, for arch-framed panoramas of the city, ocean and mountains. You can explore on your own, but you'll get a lot more out of a free, one-hour docent-guided tour: 2pm daily, plus 10:30am Monday to Friday.

★**MOXI**   MUSEUM
(Wolf Museum of Exploration + Innovation; 📞805-770-5000; www.moxi.org; 125 State St; adult/child $14/10; ⊘10am-5pm; 🅿) Part of the regeneration of this neglected strip of State St, Moxi's three floors filled with hands-on displays covering science, arts and technology themes will tempt families in, even when it's not raining outside. If all that interactivity gets too much, head to the roof terrace for views across Santa Barbara and a nerve-challenging walk across a glass ceiling.

Mission Santa Barbara   CHURCH
(📞805-682-4713; www.santabarbaramission.org; 2201 Laguna St; adult/child 5-17yr $9/4; ⊘9am-5pm, last entry 4:15pm; 🅿) California's 'Queen of the Missions' reigns above the city on a hilltop perch over a mile north of downtown. Its imposing Ionic facade, an architectural homage to an ancient Roman chapel, is topped by an unusual twin bell tower. Inside the mission's 1820 stone church, notice the striking Chumash artwork. In the cemetery the elaborate mausoleums of early California settlers stand out, while the graves of thousands of Chumash lie largely forgotten.

Architectural Foundation of Santa Barbara
WALKING

(☎ 805-965-6307; www.afsb.org; adult/child under 12yr $10/free; ⊘ 10am Sat & Sun weather permitting) Take time out of your weekend for a fascinating 90-minute guided walking tour of downtown's art, history and architecture. No reservations required; call or check the website for meet-up times and places.

Surf Happens
SURFING

(☎ 805-966-3613; http://surfhappens.com; 13 E Haley St; 2hr private lesson from $160; ⬚) Welcoming families, beginners and 'Surf Happens Sisters,' these highly reviewed classes and camps led by expert staff incorporate the Zen of surfing. In summer, you'll begin your spiritual wave-riding journey. Make reservations in advance. The office is based in downtown Santa Barbara.

⚜ Festivals & Events

Summer Solstice Celebration
FESTIVAL

(☎ 805-965-3396; www.solsticeparade.com; ⊘ late Jun) FREE Kicking off summer, this wildly popular and wacky float parade down State St feels like something out of Burning Man.

Old Spanish Days Fiesta
CULTURE, ART

(www.oldspanishdays-fiesta.org; ⊘ late Jul-early Aug) FREE The entire city fills up for this long-running – if slightly overblown – festival celebrating Santa Barbara's Spanish and Mexican colonial heritage.

🛏 Sleeping

Prepare for sticker shock: even basic motel rooms by the beach command over $200 in summer. Don't arrive without reservations and expect to find anything reasonably priced, especially not on weekends. A good selection of renovated motels are tucked between the harbor and the 101 freeway, just about walking distance to everything. Cheaper motels cluster along upper State St and Hwy 101 northbound to Goleta and southbound to Carpinteria, Ventura and Camarillo.

Santa Barbara Auto Camp
CAMPGROUND $$

(☎ 888-405-7553; http://autocamp.com/sb; 2717 De La Vina St; d $175-215; P✳🅿🐾) 🍴 Ramp up the retro chic and bed down with vintage style in one of five shiny metal Airstream trailers parked near upper State St, north of downtown. All five architect-designed trailers have unique perks, such as a claw-foot tub or extra twin-size beds for kiddos, as well as full kitchen and complimentary cruiser

bikes to borrow. Book ahead; two-night minimum may apply. Pet fee $25.

Marina Beach Motel
MOTEL $$

(☎ 805-963-9311; www.marinabeachmotel.com; 21 Bath St; r from $155; P✳🅿🐾) Family-owned since 1942, this whitewashed, one-story motor lodge that wraps around a grassy courtyard is worth a stay just for the location. Right by the beach, tidy remodeled rooms are comfy enough and some have kitchenette. Complimentary beach-cruiser bikes to borrow. Small pets OK (fee $15).

★ Hotel Californian
BOUTIQUE HOTEL $$$

(www.thehotelcalifornian.com; 36 State St; r from $400; P✳@🅿🐾) Hotel Californian is the new kid on the once-rundown block that is the lower end of State St. Spearheading the area's rehabilitation, it would be worth staying just for the prime location (next to the beach, Stearns Wharf and the Funk Zone) but its appeal goes way beyond geography. A winning architectural mix of Spanish Colonial and North African Moorish styles set a glamorous tone.

★ Belmondo El Encanto
LUXURY HOTEL $$$

(☎ 805-845-5800; www.elencanto.com; 800 Alvarado Pl; r from $475; P✳@🅿🐾🐾) Triumphantly reborn in 2013, this 1908 icon of Santa Barbara style is a hilltop hideaway for travelers who demand the very best of everything. An infinity pool gazes out at the Pacific, while

---

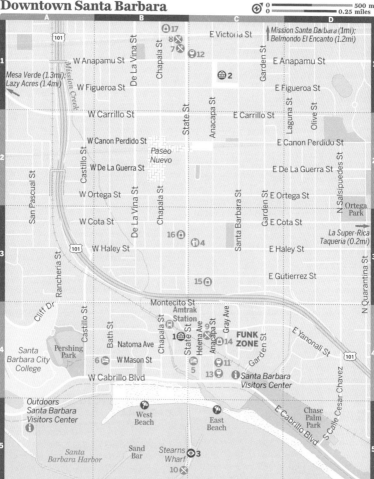

flower-filled gardens, fireplace lounges, a full-service spa and private bungalows with sun-drenched patios concoct the glamorous atmosphere perfectly fitted to SoCal socialites.

✕ Eating

Restaurants abound along downtown's State St and by the waterfront, where you'll find a few gems among the touristy claptrap. More creative kitchens are found in the Funk Zone, while east of downtown, Milpas St has great taco shops. It's wise to book well in advance (a couple of weeks) for popular places or somewhere you're particularly keen to eat.

Arigato Sushi JAPANESE $

(☑805-965-6074; www.arigatosb.com; 1225 State St; rolls from $7; ⊙5:30-10pm Sun-Thu, to 10:30pm Fri & Sat; ✿ ☑) Phenomenally popular Arigato Sushi always has people milling around waiting for a table (no reservations taken) but it's worth the wait. Traditional and more unusual sushi, including lots of vegetarian options, plus salads and a dizzying array of hot and cold starters will make you order a sake pronto just to help you get through the menu.

La Super-Rica Taqueria MEXICAN $

(☑805-963-4940; 622 N Milpas St; ⊙11am-9pm Thu-Mon) It's small, there's usually a line and

Downtown Santa Barbara

the decor is basic, but all that's forgotten once you've tried the most authentic Mexican food in Santa Barbara. The fish tacos, tamales and other Mexican staples have been drawing locals and visitors here for decades, and were loved by TV chef and author Julia Childs.

Mesa Verde　　　　　　　　　　VEGAN $$
(☏805-963-4474; http://mesaverderestaurant. com; 1919 Cliff Dr; mains $15-21; ⊙11am-9pm; ♪) ⚑ Perusing the menu is usually a quick job for vegetarians – but not at Mesa Verde. There are so many delicious, innovative all-vegan options on offer here (the tacos with jackfruit are a highlight) that meat-avoiding procrastinators will be in torment. If in doubt, pick a selection and brace yourself for flavor-packed delights. Meat-eaters welcome (and possibly converted).

**Santa Barbara
Shellfish Company**　　　　　SEAFOOD $$
(☏805-966-6676; http://shellfishco.com; 230 Stearns Wharf; dishes $4-19; ⊙11am-9pm; ♠☺) 'From sea to skillet to plate' sums up this end-of-the-wharf seafood shack that's more of a buzzing counter joint than a sit-down restaurant. Chase away the seagulls as you chow down on garlic-baked clams, crab cakes and coconut-fried shrimp at wooden picnic tables outside. Awesome lobster bisque, ocean views and the same location for almost 40 years.

Bouchon　　　　　　　　　CALIFORNIAN $$$
(☏805-730-1160; www.bouchonsantabarbara.com; 9 W Victoria St; mains $26-36; ⊙5-9pm Sun-Thu, to 10pm Fri & Sat) ⚑ The perfect, unhurried follow up to a day in the Wine Country is to feast on the bright, flavorful California cooking at pretty Bouchon (meaning 'wine cork'). A seasonally changing menu spotlights locally grown farm produce and ranched meats that marry beautifully with almost three-dozen regional wines available by the glass. Lovebirds, book a table on the candlelit patio.

Lark　　　　　　　　　　　CALIFORNIAN $$$
(☏805-284-0370; www.thelarksb.com; 131 Anacapa St; shared plates $7-17, mains $19-48; ⊙5-10pm Tue-Sun, bar to midnight) ⚑ There's no better place in Santa Barbara County to taste the bountiful farm and fishing goodness of this stretch of SoCal coast. Named after an antique Pullman railway car, this chef-run restaurant in the Funk Zone morphs its menu with the seasons, presenting unique flavor combinations such as crispy Brussels sprouts with dates or harissa and honey chicken. Make reservations.

⊓ Drinking & Nightlife

On lower State St, most of the watering holes have happy hours, tiny dance floors and rowdy college nights. The Funk Zone's eclectic mix of bars and wine-tasting rooms provides a trendier, more sophisticated alternative.

Good Lion　　　　　　　　COCKTAIL BAR
(☏805-845-8754; www.goodlioncocktails.com; 1212 State St; ⊙4pm-1am) Grab a cocktail at the beautiful blue-tiled bar, then grab a book from the shelves and settle into a leather banquette in this petite place that has a cool Montmartre-turn-of-the-20th-century feel (candles on the tables and absinthe in many of the cocktails helps with the Parisian atmosphere).

Municipal Winemakers　　　　　　　BAR
(☏805-931-6864; www.municipalwinemakers.com; 22 Anacapa St; tastings $12; ⊙11am-8pm Sun-Wed, to 11pm Thu-Sat; ☺) Dave, the owner of Municipal Winemakers, studied the vine arts in Australia and France before applying his knowledge in this industrially decorated tasting room and bar. Pale Pink rosé is a staple and hugely popular – enjoy a bottle on the large patio. For food, you can't beat the cheese plate, or at weekends a burger van parks outside.

Brass Bear CRAFT BEER

(📞805-770-7651; www.brassbearbrewing.com; 28 Anacapa St; ☺noon-9pm Wed & Sun-Mon, to 10pm Thu, to 11pm Fri & Sat; 🖶 🐾) Large glasses of wine and beer and a great grilled cheese make this cozy place, located up an alley off Anacapa, a worthy detour. Friendly staff add to the convivial atmosphere. Just be careful not to drink too much and end up taking some of the for-sale art on the walls home with you.

🛍 Shopping

REI SPORTS & OUTDOORS

(📞805-560-1938; www.rei.com; 321 Anacapa St; ☺10am-9pm Mon-Fri, to 7pm Sat, to 6pm Sun) If you forgot your tent or rock-climbing carabiners at home, the West Coast's most popular independent co-op outdoor retailer is the place to pick up outdoor recreation gear, active clothing, sport shoes and topographic maps.

Channel Islands Surfboards SPORTS & OUTDOORS

(📞805-966-7213; www.cisurfboards.com; 36 Anacapa St; ☺10am-7pm Mon-Sat, 11am-5pm Sun) Are you ready to take home a handcrafted, Southern California–born surfboard? Down in the Funk Zone, this surf shack is the place for innovative pro-worthy board designs, as well as surfer threads and beanie hats.

ℹ Information

MEDICAL SERVICES

Santa Barbara Cottage Hospital (📞805-682-7111; www.cottagehealthsystem.org; 400 W Pueblo St; ☺24hr) Emergency room (ER) open 24 hours.

TOURIST INFORMATION

Outdoors Santa Barbara Visitors Center (📞805-456-8752; http://outdoorsb.sbmm.org; 4th fl, 113 Harbor Way; ☺11am-5pm) In the same building as the maritime museum, this volunteer-staffed visitor center offers info on Channel Islands National Park and a harbor-view deck.

Santa Barbara Visitors Center (📞805-568-1811, 805-965-3021; www.santabarbaraca.com; 1 Garden St; ☺9am-5pm Mon-Sat, 10am-5pm Sun, closes 1hr earlier Nov-Jan) Pick up maps and brochures while consulting with the helpful but busy staff. The website offers free downloadable DIY touring maps and itineraries, from famous movie locations to wine trails, art galleries and outdoors fun. Self-pay metered parking lot nearby.

Los Padres National Forest Headquarters (📞805-968-6640; www.fs.usda.gov/lpnf; 6750 Navigator Way, Goleta; ☺8am-noon & 1-4:30pm Mon-Fri) HQ for the whole Los Padres National Forest. Pick up maps, recreation passes etc.

CENTRAL COAST

Pismo Beach

📞805 / POP 7861

Backed by a wooden pier that stretches toward the setting sun, Pismo Beach is where James Dean once trysted with Pier Angeli. Fronted by an invitingly wide, sandy beach, this 1950s-retro town feels like somewhere straight out of *Rebel Without a Cause* or *American Graffiti*. If you're looking for a sand-and-surf respite from coastal road tripping, break your journey here. Pismo likes to call itself the 'Clam Capital of the World,' but these days the beach is pretty much clammed out. You'll have better luck catching something fishy off the pier, where you can rent rods. To rent a wet suit, body board or surfboard, cruise nearby surf shops.

◉ Sights & Activities

Sunset Drive-In CINEMA

See p22.

Pismo Beach Monarch Butterfly Grove PARK

(📞805-773-5301; www.monarchbutterfly.org; Hwy 1; ☺sunrise-sunset; 🖶) 🎫 **FREE** From November through February, over 25,000 black-and-orange monarchs make their winter home here. Forming dense clusters in the tops of eucalyptus trees, they might easily be mistaken for leaves. Between 10am and 4pm during the roosting season, volunteers can tell you all about the insects' incredible journey, which outlasts any single generation of butterflies. Look for a gravel parking pullout on the ocean side of Pacific Blvd (Hwy 1), just south of Pismo State Beach's North Beach Campground.

Central Coast Kayaks KAYAKING

(📞805-773-3500; www.centralcoastkayaks.com; 1879 Shell Beach Rd, Shell Beach; kayak or SUP set rental $20-25, classes $60-75, tours $60-120; ☺9am-4:30pm Mon-Tue & Thu-Fri, to 5pm Sat-Sun) Paddle out among sea otters and seals and through mesmerizing sea caves, rock grottos, arches and kelp forests. Wet suits, paddle jackets and booties available (small surcharge applies) with kayak rentals.

🛏 Sleeping

Pismo Beach has dozens of motels, but rooms fill up quickly and prices skyrocket in summer, especially on weekends. Resorts and hotels roost on cliffs north of town via Price St and Shell Beach Rd, while motels cluster near the beach and along Hwy 101.

Pismo State Beach – North Beach Campground
CAMPGROUND $

(📕 reservations 800-444-7275; www.reserveam
erica.com; 399 S Dolliver St; tent & RV sites $40;
🐾) About a mile south of downtown Pismo
Beach, off Hwy 1, the state park's North Beach
Campground is shaded by eucalyptus trees
and has over 170 well-spaced, grassy sites with
fire pits. The campground offers easy beach
access, flush toilets and coin-op hot showers.

Pismo Lighthouse Suites
HOTEL $$

(📕 805-773-2411; www.pismolighthousesuites.com;
2411 Price St; ste from $239; P ⇨ @ 🛜 🛂 🐾) With
everything a vacationing family needs – from
kitchenettes to a life-sized chessboard, a put-
ting green, table tennis and badminton courts –
this contemporary all-suites hotel right on the
beach is hard to tear yourself away from. Ask
about off-season discounts and check out the
on-site spa services. Pet fee $50.

Sandcastle Inn
HOTEL $$$

(📕 805-773-2422; www.sandcastleinn.com; 100
Stimson Ave; r $305; 🛜) Many of these Eastern
Seaboard–styled rooms are mere steps from
the sand. The top-floor ocean-view patio is
perfect for cracking open a bottle of wine at
sunset or after dark by the fireplace.

🍴 Eating & Drinking

Doc Burnstein's Ice Cream Lab
ICE CREAM $

(📕 805-474-4068; www.docburnsteins.com; 114 W
Branch St, Arroyo Grande; snacks $4-12; ⊙ 11am-
9:30pm Sun-Thu, to 10:30pm Fri & Sat, reduced
hours in winter; 👶) In Pismo's neighboring
Arroyo Grande, Doc's scoops up fantastical
flavors like Merlot raspberry truffle and the
'Elvis Special' (peanut butter with banana
swirls). Live ice-cream lab shows start at 7pm
sharp on Wednesday. From Hwy 101 southbound, exit at Grand Ave.

Frutiland La Casa Del Sabor
MEXICAN $$

(📕 805-541-3663; www.facebook.com/frutiland.fruti
land; 803 E Grand Ave, Arroyo Grande; mains $8-14;
⊙ 10am-6pm) Oversized, overstuffed Mexican
tortas (sandwiches) will feed two, and there
are two dozen varieties to choose from. Or or-
der a platter of blue-corn-tortilla fish tacos with
a mango or papaya *agua fresca* (fruit drink).
To find this taco shack in Arroyo Grande, exit
Hwy 101 southbound at Halcyon Rd.

⭐ Ember
CALIFORNIAN $$$

(📕 805-474-7700; www.emberwoodfire.com; 1200
E Grand Ave, Arroyo Grande; shared dishes $12-26,
mains $26-36; ⊙ 4-9pm Wed-Thu & Sun, to 10pm Fri
& Sat) 🍴 Chef Brian Collins, who once cooked

Pismo Beach
PRODESIGN STUDIO/SHUTTERSTOCK ©

at Alice Waters' revered Chez Panisse, has
returned to his roots in SLO County. Out of
the heart-warming wood-burning oven comes
savory flatbreads, artfully charred squid and
hearty red-wine-smoked short ribs. No reservations, so show up at 4pm or after 7:30pm,
or be prepared for a very long wait for a table.

Taste of the Valleys
WINE BAR

(📕 805-773-8466; www.pismowineshop.com; 911
Price St; ⊙ noon-9pm Mon-Sat, to 8pm Sun) Inside
a wine shop stacked floor to ceiling with hand-
picked vintages from around California and
beyond, ask for a taste of anything they've got
open, or sample from a quite astounding list
of more than 1000 wines poured by the glass.

Boardroom
BAR

(📕 805-295-6222; www.theboardroompismobeach.
com; 160 Hinds Ave; ⊙ 2-10pm Mon-Wed, noon-10pm
Sun & Thu, noon-1am Fri-Sat; 🛜) An exemplary
range of craft beers – mainly from the West
Coast of the US – combines with knowledgeable and friendly bartenders at this easygoing
bar with a surfing ambience. Get to know the
locals over a game of darts, maximize your
travel budget during happy hour from 4pm
to 6pm, and fill up on pizza, salads and panini.

ℹ️ Information

Pismo Beach Visitors Information Center
(📕 805-773-4382; www.classiccalifornia.com;
581 Dolliver St; ⊙ 9am-5pm Mon-Fri, 10am-2pm
Sat) Free maps and brochures. A smaller kiosk
on the pier is open from 11am to 4pm on Sunday.

Monterey

📞 831 / POP 27,810

Working-class Monterey is all about the sea. What draws many visitors is a world-class aquarium overlooking **Monterey Bay National Marine Sanctuary**, which protects dense kelp forests and a sublime variety of marine life, including seals and sea lions, dolphins and whales. The city itself possesses the best-preserved historical evidence of California's Spanish and Mexican periods, with many restored adobe buildings. An afternoon's wander through downtown's historic quarter promises to be more edifying than time spent in the tourist ghettos of Fisherman's Wharf and Cannery Row.

◉ Sights

Monterey Bay Aquarium   AQUARIUM
See p23.

**Monterey State
Historic Park**   HISTORIC SITE
(📞info 831-649-7118; www.parks.ca.gov) FREE
Old Monterey is home to an extraordinary assemblage of 19th-century brick and adobe buildings, administered as Monterey State Historic Park, and all found along a 2-mile self-guided walking tour portentously called the 'Path of History.' You can inspect dozens of buildings, many with charming gardens; expect some to be open while others aren't, according to a capricious schedule dictated by unfortunate state-park budget cutbacks.

🛏 Sleeping

HI Monterey Hostel   HOSTEL $
(📞831-649-0375; www.montereyhostel.org; 778 Hawthorne St; dm with shared bathdm $30-40; ☺check-in 4-10pm; @🛜) Four blocks from Cannery Row and the aquarium, this simple, clean hostel houses single-sex and mixed dorms, as well as private rooms accommodating up to five people (check online for rates). Budget backpackers stuff themselves silly with make-your-own-pancake breakfasts. Reservations strongly recommended. Take MST bus 1 from downtown's Transit Plaza.

Hotel Abrego   BOUTIQUE HOTEL $$
(📞831-372-7551; www.hotelabrego.com; 755 Abrego St; r from $144; 🛜🏊) At this downtown Monterey boutique hotel, most of the spacious, clean-lined contemporary rooms have gas fireplaces and chaise lounges. Work out in the fitness studio, take a dip in the recently redeveloped outdoor pool or warm up in the hot tub. A new fire pit is a cozy addition for cooler Monterey evenings.

Monterey Hotel   HISTORIC HOTEL $$
(📞831-375-3184; www.montereyhotel.com; 406 Alvarado St; r $131-275; 🛜) In the heart of downtown and a short walk from Fisherman's Wharf, this 1904 edifice harbors five-dozen smallish but renovated rooms and suites with Victorian-styled furniture and plantation shutters. No elevator. A recently added boutique spa offers massage and beauty treatments.

★Jabberwock   B&B $$$
(📞831-372-4777; www.jabberwockinn.com; 598 Laine St; r $249-339; @🛜) Barely visible through a shroud of foliage, this 1911 arts-and-crafts house hums a playful *Alice in Wonderland* tune through seven immaculate rooms, a few with fireplaces and Jacuzzis. Over afternoon tea and cookies or evening wine and hors d'oeuvres, ask the genial hosts about the house's many salvaged architectural elements. Weekends are more expensive and have a two-night minimum.

🍴 Eating

Old Monterey Marketplace   MARKET $
(www.oldmonterey.org; Alvarado St, btwn Del Monte Ave & Pearl St; ☺4-7pm Tue Sep-May, to 8pm Jun-Aug; 🅿) 🌿 Rain or shine, head downtown on Tuesdays for farm-fresh fruit and veggies, artisan cheeses, international food stalls and a scrumptious 'baker's alley.'

Zab Zab   NORTHERN THAI $
(📞831-747-2225; www.zabzabmonterey.com; 401 Lighthouse Ave; mains $11-15; ☺11am-2:30pm & 5-9pm Tue-Fri, noon-9pm Sat-Sun; 🍴) Our pick of Lighthouse Ave's ethnic eateries, Zab Zab channels the robust flavors of northeast Thailand. The bijou cottage interior is perfect in cooler weather, but during summer the best spot is on the deck surrounded by a pleasantly overgrown garden. For fans of authentic Thai heat, go for the Kai Yang grilled chicken. Lunch boxes ($11 to $13) are good value.

LouLou's Griddle in the Middle   AMERICAN $$
(📞831-372-0568; www.loulousgriddle.com; Municipal Wharf 2; mains $8-17; ☺7:30am-4pm Sun, Mon, Wed & Thu, to 6pm Fri-Sat, closed Tue; 🅿🏊) Stroll down the municipal wharf to this zany diner, best for breakfasts of ginormous pancakes and omelets with Mexican *pico de gallo* salsa or fresh seafood for lunch. Breezy outdoor tables are dog-friendly, or secure a spot at the counter and chat with the friendly chefs.

Montrio Bistro
CALIFORNIAN **$$$**

(📞831-648-8880; www.montrio.com; 414 Calle Principal; shared plates $12-30, mains $25-44; ☺4:30-10pm Sun-Thu, to 11pm Fri & Sat) 🍴 Inside a 1910 firehouse, Montrio combines leather walls and iron trellises, and the tables have butcher paper and crayons for kids. The eclectic seasonal menu mixes local, organic fare with Californian, Asian and European flair, including tapas-style shared plates and mini desserts.

🍷 Drinking & Entertainment

★ Alvarado Street Brewery
CRAFT BEER

(📞831-655-2337; www.alvaradostreetbrewery.com; 426 Alvarado St; ☺11:30am-10pm Sun-Wed, to 11pm Thu-Sat) Vintage beer advertising punctuates Alvarado Street's brick walls, but that's the only concession to earlier days at this excellent craft-beer pub. Innovative brews harness new hop strains, sour and barrel-aged beers regularly fill the taps, and superior bar food includes Thai-curry mussels and truffle-crawfish mac 'n' cheese. In summer, adjourn to the alfresco beer garden out back.

East Village Coffee Lounge
CAFE, LOUNGE

(📞831-373-5601; www.facebook.com/eastvillage monterey; 498 Washington St; ☺6am-10pm Mon-Fri, from 7am Sat & Sun; 🛜) Downtown Monterey coffee shop on a busy corner brews with fair-trade, organic beans. At night, it pulls off a big-city lounge vibe with film, open-mike and live-music nights and an all-important booze license. Check the Facebook page for event listings.

Sardine Factory Lounge
LOUNGE

(📞831-373-3775; www.sardinefactory.com; 701 Wave St; ☺5pm-midnight) The legendary restaurant's fireplace lounge pours wines by the glass, delivers filling appetizers to your table and has a live piano player most nights.

Osio Cinema
CINEMA

(📞831-644-8171; http://osiotheater.com; 350 Alvarado St; adult $10, before 6pm $7; 🛜) Downtown Monterey cinema screens indie dramas, cutting-edge documentaries and offbeat Hollywood films. Drop by its Cafe Lumiere for locally roasted coffee, loose-leaf tea, decadent cheesecake and wi-fi.

🛍 Shopping

Wharf Marketplace
FOOD & DRINKS

(📞831-649-1116; www.thewharfmarketplace.com; 290 Figueroa St; ☺7am-7pm) 🍴 Inside an old railway station, this gourmet-food emporium

MONTEREY WHALE-WATCHING

You can spot whales off the coast of Monterey Bay year-round. The season for blue and humpback whales runs from April to early December, while gray whales pass by from mid-December through March. Tour boats depart from Fisherman's Wharf and **Moss Landing** (📞info 831-917-1042, tickets 888-394-7810; www.sanctuarycruises.com; 7881 Sandholdt Rd; tours $45-55; 👶) 🍴. Reserve trips at least a day in advance; be prepared for a bumpy, cold ride.

carries bountiful farm goodness, artisanal products and wine from Monterey County and beyond. It's a good spot for a leisurely breakfast, too.

Old Capitol Books
BOOKS

(📞831-333-0383; www.oldcapitolbooks.com; 559 Tyler St; ☺10am-6pm Wed-Mon, to 7pm Tue) Tall shelves of new, used and antiquarian books, including rare first editions, California titles and John Steinbeck's works.

ℹ️ Information

Monterey Visitors Center (📞831-657-6400; www.seemonterey.com; 401 Camino el Estero; ☺9am-6pm Mon-Sat, to 5pm Sun, closes 1hr earlier Nov-Mar) Free tourist brochures; ask for a *Monterey County Literary & Film Map*. Also a handy accommodation-booking service.

Santa Cruz

📞831 / POP 62,864

Santa Cruz has marched to its own beat since long before the Beat Generation. It's counterculture central, a touchy-feely, new-agey city famous for its leftie-liberal politics and easygoing ideology. It's still cool to be a hippie or a stoner here, although some of the far-out-looking freaks are just slumming Silicon Valley millionaires and trust-fund babies. Santa Cruz is a city of madcap fun, with a vibrant but chaotic downtown. On the waterfront is the famous beach boardwalk, and in the hills redwood groves embrace the University of California, Santa Cruz (UCSC) campus.

◎ Sights & Activities

One of the best things to do in Santa Cruz is simply stroll, shop and watch the sideshow along **Pacific Avenue** downtown. A 15-minute walk away is the beach and **Municipal Wharf**,

81

where seafood restaurants, gift shops and barking sea lions compete for attention. Ocean-view **West Cliff Drive** follows the waterfront southwest of the wharf, paralleled by a paved recreational path. Year-round, water temperatures average under 60°F, meaning that without a wet suit, body parts quickly turn blue. Surfing is incredibly popular, especially at experts-only **Steamer Lane** and beginners' Cowell's, both off W Cliff Dr. Other favorite surf spots include **Pleasure Point Beach**, on E Cliff Dr toward Capitola, and Manresa State Beach off Hwy 1 southbound.

★ **Santa Cruz Beach Boardwalk**
See p23.

★ **Seymour Marine Discovery Center**   MUSEUM
(☑ 831-459-3800; http://seymourcenter.ucsc.edu; 100 Shaffer Rd; adult/child 3-16yr $8/6; ⊙ 10am-5pm Tue-Sun; Ⓟ 🖈) 🖎 This kids' educational center is part of UCSC's Long Marine Laboratory. Interactive natural-science exhibits include tidal touch pools and aquariums, while

outside you can gawk at the world's largest blue-whale skeleton. Guided one-hour tours happen at 1pm, 2pm and 3pm daily, with a special 30-minute tour for families with younger children at 11am; sign up for tours in person an hour in advance (no reservations).

Richard Schmidt Surf School   SURFING
(☑ 831-423-0928; www.richardschmidt.com; 849 Almar Ave; 2hr group/1hr private lesson $90/120; 🖈) Award-winning surf school can get you out there, all equipment included. Summer surf camps hook adults and kids alike.

Santa Cruz Food Tour   FOOD
(☑ 866-736-6343; www.santacruzfoodtour.com; per person $59; ⊙ 2:30-6pm Fri & Sat) Combining Afghan flavors, a farm-to-table bistro, vegan cupcakes and artisan ice cream, these highly recommended walking tours also come with a healthy serving of local knowledge and interesting insights into Santa Cruz history, culture and architecture. Sign up for a tour when you first arrive in town to get your bearings in the tastiest way possible.

SANTA CRUZ BEACHES
••

Sun-kissed Santa Cruz has warmer beaches than San Francisco or Monterey. *Baywatch* it isn't, but 29 miles of coastline reveal a few Hawaii-worthy beaches, craggy coves, some primo surf spots and big sandy stretches where your kids will have a blast. Fog may ruin many a summer morning; it often burns off by the afternoon.

Main Beach *The* scene in Santa Cruz, with a huge sandy stretch, volleyball courts and swarms of people. Park on E Cliff Dr and walk across the *Lost Boys* trestle to the beach boardwalk (p23).

Manresa State Beach (☑ 831-724-3750; www.parks.ca.gov; San Andreas Rd, Watsonville; per car $10; ⊙ 8am-sunset) Near Watsonville, the La Selva Beach exit off Hwy 1 leads here to this sparsely populated beach.

Seacliff State Beach (☑ 831-685-6442; www.parks.ca.gov; State Park Rd, Aptos; per car $10; ⊙ 8am-sunset) Seacliff State Beach harbors a 'cement boat,' a quixotic freighter built of concrete that floated OK, but ended up here as a coastal fishing pier. During huge storms in February 2017, the boat actually broke apart but remains *in situ*.

Natural Bridges State Beach (☑ 831-423-4609; www.parks.ca.gov; 2531 W Cliff Dr; per car $10; ⊙ 8am-sunset; Ⓟ 🖈) Best for sunsets, this family favorite has lots of sand, tide pools and monarch butterflies from mid-October through mid-February.

Twin Lakes State Beach (www.parks.ca.gov; E Cliff Dr & 9th Ave; ⊙ 8am-sunset; 🖈) Big beach with bonfire pits and a lagoon, good for kids and often fairly empty. It's off E Cliff Dr.

Sunset State Beach (☑ 831-763-7062; www.parks.ca.gov; San Andreas Rd, Watsonville; per car $10; ⊙ 8am-sunset) The La Selva Beach exit off Hwy 1, near Watsonville, brings you here, where you can have miles of sand and surf almost all to yourself.

Its Beach (🐾) The only official off-leash beach for dogs (before 10am and after 4pm) in Santa Cruz is just west of the lighthouse. The field across the street is another good romping ground.

Cowell's Beach Popular Santa Cruz surfing beach off W Cliff Dr.

📛 Sleeping

Santa Cruz does not have enough beds to satisfy demand: expect high prices at peak times for nothing-special rooms. Places near the beach boardwalk range from friendly to frightening. For a decent motel, cruise Ocean St inland or Mission St (Hwy 1).

★ Adobe on Green B&B   B&B $$
(☑ 831-469-9866; www.adobeongreen.com; 103 Green St; r $179; P 🅿 🐾 🛜) 🔌 Peace and quiet are the mantras at this place, a short walk from Pacific Ave. The hosts are practically invisible, but their thoughtful touches are everywhere, from boutique-hotel amenities in spacious, stylish and solar-powered rooms to breakfast spreads from their organic gardens.

Pacific Blue Inn   B&B $$$
(☑ 831-600-8880; www.pacificblueinn.com; 636 Pacific Ave; r $189-289; P 🅿 🐾 🛜 🐕) 🔌 This downtown courtyard B&B is an eco-conscious gem, with water-saving fixtures, and renewable and recycled building materials. Refreshingly elemental rooms have pillow-top beds, electric fireplaces and flat-screen TVs with DVD players. Free parking and loaner bikes. Pet fee $50.

🍴 Eating & Drinking

Santa Cruz's downtown overflows with bars, lounges and coffee shops. Heading west on Mission St (Hwy 1), craft breweries and wine-tasting rooms fill the raffish industrial ambience of the Smith St and Ingalls St courtyards.

★ Penny Ice Creamery   ICE CREAM $
(☑ 831-204-2523; www.thepennyicecreamery.com; 913 Cedar St; snacks $3-5; ⏰ noon-11pm; 🅿) 🔌 With a cult following, this artisan ice-cream shop crafts zany flavors such as bourbon-candied ginger, lemon-verbena–blueberry and ricotta apricot all from scratch using local, organic and wild-harvested ingredients. Even plain old vanilla is special: it's made using Thomas Jefferson's original recipe. Also at a downtown kiosk (1520 Pacific Ave; ⏰ noon-6pm) and near Pleasure Point (820 41st Ave; ⏰ noon-9pm Sun-Thu, to 10pm Fri & Sat).

Santa Cruz Farmers Market   MARKET $
(☑ 831-454-0566; www.santacruzfarmersmarket. org; cnr Lincoln & Center Sts; ⏰ 1:30-6:30pm Wed; 🅿 🅿) 🔌 Organic produce, baked goods and arts-and-crafts and food booths all give you an authentic taste of the local vibe. Shorter fall and winter hours.

Assembly   CALIFORNIAN $$
(☑ 831-824-6100; www.assembly.restaurant; 1108 Pacific Ave; brunch & lunch $12-16, dinner mains $22-28; ⏰ 11:30am-9pm Mon & Wed-Thu, to 10pm Fri, 10am-10pm Sat-Sun; 🅿) 🔌 Farm-to-table and proudly regional flavors feature at this excellent bistro in downtown Santa Cruz. Assembly's Californian vibe belies real culinary nous in the kitchen. Don't miss trying the Scotch olives and meatballs with a tasting flight of local craft beers.

Verve Coffee Roasters   CAFE
(☑ 831-600-7784; www.vervecoffee.com; 1540 Pacific Ave; ⏰ 6:30am-9pm; 🛜) To sip finely roasted artisan espresso or a cup of rich pour-over coffee, join the surfers and hipsters at this industrial-zen cafe. Single-origin brews and house blends rule. It's been so successful around their home patch that it's also opened satellite cafes in Los Angeles and Tokyo.

Lupulo Craft Beer House   CRAFT BEER
(☑ 831-454-8306; www.lupulosc.com; 233 Cathcart St; ⏰ 11:30am-10pm Sun-Thu, to 11:30pm Fri-Sat) Named after the Spanish word for hops, Lupulo Craft Beer House is an essential downtown destination for traveling beer fans, with almost 400 bottled and canned beers. Modern decor combines with an ever-changing tap list and good bar snacks such as empanadas, tacos and charcuterie plates.

☆ Entertainment

Moe's Alley   LIVE MUSIC
(☑ 831-479-1854; www.moesalley.com; 1535 Commercial Way; admission varies by gig) In a way-out industrial wasteland, this joint puts on live sounds almost every night: jazz, blues, reggae, roots, salsa and acoustic world-music jams.

Catalyst   LIVE MUSIC
(☑ 831-423-1338; www.catalystclub.com; 1011 Pacific Ave; admission varies by gig) Over the years, this stage for local bands has seen big-time national acts perform, from Queens of the Stone Age to Snoop Dogg. Expect loads of punk attitude and look forward to gigs ranging from classic reggae acts to the occasional Ned Flanders–inspired thrash-metal band (c'mon down Okilly Dokilly...).

🛈 Information

Santa Cruz Visitor Center (☑ 831-425-1234; www.santacruzca.org; 303 Water St; ⏰ 9am-noon & 1-4pm Mon-Fri, 11am-3pm Sat & Sun) Free public internet terminal, maps and brochures.

San Francisco & the Bay Area

Grab your coat and a handful of glitter, and enter San Francisco, the land of fog and fabulousness. Meanwhile, the surrounding Bay Area encompasses a bonanza of natural vistas and wildlife.

SAN FRANCISCO

POP 870,887

Get to know the capital of weird from the inside out, from mural-lined alleyways named after poets to clothing-optional beaches on a former military base. But don't be too quick to dismiss San Francisco's wild ideas. Biotech, gay rights, personal computers, cable cars and organic fine dining were once considered outlandish too, before San Francisco introduced these underground ideas into the mainstream decades ago. San Francisco's morning fog erases the boundaries between land and ocean, reality and infinite possibility.

⊙ Sights

⊙ Downtown, Civic Center & SoMa

★**Ferry Building**
See p31.

★**San Francisco Museum of Modern Art**   MUSEUM
(SFMOMA; ☑ 415-357-4000; www.sfmoma.org; 151 3rd St; adult/under 18yr/student $25/free/$19; ⊙ 10am-5pm Fri-Tue, to 9pm Thu, public spaces from 9am; ♿; ⛉ 5, 6, 7, 14, 19, 21, 31, 38, Ⓜ Montgomery, Ⓑ Montgomery) The expanded SFMOMA is a mind-boggling feat, tripled in size to accommodate a sprawling collection of modern masterworks and 19 concurrent exhibitions over 10 floors – but, then again, SFMOMA has defied limits ever since its 1935 founding. The museum was a visionary early investor in then-emerging art forms, including photography, installations, video, performance art, and (as befits a global technology hub) digital art and industrial design. Even during the Depression, SFMOMA envisioned a world of vivid possibilities, starting in San Francisco.

★**Asian Art Museum**   MUSEUM
(☑ 415-581-3500; www.asianart.org; 200 Larkin St; adult/student/child $15/10/free, 1st Sun of month free; ⊙ 10am-5pm Tue, Wed & Fri-Sun, to 9pm Thu; ♿; Ⓜ Civic Center, Ⓑ Civic Center) Imaginations race from ancient Persian miniatures to cutting-edge Japanese minimalism across three floors spanning 6000 years of Asian art. Besides the largest collection outside Asia – 18,000 works – the museum offers excellent programs for all ages, from shadow-puppet shows and tea tastings with star chefs to mixers with cross-cultural DJ mash-ups.

Contemporary Jewish Museum   MUSEUM
(☑ 415-344-8800; www.thecjm.org; 736 Mission St; adult/student/child $14/12/free, after 5pm Thu $5;

⊙ 11am-5pm Mon, Tue & Fri-Sun, to 8pm Thu; ▣; 🚇 14, 30, 45, Ⓑ Montgomery, Ⓜ Montgomery) That upended blue-steel box miraculously balancing on one corner isn't sculpture but the Yerba Buena Lane entry to the Contemporary Jewish Museum – an institution that upends conventional ideas about art and religion. Exhibits here are compelling explorations of Jewish ideals and visionaries, including writer Gertrude Stein, rock promoter Bill Graham, cartoonist Roz Chast and filmmaker Stanley Kubrick.

Luggage Store Gallery   GALLERY
(📞 415-255-5971; www.luggagestoregallery.org; 1007 Market St; ⊙ noon-5pm Wed-Sat; 🚇 5, 6, 7, 21, 31, Ⓜ Civic Center, Ⓑ Civic Center) Like a dandelion pushing through sidewalk cracks, this plucky nonprofit gallery has brought signs of life to one of the Tenderloin's toughest blocks for two decades. By giving SF street artists a gallery platform, the Luggage Store helped launch graffiti-art star Barry McGee, muralist Rigo and street photographer Cheryl Dunn. Find the graffitied door and climb to the 2nd-floor gallery, which rises above the street without losing sight of it.

SF Camerawork   GALLERY
(📞 415-487-1011; www.sfcamerawork.org; 1011 Market St, 2nd fl; ⊙ noon-6pm Tue-Sat; 🚇 6, 7, 9, 21, Ⓑ Civic Center, Ⓜ Civic Center) FREE Since 1974, this nonprofit art organization has championed experimental photo-based imagery beyond classic B&W prints and casual digital snapshots. Since moving into this spacious new Market St gallery, Camerawork's far-reaching exhibitions have examined memories of love and war in Southeast Asia, taken imaginary holidays with slide shows of vacation snapshots scavenged from the San Francisco Dump and showcased SF-based artist Sanaz Mazinani's mesmerizing Islamic-inspired photo montages made of tiny Trumps.

Diego Rivera's
Allegory of California Fresco   PUBLIC ART
(www.sfcityguides.org/desc.html?tour=96; 155 Sansome St; tours free; ⊙ tours by reservation with SF City Guides 3pm 1st & 3rd Mon of month; Ⓑ Montgomery, Ⓜ Montgomery) FREE Hidden inside San Francisco's Stock Exchange tower is a priceless treasure: Diego Rivera's 1930–31 *Allegory of California* fresco. Spanning a two-story stairwell between the 10th and 11th floors, the fresco shows California as a giant golden goddess offering farm-fresh produce, while gold miners toil beneath her

and oil refineries loom on the horizon. Rivera's *Allegory* is glorious, but cautionary – while Californian workers, inventors and dreamers go about their business, the pressure gauge in the left-hand corner is entering the red zone.

⊙ North Beach & Chinatown

Waverly Place   STREET
(🚇 1, 30, 🚋 California, Powell-Mason) Grant Ave may be the economic heart of Chinatown, but its soul is Waverly Pl, lined with historic clinker-brick buildings and flag-festooned temple balconies. Through good times and bad, Waverly Pl stood its ground, and temple services have been held here since 1852 – even after San Francisco's 1906 earthquake and fire, when altars were still smoldering.

Chinatown Alleyways   AREA
(btwn Grant Ave, Stockton St, California St & Broadway; 🚇 1, 30, 45, 🚋 Powell-Hyde, Powell-Mason, California) The 41 historic alleyways packed into Chinatown's 22 blocks have seen it all since 1849: gold rushes and revolution, incense and opium, fire and icy receptions. In clinker-brick buildings lining these narrow backstreets, temple balconies jut out over bakeries, laundries and barbers – there was nowhere to go but up in Chinatown after 1870, when laws limited Chinese immigration, employment and housing. Chinatown Alleyway Tours (p93) and Chinatown Heritage Walking Tours (📞 415-986-1822; www.

GOLDEN GATE BRIDGE
....
Hard to believe the Navy almost nixed SF's signature art-deco landmark (📞 toll information 877-229-8655; www.goldengatebridge.org/visitors; Hwy 101; northbound free, southbound $6.50-7.50; 🚇 28, all Golden Gate Transit buses) by architects Gertrude and Irving Morrow and engineer Joseph B Strauss. Photographers, take your cue from Hitchcock: seen from Fort Point (📞 415-556-1693; www.nps.gov/fopo; Marine Dr; ⊙ 10am-5pm Fri-Sun; Ⓟ; 🚇 28) FREE, the 1937 bridge induces a thrilling case of vertigo. Fog aficionados prefer Marin's Vista Point, watching gusts billow through bridge cables like dry ice at a Kiss concert. For the full effect, hike or bike the 2-mile span.

Alcatraz

cccsf.us; Chinese Culture Center, Hilton Hotel, 3rd fl, 750 Kearny St; group tour adult $25-30, student $15-20, private tour 1-4 people $60; ⊙ tours 10am, noon & 2pm Tue-Sat; 🚻) offer community-supporting, time-traveling strolls through defining moments in American history.

City Lights Books   CULTURAL CENTER
(📞 415-362-8193; www.citylights.com; 261 Columbus Ave; ⊙ 10am-midnight; 🚻; 🚌 8, 10, 12, 30, 41, 45, 🚋 Powell-Mason, Powell-Hyde) Free speech and free spirits have flourished here since 1957, when City Lights founder and poet Lawrence Ferlinghetti and manager Shigeyoshi Murao won a landmark ruling defending their right to publish Allen Ginsberg's magnificent epic poem *Howl*. Celebrate your freedom to read freely in the designated Poet's Chair upstairs overlooking Jack Kerouac Alley, load up on zines on the mezzanine and entertain radical ideas downstairs in the new Pedagogies of Resistance section.

★ Coit Tower   PUBLIC ART
(📞 415-249-0995; www.sfrecpark.org; Telegraph Hill Blvd; nonresident elevator fee adult/child $8/5; ⊙ 10am-6pm Apr-Oct, to 5pm Nov-Mar; 🚌 39) The exclamation mark on San Francisco's skyline is Coit Tower, with 360-degree views of downtown and wraparound 1930s Works Progress Administration (WPA) murals glorifying SF workers. Initially denounced as communist, the murals are now a national landmark. For a wild-parrot's panoramic view of San Francisco 210ft above the city, take the elevator to the tower's open-air platform. To glimpse seven recently restored murals up a hidden stairwell on the 2nd floor, join the 11am tour Wednesday or Saturday (free; donations welcome).

Beat Museum   MUSEUM
(📞 800-537-6822; www.kerouac.com; 540 Broadway; adult/student $8/5, walking tours $25; ⊙ museum 10am-7pm, walking tours 2-4pm Sat; 🚌 8, 10, 12, 30, 41, 45, 🚋 Powell-Mason) The closest you can get to the complete Beat experience without breaking a law. The 1000-plus artifacts in this museum's literary-ephemera collection include the sublime (the banned edition of Ginsberg's *Howl*, with the author's own annotations) and the ridiculous (those Kerouac bobblehead dolls are definite head-shakers). Downstairs, watch Beat-era films in ramshackle theater seats redolent with the odors of literary giants, pets and pot. Upstairs, pay your respects at shrines to individual Beat writers.

Chinese Historical Society of America   MUSEUM
(CHSA; 📞 415-391-1188; www.chsa.org; 965 Clay St; adult/student/child $15/10/free; ⊙ noon-5pm Tue-Fri, 10am-4pm Sat & Sun; 🚻; 🚌 1, 8, 30, 45, 🚋 California, Powell-Mason, Powell-Hyde) **FREE** Picture what it was like to be Chinese in America during the gold rush, transcontinental railroad construction or Beat heyday in this 1932 landmark, built as Chinatown's YWCA by Julia Morgan (chief architect of Hearst Castle). CHSA historians unearth fascinating artifacts, from 1920s silk *qipao*

dresses to Chinatown miniatures created by set designer Frank Wong. Exhibits reveal once-popular views of Chinatown, including the sensationalist opium-den exhibit at San Francisco's 1915 Panama-Pacific International Expo inviting fairgoers to 'Go Slumming' in Chinatown.

⊙ The Marina, Fisherman's Wharf & the Piers

★ Alcatraz   HISTORIC SITE

(☑ Alcatraz Cruises 415-981-7625; www.nps.gov/alcatraz; tours adult/child 5-11yr day $37.25/23, night $44.25/26.50; ⊙ call center 8am-7pm, ferries depart Pier 33 half-hourly 8:45am-3:50pm, night tours 5:55pm & 6:30pm; ⛴) Alcatraz: for over 150 years, the name has given the innocent chills and the guilty cold sweats. Over the decades, it's been the nation's first military prison, a forbidding maximum-security penitentiary and disputed territory between Native American activists and the FBI. No wonder that first step you take onto 'the Rock' seems to cue ominous music: dunh-dunh-dunnnnh!

★ Exploratorium   MUSEUM

(☑ 415-528-4444; www.exploratorium.edu; Pier 15; adult/child $30/20, 6-10pm Thu $15; ⊙ 10am-5pm Tue-Sun, over 18yr only 6-10pm Thu; P ⛴; M E, F) ✐ Is there a science to skateboarding? Do toilets really flush counterclockwise in Australia? Find out things you'll wish you learned in school at San Francisco's hands-on science museum. Combining science with art and investigating human perception, the Exploratorium nudges you to question how you perceive the world around you. The setting is thrilling: a 9-acre, glass-walled pier jutting straight into San Francisco Bay, with large outdoor portions you can explore free of charge, 24 hours a day.

Maritime National Historical Park   HISTORIC SITE

(☑ 415-447-5000; www.nps.gov/safr; 499 Jefferson St, Hyde St Pier; 7-day ticket adult/child $10/free; ⊙ 9:30am-5pm Oct-May, to 5:30pm Jun-Sep; ⛴; ⛴ 19, 30, 47, ⛴ Powell-Hyde, M F) Four historic ships are floating museums at this maritime national park, Fisherman's Wharf's most authentic attraction. Moored along Hyde St Pier, standouts include the 1891 schooner *Alma*, which hosts guided sailing trips in summer; 1890 steamboat *Eureka*; paddle-wheel tugboat *Eppleton Hall*; and iron-hulled *Balclutha*, which brought coal to San

Francisco. It's free to walk the pier; pay only to board ships.

Baker Beach   BEACH

(☑ 10am-5pm 415-561-4323; www.nps.gov/prsf; ⊙ sunrise-sunset; P; ⛴ 29, PresidiGo Shuttle) Picnic amid wind-sculpted pines, fish from craggy rocks or frolic nude at mile-long Baker Beach, with spectacular views of the Golden Gate. Crowds come weekends, especially on fog-free days; arrive early. For nude sunbathing (mostly straight girls and gay boys), head to the north. Families in clothing stick to the south, nearer parking. Mind the currents and the c-c-cold water.

Musée Mécanique   AMUSEMENT PARK

(☑ 415-346-2000; www.museemechanique.org; Pier 45, Shed A; ⊙ 10am-8pm; ⛴; ⛴ 47, ⛴ Powell-Mason, Powell-Hyde, M E, F) A flashback to penny arcades, the Musée Mécanique houses a mind-blowing collection of vintage mechanical amusements. Sinister, freckle-faced Laffing Sal has creeped out kids for over a century, but don't let this manic mannequin deter you from the best arcade west of Coney Island. A quarter lets you start brawls in Wild West saloons, peep at belly dancers through a vintage Mutoscope and even learn a cautionary tale about smoking opium.

Crissy Field   PARK

(☑ 415-561-4700; www.crissyfield.org; 1199 East Beach; P; ⛴ 30, PresidiGo Shuttle) War is for the birds at Crissy Field, a military airstrip turned waterfront nature preserve with knockout Golden Gate views. Where military aircraft once zoomed in for landings, bird-watchers now huddle in the silent rushes of a reclaimed tidal marsh. Joggers pound beachside trails and the only security alerts are raised by puppies suspiciously sniffing surfers. On foggy days, stop by the certified-green **Warming Hut** (☑ 415-561-3042; www.parksconservancy.org/visit/eat/warming-hut.html; 983 Marine Dr; items $4-9; ⊙ 9am-5pm; P ⛴; ⛴ PresidiGo Shuttle) ✐ to browse regional-nature books and warm up with fair-trade coffee.

Pier 39   PIER

(☑ 415-705-5500; www.pier39.com; cnr Beach St & the Embarcadero; P ⛴; ⛴ 47, ⛴ Powell-Mason, M E, F) The focal point of Fisherman's Wharf isn't the waning fishing fleet but the carousel, carnival-like attractions, shops and restaurants of Pier 39 – and, of course, the famous **sea lions**. Developed in the 1970s to revitalize tourism, the pier draws thousands

Alcatraz

A HALF-DAY TOUR

Book a ferry from Pier 33 and ride 1.5 miles across the bay to explore America's most notorious former prison. The trip itself is worth the money, providing stunning views of the city skyline. Once you've landed at the ❶ **Ferry Dock & Pier**, you begin the 580-yard walk to the top of the island and prison; if you need assistance to reach the top, there's a twice-hourly tram.

As you climb toward the ❷ **Guardhouse**, notice the island's steep slope; before it was a prison, Alcatraz was a fort. In the 1850s, the military quarried the rocky shores into near-vertical cliffs. Ships could then only dock at a single port, separated from the main buildings by a sally port (a drawbridge and moat in what became the guardhouse). Inside, peer through floor grates to see Alcatraz' original prison.

Volunteers tend the brilliant ❸ **Officer's Row Gardens** an orderly counterpoint to the overgrown rose bushes surrounding the burned-out shell of the ❹ **Warden's House**. At the top of the hill, by the front door of the ❺ **Main Cellhouse**, beautiful shots unfurl all around, including a view of the ❻ **Golden Gate Bridge**. Above the main door of the administration building, notice the ❼ **historic signs & graffiti**, before you step inside the dank, cold prison to find the ❽ **Frank Morris cell**, former home to Alcatraz' most notorious jail-breaker.

TOP TIPS

➡ Book at least one month prior for self-guided daytime visits, longer for ranger-led night tours. For info on garden tours, see www.alcatraz gardens.org.

➡ Be prepared to hike; a steep path ascends from the ferry landing to the cell block. Most people spend two to three hours on the island. You need only reserve for the outbound ferry; take any ferry back.

➡ There's no food (just water) but you can bring your own; picnicking is allowed at the ferry dock only. Dress in layers as weather changes fast and it's usually windy.

ADRIEN_G/SHUTTERSTOCK ©

Historic Signs & Graffiti

During their 1969–71 occupation, Native Americans graffitied the water tower: 'Home of the Free Indian Land.' Above the cellhouse door, examine the eagle-and-flag crest to see how the red-and-white stripes were changed to spell 'Free.'

DOPTIS/SHUTTERSTOCK ©

Warden's House

Fires destroyed the warden's house and other structures during the Indian Occupation. The government blamed the Native Americans; the Native Americans blamed agents provocateurs acting on behalf of the Nixon Administration to undermine public sympathy.

Parade Grounds

Officer's Row Gardens

In the 19th century soldiers imported topsoil to beautify the island with gardens. Well-trusted prisoners later gardened – Elliott Michener said it kept him sane. Historians, ornithologists and archaeologists choose today's plants.

Main Cellhouse

During the mid-20th century, the maximum-security prison housed the day's most notorious troublemakers, including Al Capone and Robert Stroud, the 'Birdman of Alcatraz' (who actually conducted his ornithology studies at Leavenworth).

View of Golden Gate Bridge

The Golden Gate Bridge stretches wide on the horizon. Best views are from atop the island at Eagle Plaza, near the cellhouse entrance, and at water level along the Agave Trail (September to January only).

Power House

Recreation Yard

Water Tower

Officers' Club

6

5

8

Guardhouse

Alcatraz' oldest building dates to 1857 and retains remnants of the original drawbridge and moat. During the Civil War the basement was transformed into a military dungeon – the genesis of Alcatraz as prison.

7

Lighthouse

3

4

2

Guard Tower

Frank Morris Cell

Peer into cell 138 on B-Block to see a recreation of the dummy's head that Frank Morris left in his bed as a decoy to aid his notorious – and successful – 1962 escape from Alcatraz.

1

Ferry Dock & Pier

A giant wall map helps you get your bearings. Inside nearby Bldg 64, short films and exhibits provide historical perspective on the prison and details about the Indian Occupation.

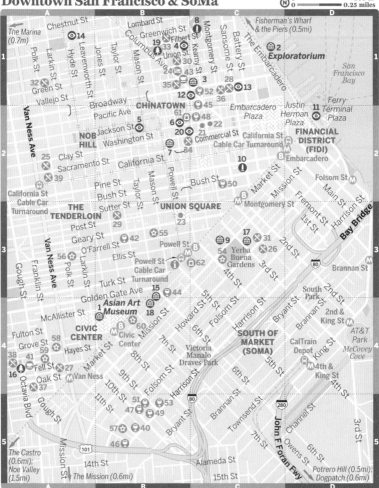

of tourists daily, but it's really just a big outdoor shopping mall. On the plus side, its visitors center rents strollers, stores luggage and has free phone-charging stations.

👁 Nob Hill, Russian Hill & Fillmore

Lombard Street   STREET
(🚋 Powell-Hyde) You've seen the eight switchbacks of Lombard St's 900 block in a thousand photographs. The tourist board has dubbed it 'the world's crookedest street,' which is factually incorrect: Vermont St in

Potrero Hill deserves that award, but Lombard is much more scenic, with its redbrick pavement and lovingly tended flowerbeds. It wasn't always so bent; before the arrival of the car it lunged straight down the hill.

Cable Car Museum   HISTORIC SITE
(📞 415-474-1887; www.cablecarmuseum.org; 1201 Mason St; donations appreciated; ⊙ 10am–6pm Apr-Sep, to 5pm Oct-Mar; 🚼; 🚋 Powell-Mason, Powell-Hyde) **FREE** Hear that whirring beneath the cable-car tracks? That's the sound of the cables that pull the cars, and they all connect inside the city's long-functioning cable-car

Downtown San Francisco & SoMa

barn. Grips, engines, braking mechanisms... if these warm your gearhead heart, you'll be besotted with the Cable Car Museum.

⊙ The Castro & Noe Valley

Castro Theatre   THEATER
(☑ 415-621-6120; www.castrotheatre.com; 429 Castro St; ⊙ Tue-Sun; Ⓜ Castro St) The city's grandest movie palace opened in 1922. The Spanish-Moorish exterior yields to mishmash styles inside, from Italianate to Oriental. Ask nicely and staff may let you take a peek, or come for the nightly cult or classic **films**

(adult/child $11/8.50), or one of the many film festivals – check calendars online. At evening shows, arrive early to hear the organist play before the curtain rises.

Barbie-Doll Window   PUBLIC ART
(4099 19th St; ⓐ 24, Ⓜ Castro) No first-time loop through the Castro would be complete without a peek at the Barbie-Doll Window – better called the Billy-Doll Window, a gay spin-off of Barbie, notable for its shockingly huge penis. Dolls are dressed – well, some of them – in outrageous costumes and arranged in miniature protest lines, complete with signs. One of them says it best: 'It's Castro, Bitch.'

91

GOLDEN GATE PARK

When San Franciscans refer to 'the park,' there's only one that gets the definite article. Everything they hold dear is in Golden Gate Park (www.golden-gate-park.com; btwn Stanyan St & Great Hwy; P H B; 5, 7, 18, 21, 28, 29, 33, 44, M N) FREE, including free spirits, free music, Frisbee and bison.

At the east end you can join year-round drum circles at Hippie Hill, sweater-clad athletes at the historic Lawn Bowling Club, toddlers clinging for dear life onto the 100-year-old carousel and meditators in the contemplative AIDS Memorial Grove. To the west, turtles paddle past model yachts at Spreckels Lake, offerings are made at pagan altars behind the baseball diamond and free concerts are held in the Polo Fields, site of 1967's hippie Human Be-In. This scenery seems far-fetched now, but impossible when proposed in 1866. When New York's Central Park architect Frederick Law Olmsted balked at transforming 1017 acres of dunes into the world's largest developed park, San Francisco's green scheme fell to tenacious young civil engineer William Hammond Hall. He insisted that park features should include botanical gardens (Strybing Arboretum; 415-661-1316; www.strybing.org; 1199 9th Ave; adult/child $8/2, before 9am daily & 2nd Tue of month free; 7:30am-7pm Mar-Sep, to 6pm Oct–mid-Nov & Feb, to 5pm mid-Nov–Jan, last entry 1hr before closing, bookstore 10am-4pm; H; 6, 7, 44, M N) , a dedicated buffalo paddock (www.golden-gate-park.com/buffalo-paddock.html; sunrise-sunset; 5, 21) FREE and waterfalls at Stow Lake (www.sfrecpark.org; sunrise-sunset; H; 7, 44, M N). Sundays, when John F Kennedy Dr closes to traffic around 9th Ave, don't miss roller disco and lindy-hopping in the park.

Also in the park is the de Young Museum (415-750-3600; http://deyoung.famsf.org; 50 Hagiwara Tea Garden Dr; adult/child $15/free, 1st Tue of month free; 9:30am-5:15pm Tue-Sun, to 8:45pm Fri Apr-Nov; H; 5, 7, 44, M N) – follow sculptor Andy Goldsworthy's artificial fault line in the sidewalk into Herzog & de Meuron's sleek, copper-clad building that's oxidizing green to blend into the park. You can also visit the California Academy of Sciences (415-379-8000; www.calacademy.org; 55 Music Concourse Dr; adult/student/child $35/30/25; 9:30am-5pm Mon-Sat, from 11am Sun; P H; 5, 6, 7, 21, 31, 33, 44, M N) . Architect Renzo Piano's 2008 landmark LEED-certified green building houses 40,000 weird and wonderful animals in a four-story rainforest, split-level aquarium and planetarium all under a 'living roof' of California wildflowers.

Harvey Milk & Jane Warner Plazas SQUARE
(cnr Market & Castro Sts; M Castro St) A huge rainbow flag flaps above Castro and Market Sts, officially Harvey Milk Plaza. Look closer and spot a plaque honoring the man whose legacy is gay civic pride and political clout. Across Castro, by the F-train terminus, is Jane Warner Plaza, where ragtag oddballs and kids too young for the bars congregate at public tables and chairs.

○ The Mission, Dogpatch & Potrero Hill

Anglim Gilbert Gallery GALLERY
(415-528-7258; http://anglimgilbertgallery.com; 1275 Minnesota St, 2nd fl; 11am-6pm Tue-Sat; 48, T) FREE The Bay Area hits the big time here, with gallerist Ed Gilbert continuing Anglim's 30-year legacy of launching art movements from Beat assemblage to Bay Area conceptualists. Major gallery artists range from political provocateur Enrique Chagoya to sublime

sculptor Deborah Butterfield, yet shows here maintain a hair-raising edge, such as an upraised fist pushed through gallery walls in David Huffman's *Panther*. Check the website for concurrent Anglim Gilbert shows at the gallery's downtown location at 14 Geary St.

826 Valencia CULTURAL CENTER
(415-642-5905; www.826valencia.org; 826 Valencia St; noon-6pm; H; 14, 33, 49, B 16th St Mission, M J) Avast, ye scurvy scalawags! If ye be shipwrecked without yer eye patch or McSweeney's literary anthology, lay down ye doubloons and claim yer booty at this here nonprofit Pirate Store. Below decks, kids be writing tall tales for dark nights a'sea, and ye can study writing movies and science fiction and suchlike, if that be yer dastardly inclination. Arrrr!

Dolores Park PARK
(http://sfrecpark.org/destination/mission-dolores-park; Dolores St, btwn 18th & 20th Sts; 6am-10pm; H B; 14, 33, 49, B 16th St Mission, M J) Semi-

professional tanning and taco picnics: welcome to San Francisco's sunny side. Dolores Park has something for everyone, from street ball and tennis to the Mayan-pyramid playground (sorry, kids: no blood sacrifices allowed). Political protests and other favorite local sports happen year-round, and there are free movie nights and mime troupe performances in summer. Climb to the upper southwestern corner for superb views of downtown, framed by palm trees.

★ **Balmy Alley**   PUBLIC ART

(☑415-285-2287; www.precitaeyes.org; btwn 24th & 25th Sts; ☑10, 12, 14, 27, 48, Ⓑ24th St Mission) Inspired by Diego Rivera's 1930s San Francisco murals and provoked by US foreign policy in Central America, 1970s Mission *muralistas* (muralists) led by Mia Gonzalez set out to transform the political landscape, one mural-covered garage door at a time. Today, Balmy Alley murals span three decades, from an early memorial for El Salvador activist Archbishop Óscar Romero to a homage to Frida Kahlo, Georgia O'Keeffe and other trailblazing female modern artists.

Creativity Explored   GALLERY

(☑415-863-2108; www.creativityexplored.org; 3245 16th St; donations welcome; ☺10am-3pm Mon-Wed & Fri, to 7pm Thu, noon-5pm Sat & Sun; 🚼; ☑14, 22, 33, 49, Ⓑ16th St Mission, Ⓜ J) Brave new worlds are captured in celebrated artworks destined for museum retrospectives, international shows, and even Marc Jacobs handbags and CB2 pillowcases – all by local artists with developmental disabilities, who create at this nonprofit center. Intriguing themes range from monsters to Morse code, and openings are joyous celebrations with the artists, their families and rock-star fan base.

Galería de la Raza   GALLERY

(☑415-826-8009; www.galeriadelaraza.org; 2857 24th St; donations welcome; ☺during exhibitions noon-6pm Wed-Sat; 🚼; ☑10, 14, 33, 48, 49, Ⓑ24th St Mission) Art never forgets its roots at this nonprofit that has showcased Latino art since 1970. Culture and community are constantly being redefined here, from contemporary Mexican photography and group shows exploring Latin gay culture to performances capturing community responses to Mission gentrification. Outside is the Digital Mural Project, where, in place of the usual cigarette advertisements, a billboard features slogans like 'Abolish borders!' in English, Arabic and Spanish.

🏃 **Activities**

Oceanic Society Expeditions   CRUISE

(☑415-256-9604; www.oceanicsociety.org; 3950 Scott St; whale-watching trips per person $128; ☺office 9am-5pm Mon-Fri, to 2pm Sat; ☑30) The Oceanic Society runs top-notch, naturalist-led, ocean-going weekend boat trips – sometimes to the Farallon Islands – during both whale-migration seasons. Cruises depart from the yacht harbor and last all day. Kids must be 10 years or older. Reservations required.

Kabuki Springs & Spa   SPA

(☑415-922-6000; www.kabukisprings.com; 1750 Geary Blvd; adult $25; ☺10am-9:45pm, co-ed Tue, women only Wed, Fri & Sun, men only Mon, Thu & Sat; ☑22, 38) This favorite urban retreat recreates communal, clothing-optional Japanese baths. Salt-scrub in the steam room, soak in the hot pool, then cold-plunge and reheat in the sauna. Rinse and repeat. Silence is mandatory, fostering a meditative mood – if you hear the gong, it means Shhhh! Men and women alternate days, except on co-ed Tuesdays (bathing suits required Tuesdays).

Basically Free Bike Rentals   CYCLING

(☑415-741-1196; www.sportsbasement.com/annex; 1196 Columbus Ave; half-/full-day bike rentals adult from $24/32, child $15/20; ☺9am-7pm Mon-Fri, 8am-7pm Sat & Sun; 🚼; ☑F, 30, 47, 🚋Powell-Mason, Powell-Hyde) This quality bike-rental shop cleverly gives you the choice of paying for your rental or taking the cost as credit for purchases (valid for 72 hours) at sporting-goods store **Sports Basement** (☑415-437-0100; www.sportsbasement.com; 610 Old Mason St; ☺9am-9pm Mon-Fri, 8am-8pm Sat & Sun; ☑30, 43, PresidiGo Shuttle), in the Presidio en route to the Golden Gate Bridge. (If you buy too much to carry, Sports Basement staff will mount panniers or mail your stuff home.)

☞ **Tours**

Chinatown Alleyway Tours   WALKING

(☑415-984-1478; www.chinatownalleywaytours.org; Portsmouth Sq; adult/student $26/16; ☺tours 11am Sat; 🚼; ☑1, 8, 10, 12, 30, 41, 45, 🚋California, Powell-Mason, Powell-Hyde) Teenage Chinatown residents guide you on two-hour tours through backstreets that have seen it all – Sun Yat-sen plotting China's revolution, forty-niners squandering fortunes on opium, services held in temple ruins after the 1906 earthquake. Your presence here helps the community remember its history and shape its future – Chinatown Alleyway Tours is a

HAIGHT & ASHBURY

This legendary intersection (🚌 6, 7, 33, 37, 43) was the epicenter of the psychedelic '60s, and 'Hashbury' remains a counter-culture magnet. On average Saturdays here you can sign Green Party petitions, commission a poem and hear Hare Krishna on keyboards and Bob Dylan on banjo. The clock overhead always reads 4:20 – better known in herbal circles as International Bong-Hit Time. A local clockmaker recently fixed the clock; within a week it was stuck again at 4:20.

nonprofit youth-led program of the Chinatown Community Development Center.

Precita Eyes
Mission Mural Tours   WALKING
(🗹 415-285-2287; www.precitaeyes.org; 2981 24th St; adult $15-20, child $3; 🚹; 🚌 12, 14, 48, 49, 🅱 24th St Mission) Muralists lead weekend walking tours covering 60 to 70 Mission murals within a six- to 10-block radius of mural-bedecked Balmy Alley (p93). Tours last 90 minutes to two hours and 15 minutes (for the more in-depth Classic Mural Walk). Proceeds fund mural upkeep at this community arts nonprofit.

Emperor Norton's
Fantastic Time Machine   WALKING
(🗹 415-644-8513; www.emperornortontour.com; $20; ⊘ 11am & 2:30pm Thu & Sat, 11am Sun; 🚌 30, 38, 🅱 Powell St, 🅼 Powell St, 🚋 Powell-Mason, Powell-Hyde) Huzzah, San Francisco invented time-travel contraptions! They're called shoes, and you wear them to follow the self-appointed Emperor Norton (aka historian Joseph Amster) across 2 miles of the most dastardly, scheming, uplifting and urban-legendary terrain on Earth...or at least west of Berkeley. Sunday waterfront tours depart from the Ferry Building; all others depart from Union Square's Dewey Monument. Cash only.

⭐ Festivals & Events

SF Pride Celebration   LGBT
(⊘ Jun) A day isn't enough to do SF proud: June begins with the San Francisco LGBTQ Film Festival (www.frameline.org; tickets $10-35; ⊘ Jun) and goes out in style over the last weekend with Saturday's Dyke March (www.thedykemarch.org) to the Castro's Pink Party and the joyous, million-strong Pride Parade (www.sfpride.org; ⊘ last Sun Jun) on Sunday.

Stern Grove Festival   MUSIC
(www.sterngrove.org) Music for free among the redwood and eucalyptus trees every summer since 1938. Stern Grove's 2pm Sunday concerts include hip-hop, world music and jazz, but the biggest events are performances by the SF Ballet, SF Symphony and SF Opera.

Hardly Strictly Bluegrass   MUSIC
(www.hardlystrictlybluegrass.com; ⊘ Oct) The West goes wild for free bluegrass at Golden Gate Park, with three days of concerts by 100-plus bands and seven stages of headliners.

Litquake   LITERATURE
(www.litquake.org; ⊘ 2nd week Oct) Stranger-than-fiction literary events take place during SF's outlandish literary festival, with authors leading lunchtime story sessions and spilling trade secrets over drinks at the legendary Lit Crawl.

Día de los Muertos   FESTIVAL
(Day of the Dead; www.dayofthedeadsf.org; ⊘ 2 Nov) Zombie brides and Aztec dancers in feather regalia party to wake the dead on Día de los Muertos, paying their respects to the dead at altars along the Mission processional route.

🛌 Sleeping

HI San Francisco
Fisherman's Wharf   HOSTEL $
(🗹 415-771-7277; www.sfhostels.com; Fort Mason, Bldg 240; dm $30-53, r $116-134; 🅿 @ 🛜; 🚌 28, 30, 47, 49) Trading downtown convenience for a glorious park-like setting with million-dollar waterfront views, this hostel occupies a former army-hospital building, with bargain-priced private rooms and dorms (some co-ed) with four to 22 beds (avoid bunks one and two – they're by doorways). Huge kitchen. No curfew, but no heat during daytime: bring warm clothes. Limited free parking.

Metro Hotel   HOTEL $
(🗹 415-861-5364; www.metrohotelsf.com; 319 Divisadero St; r $107; @ 🛜; 🚌 6, 24, 71) Trendy Divisadero St offers boutiques and restaurants galore, and the Metro Hotel has a prime position – some rooms overlook the garden patio of top-notch Ragazza Pizzeria. Rooms are cheap and clean, if bland – if possible, get the one with the SF mural. Some have two double beds; one room sleeps six ($150). The hotel's handy to the Haight and has 24-hour reception; no elevator.

Hotel Bohème   BOUTIQUE HOTEL $$
(🗹 415-433-9111; www.hotelboheme.com; 444 Columbus Ave; r $235–295; ⊛ @ 🛜; 🚌 10, 12, 30, 41,

45) Eclectic, historic and unabashedly poetic, this quintessential North Beach boutique hotel has jazz-era color schemes, pagoda-print upholstery and photos from the Beat years on the walls. The vintage rooms are small-ish, some face noisy Columbus Ave (quieter rooms are in back) and bathrooms are teensy, but novels beg to be written here – especially after bar crawls. No elevator or parking lot.

Inn at the Presidio   HOTEL $$
(415-800-7356; www.innatthepresidio.com; 42 Moraga Ave; r $295-380; P @ ; 43, PresidiGo Shuttle) Built in 1903 as bachelor quarters for army officers, this three-story, redbrick building in the Presidio was transformed in 2012 into a spiffy national-park lodge, styled with leather, linen and wood. Oversized rooms are plush, including feather beds with Egyptian-cotton sheets. Suites have gas fireplaces. Nature surrounds you, with hiking trailheads out back, but taxis downtown cost $25. Free parking.

Hotel Drisco   BOUTIQUE HOTEL $$$
(800-634-7277, 415-346-2880; www.hoteldrisco. com; 2901 Pacific Ave; r $338-475; @ ; 3, 24) The only hotel in Pacific Heights, a stately 1903 apartment-hotel tucked between mansions, stands high on the ridgeline. It's notable for its architecture, attentive service and chic rooms, with their elegantly austere decor, while the high-on-a-hill location is convenient only to the Marina; anywhere else requires a bus or taxi. Still, for a real boutique hotel, it's tops.

Argonaut Hotel   BOUTIQUE HOTEL $$$
(800-790-1415, 415-563-0800; www.argonaut hotel.com; 495 Jefferson St; r from $389; P ; 19, 47, 49, Powell-Hyde) Fisherman's Wharf's top hotel was built as a cannery in 1908 and has century-old wooden beams and exposed-brick walls. Rooms sport an over-the-top nautical theme, with porthole-shaped mirrors and plush, deep-blue carpets. Though all rooms have the amenities of an upper-end hotel – ultra-comfy beds, iPod docks – some are tiny with limited sunlight. Parking is $59.

Eating

Downtown, Civic Center & SoMa

farm:table   AMERICAN $
(415-292-7089; www.farmtablesf.com; 754 Post St; dishes $6-9; 7:30am-2pm Tue-Fri, 8am-3pm Sat & Sun; ; 2, 3, 27, 38) A ray of sunshine in the concrete heart of the city, this plucky little storefront showcases seasonal California organics in just-baked breakfasts and farmstead-fresh lunches. Check the menu on Twitter (@farmtable) for today's homemade cereals, savory tarts and game-changing toast – mmmm, ginger peach and mascarpone on whole-wheat sourdough. Tiny space, but immaculate kitchen and great coffee. Cash only.

★ In Situ   CALIFORNIAN, INTERNATIONAL $$
(415-941-6050; http://insitu.sfmoma.org; SFMOMA, 151 3rd St; mains $14-34; 11am-3:30pm Mon & Tue, 11am-3:30pm & 5-9pm Thu-Sun; 5, 6, 7, 14, 19, 21, 31, 38, B Montgomery, M Montgomery) The landmark gallery of modern cuisine attached to SFMOMA also showcases avant-garde masterpieces – but these ones you'll lick clean. Chef Corey Lee collaborates with star chefs worldwide, scrupulously recreating their signature dishes with California-grown ingredients so that you can enjoy Harald Wohlfahrt's impeccable anise-marinated salmon, Hiroshi Sasaki's decadent chicken thighs and Albert Adrià's gravity-defying cocoa-bubble cake in one unforgettable sitting.

★ Benu   CALIFORNIAN, FUSION $$$
(415-685-4860; www.benusf.com; 22 Hawthorne St; tasting menu $285; 6-9pm seatings Tue-Sat; 10, 12, 14, 30, 45) SF has pioneered Asian fusion cuisine for 150 years, but the pan-Pacific innovation chef-owner Corey Lee brings to the plate is gasp-inducing: foie-gras soup dumplings – what?! Dungeness crab and truffle custard pack such outsize flavor into Lee's faux–shark's fin soup, you'll swear Jaws is in there. Benu dinners are investments, but don't miss star sommelier Yoon Ha's ingenious pairings ($185).

North Beach & Chinatown

Golden Boy   PIZZA $
(415-982-9738; www.goldenboypizza.com; 542 Green St; slices $2.75-3.75; 11:30am-11:30pm Sun-Thu, to 2:30am Fri & Sat; 8, 30, 39, 41, 45, Powell-Mason) Looking for the ultimate post-bar-crawl or morning-after slice? Here you're golden. Since 1978, second-generation Sodini family *pizzaioli* (pizza makers) have perfected Genovese-style focaccia-crust pizza, achieving that mystical balance between chewy and crunchy with the ideal amount of olive oil. Go for toppings like clam and garlic or pesto, and bliss out with hot slices and draft beer at the tin-shed counter.

Molinari DELI $

(☎ 415-421-2337; www.molinarisalame.com; 373 Columbus Ave; sandwiches $10-13.50; ☺ 9am-6pm Mon-Fri, to 5:30pm Sat; ☐ 8, 10, 12, 30, 39, 41, 45, ☒ Powell-Mason) Observe quasi-religious North Beach noontime rituals: enter Molinari, and grab a number and a crusty roll. When your number's called, wisecracking staff pile your roll with heavenly fixings: milky buffalo mozzarella, tangy sun-dried tomatoes, translucent sheets of prosciutto di Parma, slabs of legendary house-cured salami, drizzles of olive oil and balsamic. Enjoy hot from the panini press at sidewalk tables.

Mister Jiu's CHINESE $$

(☎ 415-857-9688; http://misterjius.com; 28 Waverly Pl; mains $14-45; ☺ 5:30-10:30pm Tue-Sat; ☐ 30, ☒ California) Ever since the gold rush, San Francisco has craved Chinese food, powerful cocktails and hyperlocal specialties – and Mister Jiu's satisfies on all counts. Build your own banquet of Chinese classics with California twists: chanterelle chow mein, Dungeness-crab rice noodles, quail and Mission-fig sticky rice. Cocktail pairings are equally inspired – try jasmine-infused-gin Happiness ($13) with tea-smoked Sonoma-duck confit.

✖ The Marina, Fisherman's Wharf & the Piers

Off the Grid FOOD TRUCK $

(www.offthegridsf.com; Fort Mason Center, 2 Marina Blvd; items $6-14; ☺ 5-10pm Fri Apr-Oct; ☗; ☐ 22, 28) Spring through fall, some 30 food trucks circle their wagons at SF's largest mobile-gourmet hootenannies on Friday night at Fort Mason Center, and 11am to 4pm Sunday for Picnic at the Presidio on the Main Post lawn. Arrive early for the best selection and to minimize waits. Cash only.

Greens VEGETARIAN, CALIFORNIAN $$

(☎ 415-771-6222; www.greensrestaurant.com; Fort Mason Center, 2 Marina Blvd, Bldg A; mains lunch $16-19, dinner $20-28; ☺ 11:45am-2:30pm & 5:30-9pm; ☗☗; ☐ 22, 28, 30, 43, 47, 49) ✐ Career carnivores won't realize there's zero meat in the hearty black-bean chili, or in Greens' other flavor-packed vegetarian dishes, made using ingredients from a Zen farm in Marin. And, oh, what views! The Golden Gate rises just outside the window-lined dining room. The on-site cafe serves to-go lunches, but for sit-down meals, including Sunday brunch, reservations are essential.

Gary Danko CALIFORNIAN $$$

(☎ 415-749-2060; www.garydanko.com; 800 North Point St; 3-/5-course menu $86/124; ☺ 5:30-10pm; ☐ 19, 30, 47, ☒ Powell-Hyde) Gary Danko wins James Beard Awards for his impeccable Californian *haute cuisine*. Smoked-glass windows prevent passersby from tripping over their tongues at the exquisite presentations – roasted lobster with blood oranges, blushing duck breast with port-roasted grapes, lavish cheeses and trios of crèmes brûlées. Reservations a must.

✖ Nob Hill, Russian Hill & Fillmore

Swan Oyster Depot SEAFOOD $$

(☎ 415-673-1101; 1517 Polk St; dishes $10-25; ☺ 10:30am-5:30pm Mon-Sat; ☐ 1, 19, 47, 49, ☒ California) Superior flavor without the superior attitude of typical seafood restaurants. Swan's downside is an inevitable wait for the few stools at its vintage lunch counter; the upside of high turnover is incredibly fresh seafood.

La Folie FRENCH $$$

(☎ 415-776-5577; www.lafolie.com; 2316 Polk St; 3-/4-/5-course menu $100/120/140; ☺ 5:30-10pm Tue-Sat; ☐ 19, 41, 45, 47) Casually sophisticated La Folie remains one of SF's top tables – even after 30 years. Its success lies in the French-born chef-owner's uncanny ability to balance formal and playful. He's a true artist, whose cooking references classical tradition but also nods to California sensibilities. The colorful flourishes on the plate are mirrored in the *très professionnel* staff. Book a week ahead.

Acquerello CALIFORNIAN, ITALIAN $$$

(☎ 415-567-5432; www.acquerello.com; 1722 Sacramento St; 3-/4-/5-course menu $95/120/140; ☺ 5:30-9:30pm Tue-Sat; ☐ 1, 19, 47, 49, ☒ California) A converted chapel is a fitting location for a meal that'll turn Italian culinary purists into true believers in Cal-Italian cuisine. Chef Suzette Gresham's generous pastas and ingenious seasonal meat dishes include heavenly quail salad, devilish lobster *panzerotti* and venison loin chops. Suave *maître d'hôtel* Giancarlo Paterlini indulges every whim, even providing black-linen napkins if you're worried about lint.

✖ The Haight & Hayes Valley

Souvla GREEK $

(☎ 415-400-5458; www.souvlasf.com; 517 Hayes St; sandwiches & salads $11-14; ☺ 11am-10pm; ☐ 5, 21, 47, 49, Ⓜ Van Ness) Ancient Greek philosophers

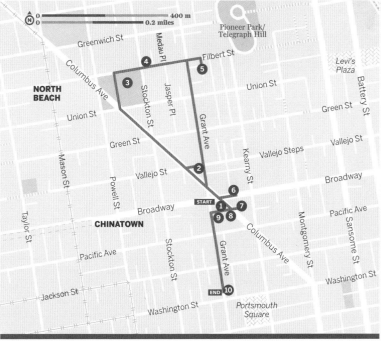

🏃 City Walk
North Beach Beat

START CITY LIGHTS BOOKS
END LI PO
LENGTH 1.5 MILES; TWO HOURS

At **❶ City Lights Books** (p86), home of Beat poetry and free speech, pick up something to inspire your journey into literary North Beach – Ferlinghetti's *San Francisco Poems* and Ginsberg's *Howl* make excellent company.

Head to **❷ Caffe Trieste** for opera on the jukebox and potent espresso in the back booth, where Francis Ford Coppola allegedly drafted *The Godfather* screenplay.

At **❸ Washington Square**, you'll spot parrots in the treetops and octogenarians in tai chi tiger stances on the lawn – pure poetry in motion. At the corner, **❹ Liguria Bakery** will give you something to write home about: focaccia hot from a 100-year-old oven.

Peaceful **❺ Bob Kaufman Alley** was named for the legendary street-corner poet, who broke a 12-year vow of silence that lasted until the Vietnam War ended, whereupon he finally walked into a North Beach cafe and recited his poem 'All Those Ships That Never

Sailed': 'Today I bring them back/Huge and transitory/And let them sail/Forever.'

Dylan jam sessions erupt in the bookshop, Allen Ginsberg spouts poetry nude in backroom documentary screenings, and onlookers grin beatifically at it all. Welcome to the **❻ Beat Museum** (p86), where visitors are all (to quote Ginsberg's *Howl*) 'angelheaded hipsters burning for the ancient heavenly connection.'

The obligatory literary bar crawl begins at **❼ Specs** (p99) amid merchant-marine memorabilia, tall tales and pitchers of Anchor Steam. *On the Road* author Jack Kerouac once blew off Henry Miller to go on a bender across the street at **❽ Vesuvio**, until bartenders ejected him into the street now named for him: **❾ Jack Kerouac Alley**. Note the words of Chinese poet Li Po embedded in the alley: 'In the company of friends, there is never enough wine.'

Follow the lead of Kerouac and Ginsberg and end your night under the laughing Buddha at **❿ Li Po** (p99) – there may not be enough wine, but there's plenty of beer.

Spaghetti at Bar Agricole
GINA FERAZZI/CONTRIBUTOR/GETTY IMAGES ©

didn't think too hard about lunch, and neither should you at Souvla. Get in line and make no-fail choices: pita or salad, wine or not. Instead of go-to gyros, try roast lamb atop kale with yogurt dressing, or tangy chicken salad with pickled onion and *mizithra* cheese. Go early/late for skylit communal seating, or head to **Patricia's Green** (http://proxysf.net; cnr Octavia Blvd & Fell St; 🚍 5, 21) with takeout.

★ **Rich Table** CALIFORNIAN $$
(📋 415-355-9085; http://richtablesf.com; 199 Gough St; mains $17-36; ⏰ 5:30-10pm Sun-Thu, to 10:30pm Fri & Sat; 🚍 5, 6, 7, 21, 47, 49, Ⓜ Van Ness) ✒ Impossible cravings begin at Rich Table, inventor of porcini doughnuts, miso-marrow-stuffed pasta and fried-chicken madeleines with caviar. Married co-chefs and owners Sarah and Evan Rich playfully riff on seasonal California fare, freestyling with whimsical off-menu amuse-bouches like trippy beet marshmallows or the Dirty Hippie: nutty hemp atop silky goat-buttermilk *panna cotta*, as offbeat and entrancing as Hippie Hill drum circles.

★ **Cala** MEXICAN, CALIFORNIAN $$$
(📋 415-660-7701; www.calarestaurant.com; 149 Fell St; ⏰ 5-10pm Mon-Wed, to 11pm Thu-Sat, 11am-3pm Sun, taco bar 11am-2pm Mon-Fri; 🚍 6, 7, 21, 47, 49, Ⓜ Van Ness) Like discovering a long-lost twin, Cala's Mexico Norte cuisine is a revelation. San Francisco's Mexican-rancher roots are deeply honored here: silky bone-marrow salsa and fragrant heritage-corn tortillas grace

a sweet potato slow-cooked in ashes. Brace yourself with mezcal margaritas for the ultimate California surf and turf: sea urchin with beef tongue. Original and unforgettable, even before Mayan-chocolate gelato with amaranth brittle.

✖ The Mission, Dogpatch & Potrero Hill

★ **La Taqueria** MEXICAN $
(📋 415-285-7117; 2889 Mission St; items $3-11; ⏰ 11am-9pm Mon-Sat, to 8pm Sun; 🚼; 🚍 12, 14, 48, 49, Ⓑ 24th St Mission) SF's definitive burrito has no saffron rice, spinach tortilla or mango salsa – just perfectly grilled meats, slow-cooked beans and tomatillo or mesquite salsa wrapped in a flour tortilla. They're purists at James Beard Award–winning La Taqueria. You'll pay extra to go without beans, because they add more meat – but spicy pickles and *crema* (sour cream) bring burrito bliss. Worth the wait, always.

★ **La Palma Mexicatessen** MEXICAN $
(📋 415-647-1500; www.lapalmasf.com; 2884 24th St; tamales, tacos & huarache $3-5; ⏰ 8am-6pm Mon-Sat, to 5pm Sun; 🚼; 🚍 12, 14, 27, 48, Ⓑ 24th St Mission) ✒ Follow the applause: that's the sound of organic tortilla-making in progress at La Palma. You've found the Mission mother lode of handmade tamales, *pupusas* (tortilla pockets) with potato and *chicharones* (pork crackling), *carnitas* (slow-roasted pork), *cotija* (Oaxacan cheese) and La Palma's own tangy tomatillo sauce. Get takeout, or bring a small army to finish that massive meal at sunny sidewalk tables.

★ **Al's Place** CALIFORNIAN $$
(📋 415-416-6136; www.alsplacesf.com; 1499 Valencia St; share plates $15-19; ⏰ 5:30-10pm Wed-Sun; 🚼; 🚍 12, 14, 49, Ⓜ J, Ⓑ 24th St Mission) ✒ The Golden State dazzles on Al's plates, featuring homegrown heirloom ingredients, pristine Pacific seafood, and grass-fed meat on the side. Painstaking preparation yields sun-drenched flavors and exquisite textures: crispy-skin cod with frothy preserved-lime dip, grilled peach melting into velvety foie gras. Dishes are half the size but thrice the flavor of mains elsewhere – get two or three, and you'll be California dreaming.

🍷 Drinking & Nightlife

No matter what you're having, SF bars, cafes and clubs are here to oblige. But why stick to your usual, when there are California wines,

Bay spirits, microbrews and local roasts to try? Adventurous drinking is abetted by local bartenders, who've been making good on gold-rush-saloon history. SF baristas take their cappuccino-foam drawings seriously and, around here, DJs invent their own software.

Pagan Idol
LOUNGE

(☑415-985-6375; www.paganidol.com; 375 Bush St; ⊘4pm-1am Mon-Fri, 6pm-1:30am Sat; Ⓑ Montgomery, ⓂF, J, K, L, M) Volcanoes erupt inside Pagan Idol every half-hour, or until there's a virgin sacrifice...what, no takers? Then order your island cocktail and brace for impact – these tiki drinks are no joke. Flirt with disaster over a Hemingway is Dead: rum, bitters and grapefruit, served in a skull. Book online to nab a hut for groups of four to six.

Bourbon & Branch
BAR

(☑415-346-1735; www.bourbonandbranch.com; 501 Jones St; ⊘6pm-2am; ⬛27, 38) 'Don't even think of asking for a cosmo' read the House Rules at this Prohibition-era speakeasy, recognizable by its deliciously misleading Anti-Saloon League sign. For award-winning cocktails in the liquored-up library, whisper the password ('books') to be ushered through the bookcase secret passageway. Reservations required for front-room booths and Wilson & Wilson Detective Agency, the noir-themed speakeasy-within-a-speakeasy (password supplied with reservations).

Bar Agricole
BAR

(☑415-355-9400; www.baragricole.com; 355 11th St; ⊘5-11pm Mon-Thu, 5pm-12am Fri & Sat, 10am-2pm & 6-9pm Sun; ⬛9, 12, 27, 47) 🍴 Drink your way to a history degree with well-researched cocktails: Whiz Bang with house bitters, whiskey, vermouth and absinthe scores high, but El Presidente with white rum, farmhouse curaçao and California-pomegranate grenadine takes top honors. This overachiever wins James Beard Award nods for spirits and eco-savvy design, plus popular acclaim for $1 oysters and $5 aperitifs during happy hour (5pm to 6pm, Monday to Sunday).

Comstock Saloon
BAR

(☑415-617-0071; www.comstocksaloon.com; 155 Columbus Ave; ⊘4pm-midnight Sun-Mon, to 2am Tue-Thu & Sat, noon-2am Fri; ⬛8, 10, 12, 30, 45, 🚋Powell-Mason) Relieving yourself in the marble trough below the bar is no longer advisable – Emperor Norton is watching from above – but otherwise this 1907 Victorian saloon brings back the Barbary Coast's glory days with authentic pisco punch and martini-precursor Martinez (gin, vermouth, bitters, maraschino liqueur). Reserve booths or back-parlor seating to hear on nights when ragtime-jazz bands play.

Li Po
BAR

(☑415-982-0072; www.lipolounge.com; 916 Grant Ave; ⊘2pm-2am; ⬛8, 30, 45, 🚋Powell-Mason, Powell-Hyde) Beat a hasty retreat to red-vinyl booths where Allen Ginsberg and Jack Kerouac debated the meaning of life under a golden Buddha. Enter the 1937 faux-grotto doorway and dodge red lanterns to place your order: Tsingtao beer or a sweet, sneaky-strong Chinese mai tai made with *baijiu* (rice liquor). Brusque bartenders, basement bathrooms, cash only – a world-class dive bar.

Specs
BAR

(Specs Twelve Adler Museum Cafe; ☑415-421-4112; 12 William Saroyan Pl; ⊘5pm-2am; ⬛8, 10, 12, 30, 41, 45, 🚋Powell-Mason) The walls here are plastered with merchant-marine memorabilia, and you'll be plastered too if you try to keep up with the salty characters holding court in back. Surrounded by seafaring mementos – including walrus genitalia over the bar – your order seems obvious: pitcher of Anchor Steam, coming right up. Cash only.

Blue Bottle Coffee Kiosk
CAFE

(www.bluebottlecoffee.net; 315 Linden St; ⊘7am-6pm Mon-Sat, from 8am Sun; ♿🐾; ⬛5, 21, 47, 49, ⓂVan Ness) Don't mock SF's coffee geekery until you've tried the elixir emerging from this back-alley garage-door kiosk. The Bay Area's Blue Bottle built its reputation with microroasted organic coffee – especially Blue Bottle–invented, off-the-menu Gibraltar, the barista-favorite drink with foam and espresso poured together into the eponymous short glass. Expect a (short) wait and seats outside on creatively repurposed traffic curbs.

%ABV
COCKTAIL BAR

(☑415-400-4748; www.abvsf.com; 3174 16th St; ⊘2pm-2am; ⬛14, 22, Ⓑ16th St Mission, ⓂJ) As kindred spirits will deduce from the name (the abbreviation for 'percent alcohol by volume'), this bar is backed by cocktail crafters who know their Rittenhouse rye from their Japanese malt whiskey. Top-notch hooch is served promptly and without pretension, including excellent Cali wine and beer on tap and original historically inspired cocktails like the Sutro Swizzle (Armagnac, grapefruit shrub, maraschino liqueur).

Trick Dog BAR

(☏ 415-471-2999; www.trickdogbar.com; 3010 20th St; ⏰ 3pm-2am; 🚍 12, 14, 49) Drink adventurously with ingenious cocktails inspired by local obsessions: San Francisco muralists, Chinese diners or conspiracy theories. Every six months, Trick Dog adopts a new theme and the entire menu changes. Arrive early for bar stools or hit the mood-lit loft for high-concept bar bites.

☆ Entertainment

SFJAZZ Center JAZZ

(☏ 866-920-5299; www.sfjazz.org; 201 Franklin St; tickets $25-120; 🚻; 🚍 5, 6, 7, 21, 47, 49, Ⓜ Van Ness) 🎷 Jazz legends and singular talents from Argentina to Yemen are showcased at North America's newest, largest jazz center. Hear fresh takes on classic jazz albums and poets riffing with jazz combos in the downstairs Joe Henderson Lab, and witness extraordinary main-stage collaborations ranging from Afro-Cuban All Stars to roots legends Emmylou Harris, Rosanne Cash and Lucinda Williams.

San Francisco Symphony CLASSICAL MUSIC

(☏ box office 415-864-6000, rush-ticket hotline 415-503-5577; www.sfsymphony.org; Grove St, btwn Franklin St & Van Ness Ave; tickets $20-150; 🚍 21, 45, 47, Ⓜ Van Ness, Ⓑ Civic Center) From the moment conductor Michael Tilson Thomas bounces up on his toes and raises his baton, the audience is on the edge of their seats for another thunderous performance by the Grammy-winning SF Symphony. Don't miss signature concerts of Beethoven and Mahler, live symphony performances with such films as *Star Trek*, and creative collaborations with artists from Elvis Costello to Metallica.

Great American Music Hall LIVE MUSIC

(☏ 415-885-0750; www.gamh.com; 859 O'Farrell St; shows $20-45; ⏰ box office 10:30am-6pm Mon-Fri & show nights; 🚻; 🚍 19, 38, 47, 49) Everyone busts out their best sets at this opulent 1907 bordello turned all-ages venue – indie rockers like the Band Perry throw down, international legends such as Salif Keita grace the stage, and John Waters hosts Christmas extravaganzas. Pay $25 extra for dinner with prime balcony seating to watch shows comfortably, or rock out with the standing-room scrum downstairs.

American Conservatory Theater THEATER

(ACT; ☏ 415-749-2228; www.act-sf.org; 405 Geary St; ⏰ box office 10am-6pm Mon, to curtain Tue-Sun; 🚍 8, 30, 38, 45, 🚋 Powell-Mason, Powell-Hyde, Ⓑ Powell, Ⓜ Powell) Breakthrough shows launch at this turn-of-the-century landmark, which has hosted ACT's productions of Tony Kushner's *Angels in America* and Robert Wilson's *Black Rider*, with William S Burroughs' libretto and music by Tom Waits. Major playwrights like Tom Stoppard, Dustin Lance Black, Eve Ensler and David Mamet premiere work here, while the ACT's new **Strand Theater** (☏ 415-749-2228; www.act-sf.org/home/box_office/strand.html; 1127 Market St; Ⓕ F, Ⓑ Civic Center, Ⓜ Civic Center) stages experimental works.

Alamo Drafthouse Cinema CINEMA

(☏ 415-549-5959; https://drafthouse.com/sf; 2550 Mission St; tickets $9-20; 🚻; 🚍 14, Ⓑ 24th St Mission) The landmark 1932 New Mission cinema, now restored to its original Timothy Pflueger–designed art-deco glory, has a new mission: to upgrade dinner-and-a-movie dates. Staff deliver microbrews and tasty fare to plush banquette seats, so you don't miss a moment of the premieres, cult revivals (especially Music Mondays) or SF favorites from *Mrs Doubtfire* to *Dirty Harry* – often with filmmaker Q&As.

🛍 Shopping

Union Square is the city's principal shopping district, with flagship stores and department stores, including international chains. Downtown shopping-district borders are (roughly) Powell St (west), Sutter St (north), Kearny St (east) and Market St (south), where the **Westfield mall** (www.westfield.com/sanfrancisco; 865 Market St; ⏰ 10am-8:30pm Mon-Sat, 11am-7pm Sun; 🚻; 🚋 Powell-Mason, Powell-Hyde, Ⓜ Powell, Ⓑ Powell) sprawls. The epicenter of the Union Square shopping area is around Post St, near Grant Ave. Stockton St crosses Market St and becomes 4th St, flanked by flagship stores and **Metreon cinema and mall** (☏ 415-369-6201; www.amctheatres.com; 101 4th St; adult/child $14.49/11.49; 🚍 14, Ⓜ Powell, Ⓑ Powell). For boutique offerings, head toward **Jackson Square** (www.jacksonsquaresf.com; around Jackson & Montgomery Sts; Ⓜ Embarcadero, Ⓑ Embarcadero) and along Commercial St.

Recchiuti Chocolates FOOD & DRINKS

(☏ 415-834-9494; www.recchiuticonfections.com; 1 Ferry Bldg, cnr Market St & the Embarcadero; ⏰ 10am-7pm Mon-Fri, 8am-6pm Sat, 10am-5pm Sun; Ⓜ Embarcadero, Ⓑ Embarcadero) No San Franciscan can resist award-winning Recchiuti: Pacific Heights parts with old money for

SOMA GAY BARS

Sailors have cruised Polk St and Tenderloin gay/trans joints since the 1940s, Castro bars boomed in the 1970s and women into women have been hitting Mission dives since the '60s – but SoMa warehouses have been the biggest weekend gay scene for decades now. From leather bars and drag cabarets to full-time LGBTIQ clubs, SoMa has it all. True, internet cruising has thinned the herd, many women still prefer the Mission and some nights are slow starters – but the following fixtures on the gay drinking scene pack at weekends.

Eagle Tavern (www.sf-eagle.com; 398 12th St; $5-10; ☺2pm-2am Mon-Fri, from noon Sat & Sun; ☐9, 12, 27, 47) Legendary leather bar with Sunday beer busts.

Oasis (☑415-795-3180; www.sfoasis.com; 298 11th St; tickets $15-35; ☐9, 12, 14, 47, Ⓜ Van Ness) SF's dedicated drag cabaret mounts outrageous shows, sometimes literally.

Lone Star Saloon (☑415-863-9999; http://lonestarsf.com; 1354 Harrison St; ☺4pm-2am Mon-Thu, from 2pm Fri, from noon Sat & Sun; ☐9, 12, 27, 47) The original bear bar makes manly men warm and fuzzy at happy hour.

Stud (www.studsf.com; 399 9th St; $5-8; ☺noon-2am Tue, 5pm-3am Thu-Sat, 5pm-midnight Sun; ☐12, 19, 27, 47) The freaks come out at night for surreal, only-in-SF theme events.

Powerhouse (☑415-522-8689; www.powerhouse-sf.com; 1347 Folsom St; free-$10; ☺4pm-2am; ☐9, 12, 27, 47) Major men-only back-patio action.

Hole in the Wall (☑415-431-4695; www.holeinthewallsaloon.com; 1369 Folsom St; ☺2pm-2am Mon-Fri, noon-2am Sat & Sun; ☐9, 12, 47) Spiritual home to gay bikers and loudmouth punks.

Club OMG (☑415-896-6473; www.clubomgsf.com; 43 6th St; free-$10; ☺5pm-2am Tue-Fri & Sun, 7pm-2am Sat; Ⓜ Powell, Ⓑ Powell) Dance in your skivvies on Skid Row.

its *fleur de sel* caramels; Noe Valley's foodie kids prefer S'more Bites to the campground variety; North Beach toasts to the red-wine-pairing chocolate box; and the Mission approves SF-landmark chocolates designed by Creativity Explored (p93) – proceeds benefit the Mission arts-education nonprofit for artists with developmental disabilities.

Heath Ceramics HOMEWARES
(☑415-399-9284; www.heathceramics.com; 1 Ferry Bldg, cnr Market St & the Embarcadero; ☺10am-7pm Mon-Fri, 8am-6pm Sat, 11am-9pm Sun; Ⓜ Embarcadero, Ⓑ Embarcadero) Odds are your favorite SF meal was served on Heath Ceramics, Bay Area chefs' tableware of choice ever since Alice Waters started using Heath's modern, hand-thrown dishes at Chez Panisse. Heath's muted colors and streamlined, mid-century designs stay true to Edith Heath's originals c 1948. Pieces are priced for fine dining, except studio seconds, sold here at weekends.

Golden Gate
Fortune Cookie Company FOOD & DRINKS
(☑415-781-3956; 56 Ross Alley; ☺9am-6pm; ☐8, 30, 45, ☐Powell-Mason, Powell-Hyde) Make a fortune at this bakery, where cookies are stamped from vintage presses – just as they were in 1909, when fortune cookies were

invented for SF's **Japanese Tea Garden** (☑415-752-1171; www.japaneseteagardensf.com; 75 Hagiwara Tea Garden Dr, Golden Gate Park; adult/child $8/2, before 10am Mon, Wed & Fri free; ☺9am-6pm Mar-Oct, to 4:45pm Nov-Feb; Ⓟ ♿; ☐5, 7, 44, ⓂN). Write your own fortunes for custom cookies (50¢ each), or get cookies with regular or risqué fortunes (pro tip: add 'in bed' to regular ones). Cash only; 50¢ tip for photos.

ⓘ Information

DANGERS & ANNOYANCES

Keep your city smarts and wits about you, especially at night in the Tenderloin, South of Market (SoMa) and the Mission.

➡ Avoid using your smart phone unnecessarily on the street – phone-snatching is a crime of opportunity and a problem in SF.

➡ The Bayview–Hunters Point neighborhood (south of Potrero Hill, along the water) is plagued by crime and violence and isn't suitable for wandering tourists.

➡ After dark, Mission Dolores Park, Buena Vista Park and the entry to Golden Gate Park at Haight and Stanyan Sts are used for drug deals and casual sex hookups.

EMERGENCY & MEDICAL SERVICES

San Francisco General Hopsital (Zuckerberg San Franciso General Hospital and Trauma

Center; ⚡emergency 415-206-8111, main hospital 415-206-8000; www.sfdph.org; 1001 Potrero Ave; ⊙24hr; 🚌9, 10, 33, 48) Best for serious trauma. Provides care to uninsured patients, including psychiatric care; no documentation required beyond ID.

University of California San Francisco Medical Center (⚡415-476-1000; www.ucsfhealth.org; 505 Parnassus Ave; ⊙24hr; 🚌6, 7, 43, Ⓜ N) ER at leading university hospital.

TOURIST INFORMATION

California Welcome Center (⚡415-981-1280; www.visitcwc.com; Pier 39, 2nd fl; ⊙9am-7pm; 🚌47, 🚋Powell-Mason, ⒻE, F) Handy resource for stroller and wheelchair rental, plus luggage storage, phone charging and ideas for broader California travel.

San Francisco Visitor Information Center (⚡415-391-2000; www.sftravel.com/visitor-information-center; lower level, Hallidie Plaza, cnr Market & Powell Sts; ⊙9am-5pm Mon-Fri, to 3pm Sat & Sun, closed Sun Nov-Apr; 🚋Powell-Mason, Powell-Hyde, ⒨Powell, ⒷPowell) Provides practical multilingual information, sells transportation passes, publishes glossy maps and booklets, and provides interactive touch screens.

❶ Getting Around

When San Franciscans aren't pressed for time, most walk, bike or ride Muni instead of taking a car or cab. Traffic is notoriously bad at rush hour, and parking is next to impossible in center-city neighborhoods. Avoid driving until it's time to leave town – or drive during off-peak hours.

For Bay Area transit options, departures and arrivals, call ⚡511 or check www.511.org. A detailed *Muni Street & Transit Map* is available free online.

BART High-speed transit to East Bay, Mission St, SF airport and Millbrae, where it connects with Caltrain.

Cable cars Frequent, slow and scenic, from 6am to 12:30am daily. Single rides cost $7; for frequent use, get a Muni Passport ($21 per day).

Muni streetcar and bus Reasonably fast, but schedules vary wildly by line; infrequent after 9pm. Fares are $2.50.

Taxi Fares are about $2.75 per mile; meters start at $3.50. Add 15% to the fare as a tip ($1 minimum). For quickest service in San Francisco, download the Flywheel app for smart phones, which dispatches the nearest taxi.

BICYCLE

Contact the **San Francisco Bicycle Coalition** (⚡415-431-2453; www.sfbike.org) for maps, information and legal matters regarding bicyclists. Bike sharing is new in SF: racks for **Bay Area Bike Share** (⚡855-480-2453; www.bayarea

bikeshare.com; 30-day membership $30) are located east of Van Ness Ave, and in the SoMa area; however, bikes come without helmets, and biking downtown without proper protection can be particularly dangerous. Bicycles can be taken on BART, but not aboard crowded trains, and never in the first car, nor in the first three cars during weekday rush hours; folded bikes are allowed in all cars at all times. On Amtrak, bikes can be checked as baggage for $5.

BOAT

With the revival of the Embarcadero and the reinvention of the Ferry Building as a gourmet dining destination, commuters and tourists alike are taking the scenic ferry across the bay.

CAR

If you can, avoid driving in San Francisco: heavy traffic is a given, street parking is harder to find than true love, and meter readers are ruthless.

THE BAY AREA

Cross the Golden Gate Bridge into Marin County and visit wizened ancient redwoods body-blocking the sun and herds of elegant tule elk prancing along the bluffs of Tomales Bay. Gray whales show some fluke off the cape of the wind-scoured Point Reyes peninsula, while hawks surf the skies in the shaggy hills of the Marin Headlands. The city of Berkeley sparked the state's locavore food movement and continues to be at the forefront of environmental and left-leaning political causes.

Berkeley

⚡510 / POP 116,770

Berkeley – the birthplace of the free-speech and disability-rights movements, and the home of the hallowed halls of the University of California, Berkeley (aka 'Cal') – is no bashful wallflower. A national hot spot of (mostly left-of-center) intellectual discourse and with one of the most vocal activist populations in the country, this infamous college town has an interesting mix of graying progressives and idealistic undergrads. It's easy to stereotype 'Beserkeley' for some of its recycle-or-else PC crankiness, but the city is often on the forefront of environmental and political issues that eventually go mainstream. Berkeley is also home to a large South Asian community, as evidenced by an abundance of sari shops on University Ave and an unusually large number of Indian, Pakistani and Nepalese restaurants.

⊙ Sights

Berkeley's downtown, centered on Shattuck Ave between University Ave and Dwight Way, has few traces of the city's tie-dyed reputation. Today it abounds with shops, restaurants and restored public buildings. The nearby arts district revolves around the acclaimed thespian stomping grounds of the Berkeley Repertory Theatre and Aurora Theatre Company and live music at the historic Freight & Salvage Coffeehouse, all on Addison St.

University of California, Berkeley   UNIVERSITY

(☑ 510-642-6000; www.berkeley.edu; ☉ hours vary; ℗; Ⓑ Downtown Berkeley) 'Cal' is one of the country's top universities, California's oldest university (1866), and home to 40,000 diverse, politically conscious students. Next to California Memorial Stadium (☑ 510-642-2730; www.californiamemorialstadium.com; 2227 Piedmont Ave; ☉ hours vary; 🚻; ⬚ AC Transit 52), the Koret Visitor Center (p106) has information and maps, and leads free campus walking tours (reservations required). Cal's landmark is the 1914 Campanile (Sather Tower; ☑ 510-642-6000; http://campanile.berkeley.edu; adult/child $3/2; ☉ 10am-3:45pm Mon-Fri, 10am-4:45pm Sat, to 1:30pm & 3-4:45pm Sun; 🚻; Ⓑ Downtown Berkeley), with elevator rides ($3) to the top and carillon concerts. The Bancroft Library (☑ 510-642-3781; www.lib.berkeley.edu/libraries/bancroft-library; University Dr; ☉ archives 10am-4pm or 5pm Mon-Fri; Ⓑ Downtown Berkeley) FREE displays the small gold nugget that started the California gold rush in 1848.

UC Berkeley Art Museum   MUSEUM

(BAMPFA; ☑ 510-642-0808; www.bampfa.berkeley.edu; 2155 Center St; adult/child $12/free; ☉ 11am-7pm Sun, Wed & Thu, to 9pm Fri & Sat; Ⓑ Downtown Berkeley) With a stainless-steel exterior wrapping around a 1930s printing plant, the museum's new location holds multiple galleries showcasing a limited number of artworks, from ancient Chinese to cutting-edge contemporary. The complex also houses a bookstore, cafe and the much-loved Pacific Film Archive (p106).

Phoebe A Hearst Museum of Anthropology   MUSEUM

(☑ 510-642-3682; http://hearstmuseum.berkeley.edu; Bancroft Way, at College Ave; adult/child $6/free; ☉ 11am-5pm Sun-Wed & Fri, to 8pm Thu, 10am-6pm Sat; ⬚ AC Transit 6, 51B) South of the Campanile in Kroeber Hall, this small museum includes exhibits from indigenous cultures around the world, including ancient Peruvian, Egyptian and African items. There's also a large collection highlighting Native Californian cultures.

Telegraph Avenue   STREET

(☉ shop & restaurant hours vary; ℗; ⬚ AC Transit 6) Telegraph Ave has traditionally been the throbbing heart of studentville in Berkeley, the sidewalks crowded with undergrads, postdocs and youthful shoppers squeezing their way past throngs of vendors, buskers and panhandlers. Street stalls hawk everything from crystals to bumper stickers to self-published tracts. Several cafes and budget eateries cater to students.

Berkeley Rose Garden   GARDENS

(☑ 510-981-6700; www.ci.berkeley.ca.us; 1200 Euclid Ave; ☉ dawn-dusk; ⬚ AC Transit 65) FREE In North Berkeley discover the Berkeley Rose Garden, with its eight terraces of colorful explosions. Here you'll find quiet benches and a plethora of almost perpetually blooming roses arranged by hue. Across the street, Cordornices Park has a children's playground with a very fun concrete slide, about 40ft long.

★ Tilden Regional Park   PARK

(☑ 510-544-2747; www.ebparks.org/parks/tilden; ☉ 5am-10pm; ℗ 🚻 ♿; ⬚ AC Transit 67) 🅿 FREE This 2079-acre park, up in the hills east of town, is Berkeley's best. It has nearly 40 miles of hiking and multiuse trails of varying difficulty, from paved paths to hilly scrambles, including part of the magnificent Bay Area Ridge Trail. There's also a miniature steam train ($3), a children's farm and environmental education center, a wonderfully wild-looking botanical garden and an 18-hole golf course. Lake Anza is good for picnics and from spring through fall you can swim ($3.50). AC Transit bus 67 runs to the park on weekends and holidays from Downtown Berkeley BART station, but only stops at the park entrance on weekdays.

UC Botanical Garden at Berkeley   GARDENS

(☑ 510-643-2755; http://botanicalgarden.berkeley.edu; 200 Centennial Dr; adult/child $10/2; ☉ 9am-5pm, last entry 4:30pm, closed 1st Tue of month; ℗ 🚻; ⬚ Bear Transit H) 🅿 With 34 acres and more than 10,000 types of plants, this garden in the hills above campus has one of the most varied collections in the USA. Flora from every continent except Antarctica are lovingly tended here, with special emphasis on Mediterranean species that grow in California, the Americas, the Mediterranean and southern Africa. On weekdays, catch the university's Bear Transit H Line shuttle ($1) from campus. Limited parking across the street from the garden costs $1 per hour. A nearby fire trail makes a woodsy walking loop around Strawberry Canyon, offering great views of town and the off-limits Lawrence Berkeley National Laboratory. Find the trailhead on the east side of Centennial Dr just southwest of the botanical garden; you'll emerge near the Lawrence Hall of Science (☑510-642-5132; www.lawrencehallofscience.org; 1 Centennial Dr; adult/child $12/10; ⊗10am-5pm Wed-Sun, daily mid-Jun–early Sep; P⊞; ⬚AC Transit 65).

Berkeley Marina   MARINA
(☑510-981-6740; www.ci.berkeley.ca.us; 201 University Ave; ⊗6am-10pm; P⊞⊠; ⬚AC Transit 81) At the west end of University Ave is the marina, frequented by squawking seagulls, silent types fishing from the pier and, especially on windy weekends, families flying colorful kites. It offers sweeping waterfront views from paved walking, cycling and running paths.

Adventure Playground   PARK
(☑510-981-6720; www.cityofberkeley.info/adventure playground; 160 University Ave; ⊗11am-5pm mid-Jun–mid-Aug, Sat & Sun only rest of year; P⊞; ⬚AC Transit 81) At the Berkeley Marina, this is a free outdoor park encouraging creativity and cooperation where supervised kids of any age can help build and paint their own structures. There's an awesome zipline too. Dress the tykes in play clothes, because they *will* get dirty.

Takara Sake   MUSEUM
(☑510-540-8250; www.takarasake.com; 708 Addison St; tasting fee $5-10; ⊗noon-6pm, last tasting 5:30pm; ⬚AC Transit 51B) Stop in to see the traditional wooden tools used for making sake and a short video of the brewing process. Tours of the factory aren't offered, but you can view elements of modern production and bottling through a window. Sake flights are poured in a spacious tasting room constructed with reclaimed wood and floor tiles fashioned from recycled glass.

🛏 Sleeping

Lodging rates spike during special university events such as graduation (mid-May) and home football games. A number of older, less expensive motels along University Ave can be handy during peak demand, as can chain motels and hotels off I-80 in Emeryville or Vallejo.

Berkeley YMCA Hotel   HOSTEL $
(☑510-848-6800; http://ymcacba.org; 2001 Allston Way; s/d with shared bath from $56/94; ⊜@🛜⊠;

B Downtown Berkeley) At the 100-year-old downtown Y building, rates for well-worn, spartan private rooms (all with shared bath) include use of the sauna, pool and fitness center and kitchen facilities. Entrance on Milvia St.

Berkeley City Club   HISTORIC HOTEL $$
(☑510-848-7800; www.berkeleycityclub.com; 2315 Durant Ave; r/ste from $215; P⊜@🛜⊠; ⬚AC Transit 51B) Designed by Julia Morgan (the architect of Hearst Castle), the 35 rooms and dazzling common areas of this refurbished 1929 historic landmark building (which is also a private club) feel like a glorious time warp into a more refined era. The hotel contains lush and serene Italianate courtyards, gardens and terraces, and a stunning indoor pool. Parking is $20.

Hotel Shattuck Plaza   HOTEL $$
(☑510-845-7300; www.hotelshattuckplaza.com; 2086 Allston Way; r from $200; P⊜❄@🛜; B Downtown Berkeley) Following a $15-million renovation and greening of this 100-year-old downtown jewel, a foyer of red Italian glass lighting and flocked Victorian-style wallpaper leads to comfortable rooms with down comforters and an airy, columned restaurant serving all meals.

★ Claremont Resort & Spa   RESORT $$$
(☑510-843-3000; www.fairmont.com/claremont -berkeley; 41 Tunnel Rd; r from $240; P⊜❄@🛜 ⊠⊠) The East Bay's classy crème de la crème, this Fairmont-owned historic hotel is a glamorous white 1915 building with elegant restaurants, a fitness center, swimming pools, tennis courts and a full-service spa. The bayview rooms are superb. It's located at the foot of the Berkeley Hills, off Hwy 13 (Tunnel Rd) near the Oakland border. Parking is $30.

🍴 Eating

Telegraph Ave is packed with cafes, pizza counters and cheap restaurants, and Berkeley's Little India runs along the University Ave corridor. Many more restaurants can be found along Shattuck Ave near the Downtown Berkeley BART station. The section of Shattuck Ave north of University Ave, nicknamed the 'Gourmet Ghetto,' is home to excellent restaurants and cafes for all budgets.

Butcher's Son   VEGAN, DELI $
(☑510-984-0818; www.thebutcherveganson.com; 1941 University Ave; mains $8-13; ⊗11am-8pm Mon & Thu-Fri, to 3pm Tue & Wed, 9am-5pm Sat & Sun; ✎; B Downtown Berkeley) What could be

more in tune with Berkeley's granola-crunchy, latter-day-hippie vibe than a vegan deli? Gorge yourself on imitation deli meats and cheeses that will scratch that itch for a fried mozzarella and meatball sandwich or hot turkey and roast beef on rye, all made without any animal products.

KoJa Kitchen FUSION $
(☏510-962-5652; www.kojakitchen.com; 2395 Telegraph Ave; items $4-10; ⏱11am-10pm; 🚌AC Transit 51B) From food truck to a brick-and-mortar shop, this Korean-Japanese fusion eatery makes addictive short-rib and braised-pork sandwiches out of garlicky fried-rice buns, with kimchi-spiked waffle fries on the side. Order ahead, or expect a wait.

Ippuku JAPANESE $$
(☏510-665-1969; www.ippukuberkeley.com; 2130 Center St; shared plates $5-20; ⏱5-10pm Tue-Thu, to 11pm Fri & Sat; 🚇Downtown Berkeley) Japanese expats gush that Ippuku reminds them of *izakaya* (Japanese gastropubs) back in Tokyo. Choose from a menu of yakitori (skewered meats and vegetables) and handmade soba noodles as you settle in at one of the traditional tatami tables (no shoes, please) or cozy booth perches. Order *shōchū*, a distilled alcohol usually made from rice or barley. Reservations essential.

La Note FRENCH $$
(☏510-843-1525; www.lanoterestaurant.com; 2377 Shattuck Ave; mains $10-25; ⏱breakfast & lunch 8am-2:30pm Mon-Fri, to 3pm Sat & Sun, dinner 6-10pm Thu-Sat; 🚇Downtown Berkeley) A rustic country-French bistro downtown, La Note serves excellent breakfasts. Wake up to a big bowl of café au lait, paired with brioche *pain perdu* or lemon-gingerbread pancakes with poached pears. Anticipate a wait on weekends.

★**Chez Panisse** CALIFORNIAN $$$
See p32.

🍸 Drinking

You'll never come up short of places to imbibe in Berkeley. Join students at bars and pubs scattered around downtown, near the university campus or along College Ave in Elmwood. Detour to industrial areas of West Berkeley to discover craft beers and a sake distillery.

Fieldwork Brewing Company BREWERY
(☏510-898-1203; http://fieldworkbrewing.com; 1160 6th St; ⏱11am-10pm Sun-Thu, to 11pm Fri & Sat; 🚌AC Transit 12) Come to this industrial

Claremont Resort & Spa
CDRIN/SHUTTERSTOCK ©

brewery taproom at the edge of town for outstanding craft beer and sit down on the outdoor patio with a tasting flight of IPAs or a glass of rich Mexican hot chocolate stout. It's dog-friendly, and there are racks to hang your bicycle inside the front door. There's a short menu of Mexican-Californian food too.

Asha Tea House CAFE
(www.ashateahouse.com; 2086 University Ave; ⏱11am-10pm Mon-Sat, to 8pm Sun; 🖥; 🚇Downtown Berkeley) 🍵 Find your bliss in this industrial-modern tea shop, where acrylic prints of verdant tea plantations overhang the bar. Handcrafted Indian chai, Japanese matcha and Hong Kong–style milk tea star on a connoisseur's drinks menu.

Albatross PUB
(☏510-843-2473; www.albatrosspub.com; 1822 San Pablo Ave; ⏱6pm-2am Sun-Tue, from 4:30pm Wed-Sat; 🚌AC Transit 51B) Berkeley's oldest pub is one of the most inviting and friendly in the city. Some serious darts are played here and board games get played around many of the worn-out tables. Sunday is trivia quiz night.

⭐ Entertainment

Berkeley's arts district, centered on Addison St between Milvia St and Shattuck Ave, anchors downtown's performing-arts scene. Berkeley also has plenty of intimate live-music venues. Cover charges usually range from $5 to $20, and several venues are all-ages or 18-and-over.

Freight & Salvage Coffeehouse   LIVE MUSIC
(📷 510-644-2020; www.thefreight.org; 2020 Addison St; tickets $5-45; ⊙ shows daily; ♿; 🅱 Downtown Berkeley) This legendary club has almost 50 years of history and is conveniently located in the downtown arts district. It features great traditional folk, country, bluegrass and world music, and welcomes all ages, with half-price tickets for patrons under 21.

Pacific Film Archive   CINEMA
(PFA; 📷 510-642-5249; www.bampfa.berkeley.edu; 2155 Center St; adult/child from $12/8; ⊙ hours vary; ♿; 🅱 Downtown Berkeley) A world-renowned film center with an ever-changing schedule of international and classic films. The spacious theater has seats comfy enough for hours-long movie marathons.

Aurora Theatre Company   THEATER
(📷 510-843-4822; www.auroratheatre.org; 2081 Addison St; tickets from $25; ⊙ box office usually 1-4pm Tue-Fri) Intimate downtown theater performs contemporary, thought-provoking plays staged with subtle aesthetics.

🛍 Shopping

University Press Books   BOOKS
(📷 510-548-0585; www.universitypressbooks.com; 2430 Bancroft Way; ⊙ 11am-7pm Mon-Fri, to 6pm Sat, noon-5pm Sun; 🚇 AC Transit 51B) Across the street from campus, this academic and scholarly bookstore stocks works by UC Berkeley professors and other academic and museum publishers, with frequent author appearances.

Down Home Music   MUSIC
(📷 510-525-2129; www.downhomemusic.com; 10341 San Pablo Ave, El Cerrito; ⊙ 11am-7pm Tue-Sun; 🚇 AC Transit 72) North of Berkeley, this world-class store for roots, blues, folk, country, jazz and world music is affiliated with the Arhoolie record label, which has been issuing landmark recordings since the early 1960s.

ℹ️ Information

MEDICAL SERVICES
Alta Bates Summit Medical Center, Ashby Campus (📷 510-204-4444; www.sutterhealth. org; 2450 Ashby Ave; ⊙ 24hr; 🚇 AC Transit 6) Has 24-hour emergency services.

TOURIST INFORMATION
UC Berkeley Koret Visitor Center (📷 510-642-5215; http://visit.berkeley.edu; 2227 Piedmont Ave; ⊙ 8:30am-4:30pm Mon-Fri, 9am-1pm Sat & Sun; 🚇 AC Transit 36) Campus maps and information available at the new visitor center on Goldman Plaza at California

Memorial Stadium (p103). Free 90-minute campus walking tours usually start at 10am daily (advance reservations required).

Visit Berkeley (📷 510-549-7040; www.visit berkeley.com; 2030 Addison St; ⊙ 9am-1pm & 2-5pm Mon-Fri; 🅱 Downtown Berkeley) Helpful Berkeley Convention & Visitors Bureau prints a free visitors guide, also available online.

ℹ️ Getting Around

Local buses, cycling and walking are the best ways to get around Berkeley.

BICYCLE
By Downtown Berkeley BART station, **Bike Station** (📷 510-548-7433; http://bikehub.com/bartbikestation; 2208 Shattuck Ave; per day/week/month $35/95/200; ⊙ 7am-9pm Mon-Fri, 11am-7pm Sat) rents bicycles with a helmet and U-lock.

BUS
AC Transit (📷 510-891-4777; www.actransit. org) operates local public buses in and around Berkeley. The one-way fare is $2.10; pay with cash (exact change required) or a Clipper card (www.clippercard.com).

The university's **Bear Transit** (📷 510-643-7701; http://pt.berkeley.edu) runs a shuttle from Downtown Berkeley BART station to various points on campus. From Bear Transit's on-campus stop at Hearst Mining Circle, the H Line runs along Centennial Dr to the upper parts of the campus. For visitors, each ride costs $1 (bring cash).

CAR & MOTORCYCLE
Drivers should note that numerous barriers have been set up to prevent car traffic from traversing residential streets at high speeds, so zigzagging is necessary in some neighborhoods.

Downtown and near the university campus, pay-parking lots are well signed. Metered street-parking spots are rarely empty.

Sebastopol

📷 707 / POP 7659

Grapes have replaced apples as the new cash crop, but Sebastopol's farm-town identity remains rooted in the apple – evidenced by the much-heralded summertime Gravenstein Apple Fair. The town center feels suburban because of traffic, but a hippie tinge gives it color. This is the refreshingly laid-back side of Wine Country and makes a good-value base for exploring the area.

⊙ Sights & Activities

Around Sebastopol, look for family-friendly farms, gardens, animal sanctuaries and pick-your-own orchards. For a countywide list, check out the Sonoma County Farm Trails Guide (www.farmtrails.org).

California Carnivores
GARDENS

(☎ 707-824-0433; www.californiacarnivores.com; 2833 Old Gravenstein Hwy S; ⊙ 10am-4pm Thu-Mon) Even vegans can't help admiring the incredible carnivorous plants (the largest collection in the US), including specimens from around the globe. Owner Peter D'Amato encourages visitors to BYOB (bring your own bugs) and watch as the plants devour them. He's also written a book with a perfect name, *The Savage Garden.*

★ Patrick Amiot
Junk Art
GALLERY

(www.patrickamiot.com; Florence Ave; P ✦) Prepare to gawk and giggle at the wacky Patrick Amiot sculptures gracing front yards along Florence Ave. Fashioned from recycled materials, a hot-rodding rat, a hectic waitress and a witch in midflight are a few of the oversized and demented lawn ornaments parading along the street. Keep an eye out and you'll notice more of these scattered throughout Sebastopol.

Spirit Works Distillery
DISTILLERY

(☎ 707-634-4793; www.spiritworksdistillery.com; 6790 McKinley St, 100, Barlow; tasting/tour $18/20; ⊙ 11am-5pm Wed-Sun) ✦ A bracing alternative to wine tasting, Spirit Works crafts superb small-batch spirits – vodka, gin, sloe gin and (soon) whiskey – from organic California red-winter wheat. The distillery abides by a 'grain-to-glass' philosophy, with milling, mashing, fermenting and distilling all done on-site. Sample and buy in the warehouse. Tours (by reservation) happen Friday to Sunday at 5pm and finish with a tasting. Bottles are $27 to $36.

Farmers Market
MARKET

(www.sebastopolfarmmarket.org; cnr Petaluma & McKinley Aves; ⊙ 10am-1:30pm Sun) Meets at the downtown plaza.

🛏 Sleeping

Fairfield Inn & Suites
HOTEL $$

(☎ 800-465-4329, 707-829-6677; www.winecountry hi.com; 1101 Gravenstein Hwy S; r $129-320; ❄ @ 🛜 🐾) Generic but modern, this hotel has little extras such as in-room refrigerators and coffee makers, plus a hot tub. Carpeting, wallpaper and furnishings were revamped throughout the hotel for a sleeker look.

Sebastopol Inn
MOTEL $$

(☎ 800-653-1082, 707-829-2500; www.sebastopol inn.com; 6751 Sebastopol Ave; r $119-388; ❄ 🛜 🐾) We like this independent, non-cookie-cutter motel for its quiet, off-street location, usually reasonable rates and good-looking, if basic, rooms. Outside are grassy areas for kids and a hot tub.

🍴 Eating

Sebastopol is a town of artists and locavores, and while its restaurant scene reflects those predilections, there are plenty of international options as well. Above all, the local produce and seafood is top-notch.

★ Handline
CALIFORNIAN $

(☎ 707-827-3744; www.handline.com; 935 Gravenstein Ave; mains $9-21; ⊙ 11am-10pm) ✦ Housed in a former Foster's Freeze, this highly anticipated seafood restaurant is over-the-counter casual but undeniably elegant. The stylish interior is defined by reclaimed wood and shoji-style paneling that opens to a tree-shaded patio. In a room designated the *tortilleria,* corn tortillas are hand-molded each day and topped with battered and fried rockfish, pickled onion and roasted summer squash.

Mom's Apple Pie
DESSERTS $

(☎ 707-823-8330; www.momsapplepieusa.com; 4550 Gravenstein Hwy N; whole pies $7-17; ⊙ 10am-6pm; ✦ ✦) Pie's the thing at this roadside bakery – and yum, that flaky crust. Apple is predictably good, especially in autumn, but the blueberry is our fave, made better with vanilla ice cream.

Hopmonk Tavern
PUB FOOD $$

(☎ 707-829-7300; www.hopmonk.com; 230 Petaluma Ave; mains $12-23; ⊙ 11:30am-9pm Mon-Thu, to 10pm Fri, 11am-10pm Sat & Sun; 🛜) Inside a converted 1903 railroad station, Hopmonk's serves 76 varieties of beer – served in type-specific glassware – that pair with a good menu of burgers, fried calamari, charcuterie platters and salads.

Zazu Kitchen & Farm
AMERICAN $$$

(☎ 707-523-4814; http://zazukitchen.com; 6770 McKinley St, 150, Barlow; mains lunch $13-18, dinner $24-29; ⊙ 5-10pm Mon & Wed, 3-10pm Thu, 11:30am-midnight Fri & Sat, 9am-10pm Sun) ✦ We love the farm-to-table ethos of Zazu – it grows its own pigs and sources everything locally – but some dishes miss and the industrial-style space gets crazy loud. Still, it does excellent pizzas, salads, housemade *salumi,* pork and bacon. Good breakfasts too.

K&L Bistro
FRENCH $$$

(☎707-823-6614; www.klbistro.com; 119 S Main St; lunch $14-20, dinner $19-29; ◷11am-11pm) K&L serves earthy provincial Cal-French bistro cooking in a convivial bar-and-grill space with sidewalk patio. Expect classics such as mussels and french fries, and grilled steaks with red-wine reduction. Reservations essential.

🍷 Drinking & Nightlife

Nightlife isn't Sebastopol's strong suit, but there are a couple of great breweries and tastings rooms at the Barlow (p29).

Woodfour Brewing Co
BREWERY

(☎707-823-3144; www.woodfourbrewing.com; 6780 Depot St, Barlow; ◷noon-7pm Wed & Thu, to 8pm Fri & Sat, 11am-6pm Sun) 🍴 Woodfour's solar-powered brewery serves about a dozen house-made beers, light on alcohol and hops, plus several sours (high-acid beer). It also has an exceptionally good menu of small plates (designed to pair with beer), from simple snacks to refined, technique-driven dishes better than any we've had at a California brewery.

Hardcore Espresso
CAFE

(☎707-823-7588; 81 Bloomfield Rd; ◷5am-7pm Mon-Fri, 6am-7pm Sat & Sun; 🛜) 🍴 Meet local hippies and artists over coffee and smoothies at this classic NorCal, off-the-grid, indoor-outdoor coffeehouse, south of downtown, that's essentially a corrugated-metal-roofed shack surrounded by umbrella tables.

Taylor Maid Farms
CAFE

(☎707-634-7129; www.taylormaidfarms.com; 6790 McKinley St, Barlow; ◷6:30am-6pm Sun-Thu, to 7pm Fri, 7am-7pm Sat) 🍴 Choose your brew method (drip, press etc) at this third-wave coffeehouse that roasts its own organic beans. Exceptional seasonal drinks include lavender lattes.

ℹ️ Information

Sebastopol Area Chamber of Commerce & Visitors Center (☎877-828-4748, 707-823-3032; www.sebastopol.org; 265 S Main St; ◷10am-5pm Mon-Fri) Maps, information and exhibits.

Petaluma

'The world's egg basket' – as the agrarian town of Petaluma has long been known – is seemingly ready to hatch. Sprawling off Hwy 101 a short drive south of Santa Rosa, Petaluma

has been grabbing headlines lately for its densely foggy and wind-whipped appellation, which winegrowers have newly dubbed 'the Petaluma Gap.' As wineries such as Keller Estate (☎707-765 2117; www.kellerestate.com; 5875 Lakeville Hwy; tour & tasting $35; ◷tour/tastings 11:30am, 1pm & 2:30pm Fri-Mon) have become more prominent, and the region's Chardonnays, Pinot Noirs and Syrahs earn a reputation for their elegance and complexity, the town, too, has been expanding its touristic offerings.

In the early 1800s, General Vallejo planted the area's first vines near his newly constructed ranch, Petaluma Adobe, which stands today as a historic state park (☎707-762-4871; www.petalumaadobe.com; 3325 Adobe Rd; adult/child $3/2; ◷10am-5pm; P). Visitors to Wine Country may also opt to settle into this up-and-coming area, where the charming downtown and its lovingly preserved Victorians are on the National Register of Historic Places, and hotels and restaurant prices are still fairly reasonable. Recommended stays include the historic Hotel Petaluma (☎707-559-3393; www.hotelpetaluma.com; 205 Kentucky St; r from $120; P❄🛜🐾), featuring its own wine-tasting room and oyster bar, and Della Fattoria Ranch Cottage (☎707-529-2701; www.dellafattoria.com; 141 Petaluma Blvd; r from $140; P🛜), a family farmstay and artisanal bakery that serves guests organic bread, butter and eggs.

The feast continues at Petaluma's delicious restaurants, including the casual but superior Cafe Zazzle (☎707-762-1700; www.zazzlecafe.com; 121 Kentucky St; mains $8-14; ◷11am-8pm Sun-Mon, to 9pm Tue-Sat), where the only thing better than the Asia- and Southwestern-inspired wraps is the friendly service. Or, for a fancier meal, make a rezzie over at industrial-chic Crocodile French Cuisine (☎707-981-8159; www.crocodilepetaluma.com; 140 2nd St; mains $19-28; ◷11:30am-9pm Mon & Wed, to 9:30pm Thu, to 10pm Fri & Sat, 5-9pm Sun) and enjoy some tender duck with a Belgian craft beer. Aspiring picnickers can stop at the old Petaluma Creamery (p29) to stock up on cheese and tri-tip BBQ sandwiches. You can also visit Green String Farm (p29) for chemical-free produce.

Point Reyes Station

📞 415 / POP 848

Though the railroad stopped coming through in 1933 and the town is small, Point Reyes Station is nevertheless the hub of western Marin County. Dominated by dairies and ranches, the region was invaded by artists in the 1960s. Today Main St is a diverting blend of art galleries, tourist shops, restaurants and cafes. The town has a rowdy saloon and the occasional smell of cattle on the afternoon breeze.

Heidrun Meadery WINERY
See p30.

Bovine Bakery BAKERY
See p29.

**Cowgirl Creamery
at Tomales Bay Foods** DELI
See p29.

Windsong Cottage Guest Yurt YURT **$$**
(☑415-663-9695; www.windsongcottage.com; 25 McDonald Lane; d $195-230; P⊖🐾) A wood-burning stove, private outdoor hot tub, comfy king bed and kitchen stocked with breakfast supplies make this round skylighted abode a slice of rural heaven.

Nick's Cove COTTAGE **$$$**
(☑415-663-1033; http://nickscove.com; 23240 Hwy 1, Marshall; cottages $250-850; P⊖🐾🐕) Fronting a peaceful cove at Tomales Bay, these water-view and waterfront vacation cottages are expensive, but oh-so romantic. Some have wood-burning fireplace, deep soaking tub, private deck and plasma TV. Two-night minimum stay on weekends and holidays. It's about a 20-minute drive north of Point Reyes Station.

Marin Sun Farms MODERN AMERICAN **$$**
(☑415-663-1800; www.marinsunfarms.com; 10905 Hwy 1; mains $14-36; ⊙11am-5pm Mon & Thu, to 8pm Fri-Sun; 🐾) 🍴 Locally raised, grass-fed meats are the specialty of this whole-animal butcher committed to sustainable agriculture and family farms and ranches. Spotlighted on the restaurant menu are *steak frites* with pan sauce, thick-cut pork chops and unbelievably delicious burgers (beef, lamb or goat) that are worth every dollar, best enjoyed with California beer, wine or mead. Reservations recommended. Expect long waits.

Marshall Store SEAFOOD **$$**
(☑415-663-1339; www.themarshallstore.com; 19225 Hwy 1, Marshall; mains $11-20; ⊙10am-5pm Mon-Fri, to 6pm Sat & Sun, closes 1hr earlier Oct-Apr;

🐾) Catapulted to fame by peripatetic chef and TV host Anthony Bourdain, this ramshackle country store lets you slurp down BBQ oysters at tables as your legs practically dangle in Tomales Bay. Smoked seafood plates and sandwiches aren't half bad either. It's a 15-minute drive north of Point Reyes Station.

Point Reyes National Seashore
☑415

Wild and beautiful Point Reyes (p30) is home to marine mammals and migratory birds as well as the site of scores of shipwrecks. It was here in 1579 that Sir Francis Drake landed to repair his ship, the *Golden Hind*. During his five-week stay he mounted a brass plaque near the shore claiming this land for England. In 1595 the first of scores of ships lost in these waters went down. The *San Augustine* was a Spanish treasure ship out of Manila, laden with luxury goods – to this day bits of its cargo still wash up on shore. Despite modern navigation, the dangerous waters here continue to claim the odd boat.

For fantastic views, head to the Point Reyes Lighthouse (p30).

Wake up to deer nibbling under a blanket of fog at one of Point Reyes' very popular backcountry campgrounds (☑reservations 877-444-6777; www.recreation.gov; tent sites $20), or stay at the pastoral youth hostel. More inns, motels and B&Bs are found in nearby Inverness, off Sir Francis Drake Blvd.

Inverness has only a couple of places to eat, scattered along Sir Francis Drake Blvd as you drive out toward the tip of the peninsula. Foodies will find many more restaurants, cafes, a bakery and a famous cheese shop in Point Reyes Station, a few miles north of Bear Valley Visitor Center.

❶ Information

At park headquarters, a mile west of Olema, **Bear Valley Visitor Center** (☑415-464-5100; www.nps.gov/pore; 1 Bear Valley Rd, Point Reyes Station; ⊙10am-5pm Mon-Fri, 9am-5pm Sat & Sun; 🐾) has information and maps. You can also get information at the Point Reyes Lighthouse and the **Kenneth Patrick Center** (☑415-669-1250; www.nps.gov/pore; 1 Drakes Beach Rd; ⊙9:30am-4:30pm Sat, Sun & holidays late Dec-late Mar or early Apr) at Drakes Beach.

North Coast & Redwoods

The jagged edge of the continent is wild, scenic and even slightly foreboding.

Point Arena

☎707

This laid-back little town of less than 450 residents combines creature comforts with relaxed, eclectic California living and is the first town up the coast where the majority of residents don't seem to be retired Bay Area refugees, but are rather a young, creative bunch who tout organic food, support their local theater and sell their fair share of dream catchers. The main street is part of scenic Hwy 1, with a small harbor at one end and a clutch of small arty shops, cafes and restaurants housed in pretty Victorian-era buildings running through the center of town. Peruse the shops and restaurants then follow the sign leading to the lighthouse at the north end of Main St, or head to the docks a mile west of town at Arena Cove and watch surfers mingle with fisherfolk and locals. Be sure to visit the Point Arena Lighthouse (p24) and take in the views.

The **Arena Theater** (☎707-882-3020; www.arenatheater.org; 214 Main St) shows mainstream, foreign and art films in a beautifully restored movie house. Sue, the ticket seller, has been in that booth for 40 years. Got a question about Point Arena? Ask Sue. The accommodation available here is around the lighthouse. For more options, stick to Mendocino or Fort Bragg. The plain, three-bedroom, kitchen-equipped former coast-guard homes at the **lighthouse** (☎707-882-2809; www.pointarenalighthouse.com; 45500 Lighthouse Rd; houses $150-250; P) offer quiet, windswept retreats.

The **Wharf Master's Inn** (☎707-882-3171; www.wharfmasters.com; 785 Iversen Ave; r $129-259; P) is a cluster of comfortable, spacious rooms on a cliff overlooking fishing boats and a stilt pier. Recently reformed, they are eminently comfortable.

Virtually all the restaurants, cafes and bars are located right on Main St running through the center of town. For live music and a chilled-out atmosphere, check out **215 Main** (www.facebook.com/215Main; 215 Main St; 2pm-2am Tue-Sun). The cutest patisserie on this stretch of coast is **Franny's Cup & Saucer** (☎707-882-2500; www.frannyscupandsaucer.com; 213 Main St; cakes from $2; 8am-4pm Wed-Sat), run by Franny and her mother, Barbara. The fresh berry tarts and creative house-made chocolates seem too beautiful to eat. The menu at **Uneda** (☎707-882-3800; www.unedaeat.com; 206 Main St; mains $16-25; 5:30-8:30pm Wed-Sat) changes nightly depending on what is fresh in the market that day. There are just nine tables so reserve ahead of time.

Mendocino

📍707 / POP 894

Leading out to a gorgeous headland, Mendocino is the North Coast's salt-washed perfect village, with B&Bs surrounded by rose gardens, white-picket fences and New England–style redwood water towers. Bay Area weekenders walk along the headland among berry bramble and wildflowers, where cypress trees stand over dizzying cliffs. The town itself is full of cute shops – no chains – and has earned the nickname 'Spendocino,' for its upscale goods.

Built by transplanted New Englanders in the 1850s, Mendocino thrived late into the 19th century, with ships transporting redwood timber from here to San Francisco. The mills shut down in the 1930s, and the town was rediscovered in the 1950s by artists and bohemians. Today the culturally savvy, politically aware, well-traveled citizens welcome visitors, but eschew corporate interlopers – don't look for a Big Mac or Starbucks. To avoid crowds, come midweek or in the low season, when the vibe is mellower – and prices more reasonable.

🔘 Sights

Mendocino is lined with all kinds of interesting galleries, which hold openings on the second Saturday of each month from 5pm to 8pm.

Kwan Tai Temple   TEMPLE
(📍707-937-5123; www.kwantaitemple.org; 45160 Albion St; ⊙by appointment) Peering in the window of this 1852 temple reveals an old altar dedicated to the Chinese god of war. Tours are available by appointment and provide a fascinating insight into the history of the area's Chinese American immigrants, dating from the mid-19th century when they worked in the lumber industry.

Point Cabrillo Light Station   LIGHTHOUSE
(📍707-937-6123; www.pointcabrillo.org; 45300 Lighthouse Rd; ⊙park sunrise-sunset, lighthouse 11am-4pm) FREE Restored in 1909, this stout lighthouse stands on a 300-acre wildlife preserve north of town, between Russian Gulch and Caspar Beach. Guided walks of the preserve leave at 11am on Sundays from May to September. You can also stay in the lighthouse keeper's house and cottages.

🏃 Activities

Wine tours, whale-watching, shopping, hiking, cycling: there's more to do in the area

than a thousand long weekends could accomplish. For navigable river and ocean kayaking, launch from tiny Albion, which hugs the north side of the Albion River mouth, 5 miles south of Mendocino.

Catch a Canoe
& Bicycles, Too!   CANOEING, CYCLING
(📍707-937-0273; www.catchacanoe.com; 44850 Comptche-Ukiah Rd, Stanford Inn by the Sea; 3hr kayak, canoe or bicycle rental adult/child $28/14; ⊙9am-5pm; 🚲) This friendly outfit rents bikes, kayaks and canoes (including redwood outriggers) for trips up the 8-mile Big River tidal estuary. Northern California's longest undeveloped estuary has no highways or buildings, only beaches, forests, marshes, streams, abundant wildlife and historic logging sites. Bring a picnic and a camera to enjoy the ramshackle remnants of century-old train trestles and majestic blue herons.

Mendocino Headlands State Park   HIKING
(📍707-937-5804; www.parks.ca.gov; Ford St) FREE Mendocino Headlands State Park surrounds the village, where trails crisscross bluffs and rocky coves. Ask at the visitor center (p113) about guided weekend walks, including spring wildflower explorations and whale-watching jaunts.

🎊 Festivals & Events

Mendocino Whale Festival   WILDLIFE
(www.mendowhale.com; ⊙early Mar) Wine and chowder tastings, whale-watching and plenty of live music.

Mendocino Music Festival   MUSIC
(www.mendocinomusic.com; ⊙mid-Jul; 🚲) Enjoy orchestral and chamber music concerts on the headlands, children's matinees and open rehearsals.

🛏 Sleeping

Standards are high in stylish Mendocino and so are prices; two-day minimums often crop up on weekends. Fort Bragg, 10 miles north, has cheaper lodgings. Only a few places have TVs. For a range of cottages and B&Bs, contact Mendocino Coast Reservations (📍707-937-5033; www.mendocinovacations.com; 45084 Little Lake St; ⊙9am-5pm).

Russian Gulch State Park   CAMPGROUND $
(📍reservations 800-444-7275; www.reserveamerica.com; tent & RV sites $35; 🅿) In a wooded canyon 2 miles north of town, with secluded drive-in sites, hot showers, a small waterfall

and the Devil's Punch Bowl (a collapsed sea arch).

★ **Didjeridoo Dreamtime Inn** B&B $$
(☎707-937-6200; www.didjeridooinn.com; 44860 Main St; r $112-160; ♨🐾✿) One of the town's more economical choices, rooms here are all different yet share the same homey, unpretentious atmosphere with tasteful artwork, antiques and parquet flooring. Several rooms have en suites, and a couple have mini hot tubs. The breakfast spread is excellent and on Sunday you are treated to some soothing live music. The front garden is a lovely place to sit.

★ **Alegria** B&B $$$
(☎707-937-5150; www.oceanfrontmagic.com; 44781 Main St; r $239-299; ♨🐾) A perfect romantic hideaway, beds have views over the coast, decks have ocean views and all rooms have wood-burning fireplaces; outside, a gorgeous path leads to a big, amber-gray beach. Friendly innkeepers also whip up amazing breakfasts. Less-expensive rooms are available across the street at bright and simple **Raku House** (☎800-780-7905; www.rakuhouse.com; 998 Main St; r $109-139; P♨🐾).

✗ Eating

With quality to rival Napa Valley, the influx of Bay Area weekenders has fostered an excellent dining scene that enthusiastically espouses organic, sustainable principles. Make reservations. Gathering picnic supplies is easy at **Harvest Market** (☎707-937-5879; www.harvestmarket.com; 10501 Lansing St; ⊙7:30am-10pm) 🌿 organic grocery store (with deli) and the **farmers market** (cnr Howard & Main St; ⊙noon-2pm Fri May-Oct).

Frankie's PIZZA $
(☎707-937-2436; www.frankiesmendocino.com; cnr Ukiah & Lansing Sts; pizza $13-16; ⊙11am-9pm; 🍴) There is no Sicilian-style simplicity to these pizzas, they are pure Californian with piled-high organic ingredients such as cremini mushrooms, Canadian bacon, roasted red peppers and pineapple (not combined, fortunately). It also serves healthy fare such as quinoa kale cakes and gluten-free falafel, plus soups, salads and Fort Bragg's famous Cowlick's ice cream.

Flow CALIFORNIAN $$
(☎707-937-3569; www.mendocinoflow.com; 45040 Main St; mains $14-20; ⊙8am-10pm; 🐾🍴) This busy place has the best views of the ocean in town from its 2nd-story perch. Brunch

is a specialty, as are Mexican-inspired small plates, artisan pizzas and a sublime local Dungeness crab chowder. Gluten-free and vegan options are available.

★ **Café Beaujolais** CALIFORNIAN $$$
(☎707-937-5614; www.cafebeaujolais.com; 961 Ukiah St; lunch mains $10-18, dinner mains $23-38; ⊙11:30am-2:30pm Wed-Sun, dinner from 5:30pm daily; P) 🌿 Mendocino's iconic, beloved country-Cal–French restaurant occupies an 1893 farmhouse restyled into a monochromatic urban-chic dining room, perfect for holding hands by candlelight. The refined, inspired cooking draws diners from San Francisco. The locally sourced menu changes with the seasons, but the Petaluma duck confit is a gourmand's delight.

🍷 Drinking & Nightlife

Have cocktails at the **Mendocino Hotel** (☎707-937-0511; www.mendocinohotel.com; 45080 Main St; r with/without bath from $185/135, ste $275; P♨🐾) or the Grey Whale Bar at the **MacCallum House Inn** (☎707-937-0289; www.maccallumhouse.com; 45020 Albion St; r & cottages from $149, water-tower ste $259-359; P♨@🐾🐾) 🌿. For boisterousness and beer, head straight to **Patterson's Pub** (www.pattersonspub.com; 10485 Lansing St; mains $13-16; ⊙10am-midnight, food to 11pm).

Dick's Place BAR
(☎707-937-6010; 45080 Main St; ⊙11:30am-2am) A bit out of place among the fancy-pants shops downtown, but an excellent spot to check out the *other* Mendocino and do shots with rowdy locals. And don't miss the retro experience of dropping 50¢ in the jukebox to hear that favorite tune.

🛍 Shopping

Mendocino's walkable streets are great for shopping, and the ban on chain stores ensures unique, often upscale gifts. There are many small galleries in town where one-of-a-kind artwork is for sale.

Twist CLOTHING
(☎707-937-1717; www.mendocinotwist.com; 45140 Main St; ⊙11am-5pm Mon-Fri, 10:30am-5:30pm Sat & Sun) 🌿 Twist stocks eco-friendly, natural-fiber clothing and lots of locally made clothing and toys.

Gallery Bookshop BOOKS
(☎707-937-2665; www.gallerybookshop.com; 319 Kasten St; ⊙9:30am-6pm) Stocks a great

selection of books on local topics, titles from California's small presses and specialized outdoor guides.

ℹ Information

Ford House Museum & Visitor Center (☑ 707-537-5397; www.mendoparks.org; 45035 Main St; ⊙ 11am-4pm) Enjoy maps, books, information and exhibits, including a scale model of 1890 Mendocino, plus a historical setting with original Victorian-period furniture and decor.

Fort Bragg

☑ 707 / POP 7302

In the past, Fort Bragg was Mendocino's ugly stepsister, home to a lumber mill, a scrappy downtown and blue-collar locals who gave a cold welcome to outsiders. Since the mill closure in 2002, the town has started to reinvent itself, slowly warming to a tourism-based economy, with the downtown continuing to develop as a wonderfully unpretentious alternative to Mendocino (even if the southern end of town is hideous). Unlike the *entire* franchise-free 180-mile stretch of Coastal Hwy 1 between here and the Golden Gate, in Fort Bragg you can get a Big Mac, grande latte or any of a number of chain-store products whose buildings blight the landscape. Don't fret. In downtown you'll find better hamburgers and coffee, old-school architecture and residents eager to show off their little town.

◉ Sights & Activities

Fort Bragg has the same banner North Coast activities as Mendocino – beachcombing, surfing, hiking – but basing yourself here is much cheaper and arguably less quaint and pretentious. The wharf lies at Noyo Harbor – the mouth of the Noyo River – south of downtown. Here you can find whale-watching cruises and deep-sea fishing trips.

★**Mendocino Coast**
Botanical Gardens   GARDENS
(☑ 707-964-4352; www.gardenbythesea.org; 18220 N Hwy 1; adult/child/senior $14/5/10; ⊙ 9am-5pm Mar-Oct, to 4pm Nov-Feb; 🅿) 🖋 This gem of Northern California displays native flora, rhododendrons and heritage roses. The succulent display alone is amazing and the organic garden is harvested by volunteers to feed area residents in need. The serpentine paths wander along 47 seafront acres south of town. Primary trails are wheelchair accessible.

★**Skunk Train**   HISTORIC TRAIN
(☑ 707-964-6371; www.skunktrain.com; 100 W Laurel St; adult/child $84/42; ⊙ 9am-3pm; 🌟) Fort Bragg's pride and joy, the vintage train got its nickname in 1925 for its stinky gas-powered steam engines, but today the historic steam and diesel locomotives are odorless. Passing through redwood-forested mountains, along rivers, over bridges and through deep mountain tunnels, the trains run from both Fort Bragg and **Willits** (E Commercial St; adult/child $54/34) to the midway point of Northspur, where they turn around.

🛏 Sleeping

Fort Bragg's lodging is cheaper than Mendocino's, but most of the motels along noisy Hwy 1 don't have air-conditioning, so you'll hear traffic through your windows. The best of the motel bunch is **Colombi Motel** (☑ 707-964-5773; www.colombimotel.com; 647 E Oak St; 1-/2-bedroom units with kitchenette from $80/85; ⊜🐾), which is in town. Most B&Bs do not have TVs.

Country Inn   B&B $$
(☑ 707-964-3737; www.beourguests.com; 632 N Main St; r $125-170; 🅿 ⊜ 🐾 🌊) This gingerbread-trimmed B&B in the middle of town is an excellent way to dodge the chain motels for a good-value stay. The lovely family hosts are welcoming and easygoing, and can offer good local tips. Breakfast can be delivered to your room and at night you can soak in a hot tub out back. There is a minimum two-night stay at weekends.

Weller House Inn   B&B $$$
(☑ 707-964-4415; www.wellerhouse.com; 524 Stewart St; r $200-310; 🅿 ⊜ 🐾) Rooms in this beautifully restored 1886 mansion have down comforters, underfloor heating, good mattresses and fine linens. The water tower is the tallest structure in town – and it has a hot tub at the top! Breakfast is in the massive redwood ballroom.

🍴 Eating

Similar to the lodging scene, the food in Fort Bragg is less spendy than Mendocino, but there are a number of truly excellent options, mainly located on or around Main St. Self-caterers should try the **farmers market** (cnr E Laurel & N Franklin Sts; ⊙ 3:30-6pm Wed May-Oct) downtown or the **Harvest Market** (☑ 707-964-7000; cnr Hwys 1 & 20; ⊙ 5am-11pm) for the best groceries.

Carson Mansion (p24), Eureka
VICTORIA DITKOVSKY/SHUTTERSTOCK ©

★ **Cucina Verona** · ITALIAN $$$
(☑707-964-6844; www.cucinaverona.com; 124
E Laurel St; mains $26-30; ⊙9am-9pm) A real-
deal Italian restaurant with no-fail tradi-
tional dishes, plus a few with a Californian
tweak, such as butternut-squash lasagna and
artichoke bruschetta. The atmosphere is as
comforting as the cuisine, with dim lighting,
a warm color scheme and unobtrusive live
music most evenings. There is an extensive
microbrewery selection on offer, as well as
local and imported wines.

ℹ Information

**Fort Bragg-Mendocino Coast Chamber of
Commerce** (☑707-961-6300; www.mendocino
coast.com; 332 S Main St; ⊙10am-5pm Mon-
Fri, to 3pm Sat; 🛜) The chamber of commerce
has lots of helpful information about this
stretch of coast and what's on. Its online guide
is also worth checking out.

Eureka

☑707 / POP 26,925

★ **Taka's Japanese Grill** JAPANESE $
(☑707-964-5204; 250 N Main St; mains $10.50-
17; ⊙11:30am-3pm & 4:30-9pm; 🅿) Although
it may look fairly run of the mill, this is an
exceptional Japanese restaurant. The owner
is a former grader at the Tokyo fish market so
the quality is tops and he makes a weekly run
to San Francisco to source freshly imported
seafood. Sushi, teriyaki dishes, noodle soups
and pan-fried noodles with salmon, beef or
chicken are just a few of the options.

Headlands Coffeehouse CAFE $
(☑707-964-1987; www.headlandscoffeehouse.com;
120 E Laurel St; mains $4-8; ⊙7am-10pm Mon-Sat,
to 7pm Sun; 🛜☑) The town's best cafe is in the
middle of the historic downtown, with high
ceilings and lots of atmosphere. The menu
gets raves for the Belgian waffles, home-
made soups, veggie-friendly salads, panini
and lasagna.

★ **Piaci Pub & Pizzeria** ITALIAN $$
(☑707-961-1133; www.piacipizza.com; 120 W Red-
wood Ave; mains $8-20; ⊙11am-9:30pm Mon-Thu,
to 10pm Fri & Sat, 4-9:30pm Sun) Fort Bragg's
must-visit pizzeria is known for its sophisticated wood-fired, brick-oven pizzas as
much as for its long list of microbrews. Try
the 'Gustoso' – with chèvre, pesto and seasonal pears, all carefully orchestrated on a
thin crust. It's tiny, loud and fun, with much
more of a bar atmosphere than a restaurant.
Expect to wait at peak times.

One hour north of Garberville, on the edge
of the giant Humboldt Bay, lies Eureka, the
largest bay north of San Francisco. With
a strip-mall sprawl surrounding a lovely
historic downtown, it wears its role as the
county seat a bit clumsily. Despite a diverse
and interesting community of artists, writers, pagans and other free-thinkers, Eureka's
wild side slips out only occasionally – the
Redwood Coast Jazz Festival has events all
over town, and summer concerts rock out
the F Street Pier – but mostly, Eureka goes
to bed early. Make for Old Town, a small
historic district with good shopping and a
revitalized waterfront. For nightlife, head to
Eureka's livelier sister up the road, Arcata.

⊙ Sights

The free *Eureka Visitors Map,* available at
tourist offices, details walking tours and scenic drives, focusing on architecture and history. **Old Town**, along 2nd and 3rd Sts from C St
to M St, was once down-and-out, but has been
refurbished into a buzzing pedestrian district.
The F Street Plaza and Boardwalk runs along
the waterfront at the foot of F St. Gallery openings fall on the first Saturday of every month.

**Humboldt Bay
National Wildlife Refuge** WILDLIFE REFUGE
See p24.

Carson Mansion HISTORIC BUILDING
See p24.

Blue Ox Millworks
& Historic Park · HISTORIC BUILDING
See p24.

Harbor Cruise · CRUISE
See p25.

Romano Gabriel
Wooden Sculpture Garden · GARDENS
(315 2nd St) The coolest thing to gawk at downtown is this collection of whimsical outsider art that's enclosed by aging glass. For 30 years, wooden characters in Gabriel's front yard delighted locals. After he died in 1977, the city moved the collection here.

Sequoia Park · PARK
(☑707-441-4263; www.sequoiaparkzoo.net; 3414 W St; park free, zoo adult/child $5/3; ☉ zoo 10am-5pm May-Sep, closed Mon Oct-Apr; P 🚼) A 77-acre old-growth redwood grove is a surprising green gem in the middle of a residential neighborhood. It has biking and hiking trails, a children's playground and picnic areas, and a small zoo, the oldest in California.

Kinetic Museum Eureka · MUSEUM
(☑707-786-3443; http://kineticgrandchampionship.com/kinetic-museum-eureka; 518 A St; admission by donation; ☉ 2:15-6:30pm Fri-Sun, also 6-9pm 1st Sat of month; 🚼) Come see the fanciful, astounding, human-powered contraptions used in the annual Kinetic Grand Championship (☑707-786-3443; www.kineticgrand championship.com; ☉ late May; 🚼) 🏁 race from Arcata to Ferndale. Shaped like giant fish and UFOs, these colorful piles of junk propel racers over roads, water and marsh during the May event.

🛏 Sleeping

Every brand of chain hotel is along Hwy 101. Room rates run high midsummer; you can sometimes find cheaper options in Arcata, to the north, or Fortuna, to the south. There is also a handful of motels that cost from $55 to $100 and have no air-conditioning; choose places set back from the road. The cheapest options are south of downtown on the suburban strip.

Inn at 2nd & C · HISTORIC HOTEL $$
(☑707-444-3344; www.theinnat2ndandc.com; 139 2nd St; r from $129, ste from $209; 🌐🛜) Formerly the Eagle House Inn, but reopened under new ownership in May 2017, this glorious Victorian hotel has been tastefully restored to combine Victorian-era decor with every possible modern amenity. The magnificent

turn-of-the-century ballroom is used for everything from theater performances to special events. There is also a yoga studio and spa room. Breakfast, tea and complimentary cocktails are additional perks.

Cornelius Daly Inn · B&B $$
(☑707-445-3638; www.dalyinn.com; 1125 H St; r with/without bath $185/130; 🌐) This impeccably maintained 1905 Colonial Revival mansion has individually decorated rooms with turn-of-the-20th-century European and American antiques. Guest parlors are trimmed with rare woods; outside are century-old flowering trees. The breakfasts reflect co-owner Donna's culinary skills with such gourmet offerings as apple-stuffed French toast.

Carter House Inns · B&B $$$
(☑707-444-8062; www.carterhouse.com; 301 L St; r $184-384; P🌐🛜) Constructed in period style, this aesthetically remodeled hotel is a Victorian lookalike. Rooms have all-modern amenities and top-quality linens; suites have in-room Jacuzzis and marble fireplaces. The same owners operate four other sumptuously decorated lodgings: a single-level house, two honeymoon hideaway cottages and a replica of an 1880s San Francisco mansion, which the owner built himself, entirely by hand.

🍴 Eating

You won't go hungry in this town, and health-conscious folk are particularly well catered to with two excellent natural-food grocery stores – North Coast Co-op (☑707-443-6027; www.northcoast.coop; cnr 4th & B Sts; ☉ 6am-9pm) and Eureka Natural Foods (☑707-442-6325; www.eurekanaturalfoods.com; 1626 Broadway St; ☉ 7am-9pm Mon-Sat, 8am-8pm Sun) – and two weekly farmers markets – one street market (cnr 2nd & F Sts; ☉ 10am-1pm Tue Jun-Oct) and one at the Henderson Center (☑707-445-3101; 2800 F St; ☉ 10am-1pm Thu Jun-Oct). The vibrant dining scene is focused in the Old Town district and has an excellent array of foodie options and price categories.

⭐ Cafe Nooner · MEDITERRANEAN $
(☑707-443-4663; www.cafenooner.com; 409 Opera Alley; mains $10-14; ☉ 11am-4pm Sun-Wed, to 8pm Thu-Sat; 🚼) Exuding a cozy bistro-style ambience with red-and-white checkered tablecloths, this perennially popular restaurant serves natural, organic and Med-inspired cuisine with choices that include a Greek-style *meze* platter, plus kebabs, salads and soups. There's a healthy kids' menu, as well.

★ **Brick & Fire** CALIFORNIAN $$
(☑707-268-8959; www.brickandfirebistro.com; 1630 F St; dinner mains $14-23; ☺11:30am-9pm Mon & Wed Fri, 5-9pm Sat & Sun; ☎) Eureka's best restaurant is in an intimate, warm-hued, bohemian-tinged setting that is almost always busy. Choose from thin-crust pizzas, delicious salads (try the pear and blue cheese) and an ever-changing selection of appetizers and mains that highlight local produce and wild mushrooms. There's a weighty wine list and servers are well versed in pairings.

★ **Restaurant 301** CALIFORNIAN $$$
(☑707-444-8062; www.carterhouse.com; 301 L St; mains $24-40; ☺5-8:30pm) *Part of the excellent Carter House Inn, Eureka's top table, romantic, sophisticated 301 serves a contemporary Californian menu, using produce from its organic gardens (tours available). The five-course tasting menu ($62, with wine pairings $107) is a good way to taste local seasonal food in its finest presentation.

🍷 Drinking & Nightlife

Eureka has some fine old bars and pubs, including live-music venues, mainly located in and around the historic center. The annual jazz festival attracts some top musicians and also includes blues concerts.

Old Town Coffee & Chocolates CAFE
(☑707-445-8600; www.oldtowncoffeeeureka.com; 211 F St; ☺7am-9pm; ☎🖐) You'll smell roasting coffee blocks before you see this place. It's a local hangout in a historic building and has board games, local art on the wall and baked goods that include savory choices like bagels with hummus, and wraps.

Speakeasy BAR
(☑707-444-2244; 411 Opera Alley; ☺4-11pm Sun-Thu, to 2am Fri & Sat) Squeeze in with the locals at this New Orleans–inspired bar with regular live blues and a convivial atmosphere.

ℹ️ Information

Eureka Chamber of Commerce (☑707-442-3738; www.eurekachamber.com; 2112 Broadway; ☺8:30am-5pm Mon-Fri; ☎) The main visitor information center is on Hwy 101.

Redwood National & State Parks

This richly forested region can be a little confusing regarding which park is where and what they all offer. The main parks in this jigsaw of mighty redwoods are: the Redwood National Park; Prairie Creek Redwoods State Park; Del Norte Coast Redwoods State Park; and Jedediah Smith Redwoods State Park. Interspersed among the parks are a number of small towns, while to the south lies Orick (population 650), which offers a few storefronts, a gas station and an excellent visitor center.

Redwood National Park

This park is the southernmost of a patchwork of state and federally administered lands under the umbrella of **Redwood National & State Parks** (☑707-465-7335; www.nps.gov/redw; Hwy 101, Orick; 🅿🖐) *FREE. After picking up a map at the visitor center, you'll have a suite of choices for hiking. A few miles north along Hwy 101, a trip inland on Bald Hills Rd will take you to Lady Bird Johnson Grove, with its 1-mile, kid-friendly loop trail, or get you lost in the secluded serenity of Tall Trees Grove.

To protect the **Tall Trees Grove**, a limited number of cars per day are allowed access; get permits at the visitor center. This can be a half-day trip itself, but you're well rewarded after the challenging approach (a 6-mile rumble on an old logging road behind a locked gate, then a moderately strenuous 4-mile round-trip hike). Another recommended hike is to **Trillium Falls** – a 2.5-mile

---

THE ENDANGERED MARBLED MURRELET

Notice how undeveloped the Redwood National & State Parks have remained? Thank the marbled murrelet, a small white and brown-black auk that nests in old-growth conifers. Loss of nesting territory due to logging has severely depleted the birds' numbers but Redwood National Park scientists have discovered that corvid predators (ravens, jays etc) are also to blame. Because corvids are attracted to food scraps left by visitors, the number of snacking, picnicking or camping humans in the park greatly affects predation on the marbled murrelet. Restrictions on development to prevent food scraps and thus protect the birds are so strict that it's nearly impossible to build anything new.

trail leading to a small waterfall, accessed from Davidson Rd at Elk Meadow. Note that during the winter, several footbridges crossing the Redwood Creek are removed due to the high waters. If you are hiking at this time of year, be sure to check with a ranger regarding the current situation before striding out.

Bright and spotless Elk Meadow Cabins (☑866-733-9637; www.redwoodadventures.com; 7 Valley Green Camp Rd, Orick; cabins $239-289; ℗ 🛜 🐾), located in a perfect mid-parks location, are equipped with kitchens and all the mod-cons. They're great if you're traveling in a group and the most comfy choice even if you're not.

ℹ️ Information

Unlike most national parks, there are no fees and no highway entrance stations at Redwood National Park, so it's imperative to pick up the free map at the park headquarters in **Crescent City** (☑707-465-7335; www.nps.gov/redw; 1111 2nd St; ⊙9am-5pm Apr-Oct, to 4pm Nov-Mar) or at the information center in Orick. Rangers here issue permits to visit Tall Trees Grove and loan bear-proof containers for backpackers.

For in-depth redwood ecology, buy the excellent official park handbook. The **Redwood Parks Association** (www.redwoodparksassociation. org) provides good information on its website, including detailed descriptions of all the park hikes.

Prairie Creek Redwoods State Park

Famous for some of the world's best virgin redwood groves and unspoiled coastline, this 14,000-acre section (www.parks.ca.gov; Newton B Drury Scenic Pkwy; per car $8; ℗ 🛉) 🐾 of Redwood National & State Parks has spectacular scenic drives and 70 miles of mainly shady hiking trails, many of which are excellent for children. Kids will enjoy the magnificent herd of elk here, which can generally be spied grazing at the Elk Prairie, signposted from the highway; the best times to be sure of seeing the elk are early morning and around sunset.

There are 28 mountain-biking and hiking trails through the park, from simple to strenuous. Only a few of these will appeal to hardcore hikers, who should take on the Del Norte Coast Redwoods. A few easy nature trails start near the visitor center, including Revelation Trail and Elk Prairie Trail. Stroll the recently reforested logging road on the Ah-Pah Interpretive Trail at the park's north end. The most challenging hike in this corner of the park is the spectacular 11.5-mile Coastal Trail, which goes through primordial redwoods and is part of the California Coastal Trail (www.

Cresent Beach, Redwood National Park

ZACK FRANK/SHUTTERSTOCK ©

californiacoastaltrail.info). Just past the Gold Bluffs Beach campground the road dead-ends at Fern Canyon, the second-busiest spot in the park, where 60ft fern-covered sheer-rock walls are so unusual that they were used in scenes from Steven Spielberg's *Jurassic Park 2: The Lost World*, as well as *Return of the Jedi*.

Just north of Orick is the turnoff for the 8-mile Newton B Drury Scenic Parkway (Hwy 101, Orick; 🛉), which runs parallel to Hwy 101 through untouched ancient redwood forests. This is a not-to-miss short detour off the freeway where you can view the magnificence of these trees.

Gorgeous Gold Bluffs Beach campground (Prairie Creek Redwoods State Park; tent sites $35) sits between 100ft cliffs and wide-open ocean, but there are some windbreaks and solar-heated showers. Look for sites up the cliff under the trees (no reservations).

Elk roam the popular Elk Prairie Campground (☑reservations 800-444-7275; www. reserveamerica.com; Prairie Creek Rd; tent & RV sites $35; ℗🐾), where you can sleep under redwoods or at the prairie's edge. There are hot showers, some hike-in sites and a shallow creek to splash in.

California Driving Guide

With jaw-dropping scenery and one of the USA's most comprehensive highway networks, California is an all-star destination for a road trip.

Driving Fast Facts

Right or left? Drive on the right
Legal driving age 16
Top speed limit 70mph on some highways.
Best bumper sticker 'Where the heck is Wall Drug?'
Best radio station National Public Radio (NPR)

DRIVER'S LICENSE & DOCUMENTS

Out-of-state and international visitors may legally drive a car in California with their home driver's license. If you're driving into the USA from Canada or Mexico, bring your vehicle's registration papers, liability insurance and home driver's license; an International Driving Permit (IDP) is a good supplement but isn't currently required.

If you're from overseas, an IDP will have more credibility with traffic police and simplify the car-rental process, especially if your license doesn't have a photo or isn't written in English. International automobile associations can issue IDPs, valid for one year, for a fee. Always carry your home license together with the IDP.

The American Automobile Association (AAA) has reciprocal agreements with some international auto clubs (eg Canada's CAA, AAA in Australia), so bring your membership card from home.

INSURANCE

California law requires liability insurance for all vehicles. When renting a car, check your home auto-insurance policy or your travel-insurance policy to see if rental cars are already covered. If not, expect to pay about $20 per day for liability insurance when renting a car.

Insurance against damage to the car itself, called Collision Damage Waiver (CDW) or Loss Damage Waiver (LDW), costs another $10 to $20 or more per day for rental cars. The deductible may require you to pay up to the first $500 for any repairs. If you decline CDW, you will be held liable for all damages up to the full value of the car.

Some credit cards cover CDW/LDW, provided you charge the entire cost of the car rental to that card. If you have an accident, you may have to pay the rental-car company first, then seek reimbursement. Most credit-card coverage isn't valid for rentals over one month or for 'exotic' models (eg convertibles, RVs).

RENTING A VEHICLE

To rent your own wheels, you'll usually need to be at least 25 years old, hold a valid driver's license and have a major credit card, *not* a check or debit card.

Road Distances (miles)

	Anaheim	Arcata	Bakersfield	Death Valley	Las Vegas	Los Angeles	Monterey	Napa	Palm Springs	Redding	Sacramento	San Diego	San Francisco	San Luis Obispo	Santa Barbara	Sth Lake Tahoe
Arcata	680															
Bakersfield	135	555														
Death Valley	285	705	235													
Las Vegas	265	840	285	140												
Los Angeles	25	650	110	290	270											
Monterey	370	395	250	495	535	345										
Napa	425	265	300	545	590	400	150									
Palm Springs	95	760	220	300	280	110	450	505								
Redding	570	140	440	565	725	545	315	190	650							
Sacramento	410	300	280	435	565	385	185	60	490	160						
San Diego	95	770	230	350	330	120	465	520	140	665	505					
San Francisco	405	280	285	530	570	380	120	50	490	215	85	500				
San Luis Obispo	225	505	120	365	405	200	145	265	310	430	290	320	230			
Santa Barbara	120	610	145	350	360	95	250	370	205	535	395	215	335	105		
Sth Lake Tahoe	505	400	375	345	460	480	285	160	485	260	100	600	185	390	495	
Yosemite	335	465	200	300	415	310	200	190	415	325	160	430	190	230	345	190

Cars

Rental-car rates generally include unlimited mileage, but expect surcharges for additional drivers and one-way rentals. Airport locations may have cheaper base rates but higher add-on fees. If you get a fly-drive package, local taxes may be extra when you pick up the car. Child and infant safety seats are legally required; reserve them (around $10 per day, or $50 per trip) when booking your car.

Some major car-rental companies offer 'green' fleets of hybrid or alternative-fuel rental cars, but they're in short supply. Make reservations far in advance and expect to pay significantly more for these models. Many companies rent vans with wheelchair lifts and hand-controlled vehicles at no extra cost, but you must also reserve these well in advance.

International car-rental companies with hundreds of branches nationwide:

Alamo (www.alamo.com)

Avis (www.avis.com)

Budget (www.budget.com)

Dollar (www.dollar.com)

Enterprise (www.enterprise.com)

Fox (www.foxrentacar.com)

Hertz (www.hertz.com)

National (www.nationalcar.com)

Thrifty (www.thrifty.com)

To find local and independent car-rental companies, check:

Car Rental Express (www.carrental express.com) Search for independent car-rental companies and specialty cars (eg hybrids).

Rent-a-Wreck (www.rentawreck.com) Often rents to younger drivers (over-18s) and those without credit cards; ask about long-term rentals.

Wheelchair Getaways (www.wheelchair getaways.com) Rents wheelchair-accessible vans across the country.

Zipcar (www.zipcar.com) Car-sharing club in dozens of cities; some foreign drivers are eligible for membership.

If you don't mind no-cancellation policies or which company you rent from, you may find better deals on car rentals through online travel discounters such as **Priceline** (www.priceline.com) and **Hotwire** (www. hotwire.com).

Motorcycles

Motorcycle rentals and insurance are very expensive, with steep surcharges for one-way rentals. Discounts may be available for three-day and weekly rentals.

Rental outfitters:

Bartels' Route 66 (☎310-578-0112, 888-434-4473; www.route66riders.com; 4161 Lincoln Blvd, Marina del Rey; ⊙10am-6pm Tue-Sat, 11am-5pm Sun) Harley-Davidson and Indian motorcycle rentals in LA's South Bay.

Dubbelju (☎866-495-2774, 415-495-2774; www.dubbelju.com; 274 Shotwell St; ⊙9am-6pm Mon-Sat) Harley-Davidson and imported motorcycle rentals in San Francisco.

Eagle Rider (☎888-900-9901, 310-321-3180; www.eaglerider.com) Motorcycle rentals in the LA and San Francisco Bay areas, San Diego, Palm Springs, Fresno and Monterey

RVs & Campervans

Popular with road-trippers, recreational vehicles (RVs, also called motorhomes) are cumbersome to drive and burn fuel at an alarming rate. They do solve transportation, accommodation and self-catering kitchen needs in one fell swoop. Even so, there are many places in national parks and scenic areas (eg narrow mountain roads) that they can't be driven

Make reservations for RVs and smaller campervans as far in advance as possible. Rental costs vary by size and model; basic rates often don't include mileage, bedding or kitchen kits, vehicle prep and cleaning or additional taxes and fees. If bringing pets is allowed, a surcharge may apply.

Rental agencies:

Cruise America (www.cruiseamerica.com) Twenty RV-rental locations statewide.

El Monte RV (www.elmonterv.com) Over a dozen RV-rental locations across California.

Happy Travel Campers (www.camperusa.com) Rents campervans in Los Angeles, San Francisco, Las Vegas and Denver.

Jucy Rentals (www.jucyusa.com) Campervan rentals in Los Angeles, San Francisco and Las Vegas.

BORDER CROSSING

California is an important agricultural state. To prevent the spread of pests and diseases, certain food items (including

---

Road Trip Websites

AUTO CLUBS

American Automobile Association (www.aaa.com) Roadside assistance, travel discounts, trip planning and maps for members.

Better World Club (www.betterworldclub.com) Eco-friendly alternative to AAA.

MAPS

America's Byways (www.fhwa.dot.gov/byways) Inspiring itineraries, maps and directions for scenic drives.

Google Maps (http://maps.google.com) Turn-by-turn driving directions with estimated traffic delays.

National Park Service (www.nps.gov) Links to individual park sites for road condition updates and free downloadable maps.

ROAD CONDITIONS & CLOSURES

511 SF Bay (www.511.org) San Francisco Bay Area traffic updates.

California Department of Transportation (CalTrans; ☎800-427-7623; www.dot.ca.gov/cgi-bin/roads.cgi) Highway conditions, construction updates and road closures.

Go511 (www.go511.com) LA and Southern California traffic updates.

ROAD RULES

California Department of Motor Vehicles (www.dmv.ca.gov) Statewide driving laws, driver's licenses and vehicle registration.

Driving Problem-Buster

What should I do if my car breaks down? Put on your hazard lights (flashers) and carefully pull over to the side of the road. Call the roadside emergency assistance number for your auto club or rental-car company. Otherwise, call information (🖉411) for the number of the nearest towing service or auto-repair shop.

What if I have an accident? If you're safely able to do so, move your vehicle out of traffic and onto the road's shoulder. For minor collisions with no major property damage or bodily injuries, be sure to exchange driver's license and auto-insurance information with the other driver, then file a report with your insurance provider or notify your car-rental company as soon as possible. For major accidents, call 🖉911 and wait for the police and emergency services to arrive.

What should I do if I'm stopped by the police? Don't get out of the car unless asked. Keep your hands where the officer can see them (ie on the steering wheel). Always be courteous. Most fines for traffic or parking violations can be handled by mail or online within a 30-day period.

What happens if my car gets towed? Call the local non-emergency police number and ask where to pick up your car. Towing and vehicle storage fees accumulate quickly, up to hundreds of dollars for just a few hours or a day, so act promptly.

meats, fresh fruit and vegetables) may not be brought into the state. Bakery items and hard-cured cheeses are admissible. If you drive across the border from Mexico or the neighboring states of Oregon, Nevada or Arizona, you may have to stop for a quick agricultural inspection.

If you're driving across the Mexican border, check the ever-changing passport and visa requirements with the **US Department of State** (http://travel.state.gov) beforehand. **US Customs and Border Protection** (http://apps.cbp.gov/bwt) tracks current wait times at every border crossing. Between San Diego and Tijuana, Mexico, San Ysidro is the world's busiest border crossing. US citizens do not require a visa for stays in Mexico of 72 hours or less in a border zone, but they do need a passport.

Unless you're planning an extended stay in Tijuana, taking a car across the Mexican border is more trouble than it's worth. Instead, leave your car on the US side of the border and walk. If you drive across, you must buy Mexican car insurance either beforehand or at the border crossing.

MAPS

Tourist information offices and visitor centers distribute free but often very basic maps. GPS navigation can't be relied upon everywhere, notably in thick forests and remote mountain, desert and canyon areas.

If you're planning on doing a lot of driving, you may want a more detailed fold-out road map or map atlas, such as DeLorme's comprehensive *California Atlas & Gazetteer* ($25). Members of the American Automobile Association (AAA) and its international auto-club affiliates (bring your membership card from home) can pick up free maps from any of AAA's California offices.

ROADS & CONDITIONS

For highway conditions, including road closures and construction updates, dial 🖉800-427-7623 or visit www.dot.ca.gov.

In places where winter driving is an issue, snow tires and tire chains may be required, especially on mountain highways. Ideally, carry your own chains and learn how to use them before you hit the road. Otherwise, chains can usually be bought (but not cheaply) on the highway, at gas stations or in nearby towns.

Most car-rental companies don't permit the use of tire chains. Driving off-road, or on unpaved roads, is also prohibited by most car-rental companies.

ROAD RULES

➡ Drive on the right-hand side of the road.
➡ Talking or texting on a cell (mobile) phone while driving is illegal.

121

Drunk Driving

The maximum legal blood-alcohol concentration for drivers is 0.08%. Penalties for 'DUI' (driving under the influence of alcohol or drugs) are severe, including heavy fines, driver's license suspension, court appearances and/or jail time. Police may give roadside sobriety checks to assess if you've been drinking or using drugs. If you fail, they'll require you to take a breath, urine or blood test to determine the level of drugs and alcohol in your body. Refusing to be tested is treated the same as if you'd taken the test and failed.

→ The use of seat belts is required for drivers, front-seat passengers and children under 16.

→ High-occupancy vehicle (HOV) lanes marked with a diamond symbol are reserved for cars with multiple occupants, but sometimes only during specific signposted hours.

→ Unless otherwise posted, the speed limit is 65mph on freeways, 55mph on two-lane undivided highways, 35mph on major city streets, and 25mph in business and residential districts. It's illegal to pass a school bus when its lights are flashing.

→ Except where signs prohibit doing so, turning right at a red light after coming to a full stop is usually permitted. Intersecting cross-traffic still has the right of way, however.

→ At four-way stop signs, cars proceed in order of arrival. If two cars arrive simultaneously, the one on the right goes first. When in doubt, politely wave the other driver ahead.

→ At intersections, U-turns are permitted unless otherwise posted.

→ When emergency vehicles approach from either direction, carefully pull over to the side of the road.

→ It's illegal to carry open containers of alcohol inside a vehicle, even empty ones. Unless containers are full and still sealed, store them in the trunk.

PARKING

Parking is plentiful and free in small towns and rural areas, but scarce and/or expensive in cities. You can pay municipal parking meters and centralized pay stations with coins (usually quarters) or sometimes credit or debit cards. When parking on the street, read all posted regulations and restrictions (eg street-cleaning hours, permit-only residential areas) and pay attention to colored curbs, or you may be ticketed and towed. Expect to pay at least $2.50 per hour or $30 overnight at a city parking garage. Flat-fee valet parking at hotels and restaurants is common in cities; tip the valet attendant at least $2 when they hand your keys back.

FUEL

Gas stations in California, nearly all of which are self-service, are everywhere, except in national parks and sparsely populated desert and mountain areas. Gas is sold in gallons (one US gallon equals 3.78L). In mid-2017, the cost for regular fuel in California averaged $3.20.

SAFETY

In rural areas, livestock sometimes graze next to unfenced roads. These areas are typically signed as 'Open Range,' with the silhouette of a steer. Where deer or other wild animals frequently appear roadside, you'll see signs with the silhouette of a leaping deer. Take these signs seriously, particularly at night or in the fog. In coastal areas, thick fog may impede driving – slow down and if it's too soupy, get off the road. Along coastal cliffs and on twisting mountain roads, watch out for falling rocks, mudslides and snow avalanches that could damage or disable your car if struck.

Warning!

As of 2016, the **US State Department** (http://travel.state.gov) has issued a travel warning about drug-trafficking violence and crime along the US–Mexico border. Travelers should exercise caution in the northern state of Baja California, including the city of Tijuana.

BEHIND THE SCENES

SEND US YOUR FEEDBACK

We love to hear from travelers – your comments help make our books better. We read every word, and we guarantee that your feedback goes straight to the authors. Visit **lonelyplanet. com/contact** to submit your updates and suggestions.

Note: We may edit, reproduce and incorporate your comments in Lonely Planet products such as guidebooks, websites and digital products, so let us know if you don't want your comments reproduced or your name acknowledged. For a copy of our privacy policy visit lonelyplanet.com/privacy.

ACKNOWLEDGMENTS

Climate map data adapted from Peel MC, Finlayson BL & McMahon TA (2007) 'Updated World Map of the Köppen-Geiger Climate Classification', *Hydrology and Earth System Sciences*, 11, 163344.

Cover photographs: Front: Convertible car in Sonoma County, Richard Price/Getty ©; Back: Redwoods in the Avenue of the Giants, Christian Heeb/AWL ©

Illustrations pp88-9 by Michael Weldon

THIS BOOK

This 2nd edition of *Pacific Coast Highways Road Trips* was researched and written by Brett Atkinson, Andrew Bender, Sara Benson, Alison Bing, Cristian Bonetto, Jade Bremner, Ashley Harrell, Josephine Quintero and John A Vlahides. The previous edition was written and researched by Andrew Bender, Sara Benson, Alison Bing, Celeste Brash, Nate Cavalieri and Adam Skolnick. This guidebook was produced by the following:

Curator Kate Mathews

Destination Editor Clifton Wilkinson

Product Editor Grace Dobell

Senior Cartographer Alison Lyall

Book Designer Mazzy Prinsep

Assisting Editors Janet Austin, Sarah Bailey, Andrew Bain, Melanie Dankel, Carly Hall, Anita Isalska, Kellie Langdon, Jodie Martire

Assisting Book Designer Meri Blazevski

Cover Researcher Brendan Dempsey-Spencer

Thanks to Elizabeth Jones, Kirsten Rawlings, Wibowo Rusli, Dan Saunders, Sarah Stocking

OUR STORY

A beat-up old car, a few dollars in the pocket and a sense of adventure. In 1972 that's all Tony and Maureen Wheeler needed for the trip of a lifetime – across Europe and Asia overland to Australia. It took several months, and at the end – broke but inspired – they sat at their kitchen table writing and stapling together their first travel guide, *Across Asia on the Cheap*. Within a week they'd sold 1500 copies. Lonely Planet was born.

Today, Lonely Planet has offices in Franklin, London, Melbourne, Oakland, Dublin, Beijing, and Delhi, with more than 600 staff and writers. We share Tony's belief that 'a great guidebook should do three things: inform, educate and amuse'.

INDEX

INDEX **S-W**

OUR WRITERS

BRETT ATKINSON

Brett Atkinson is based in Auckland, New Zealand, but is frequently on the road for Lonely Planet. He's a full-time travel and food writer specialising in adventure travel, unusual destinations, and surprising angles on more well known destinations. Since becoming a Lonely Planet author in 2005, Brett has covered areas as diverse as Vietnam, Sri Lanka, the Czech Republic, New Zealand, Morocco, California and the South Pacific.

ANDREW BENDER

Award-winning travel and food writer Andrew Bender has written three dozen Lonely Planet guidebooks (from *Amsterdam* to *Los Angeles*, *Germany* to *Taiwan* and more than a dozen titles about Japan), plus numerous articles for lonelyplanet.com. A native New Englander, he now lives in the Los Angeles area.

SARA BENSON

After graduating from college in Chicago, Sara jumped on a plane to California with one suitcase and just $100 in her pocket. She landed in San Francisco, and today she makes her home in Oakland, just across the Bay. She's an all-seasons outdoors sports nut who loves long road trips to wild, remote places.

ALISON BING

Alison has done most things travelers are supposed to do and many you definitely shouldn't, including making room for the chickens, accepting dinner invitations from cults, and trusting the camel to know the way. She has survived to tell tales for Lonely Planet, NPR, BBC Travel, the *Telegraph*, *New York Times* and other global media.

CRISTIAN BONETTO

Cristian has contributed to more than 30 Lonely Planet guides to date, including *New York City*, *Italy*, *Venice & the Veneto*, *Naples & the Amalfi Coast*, *Denmark*, *Copenhagen*, *Sweden* and *Singapore*. When not on the road, you'll find the reformed playwright and TV scriptwriter slurping espresso in his beloved hometown, Melbourne.

JADE BREMNER

Jade has been a journalist for more than a decade. She has lived in and reported on four different regions. Wherever she goes she finds action sports to try – the weirder the better – and it's no coincidence many of her favorite places have some of the best waves in the world. Jade has edited travel magazines and sections for *Time Out* and Radio Times and has been a correspondent for the *Times*, CNN and the *Independent*.

ASHLEY HARRELL

After a brief stint selling day spa coupons door-to-door in South Florida, Ashley decided she'd rather be a writer. She went to journalism grad school and convinced a newspaper to hire her. Fueling her zest for storytelling and the unknown, she traveled widely and moved often, from a tiny NYC apartment to a vast California ranch to a jungle cabin in Costa Rica, where she started writing for Lonely Planet.

JOSEPHINE QUINTERO

Josephine first got her taste of not-so-serious travel when she slung a guitar on her back and traveled in Europe in the early '70s. Since then, she has been an editor for the now defunct *Go* airlines inflight magazine and still writes two monthly columns (Malaga and Gibraltar) for Easyjet's magazine, as well as a bimonthly column on Seville for a Belgian airline.

JOHN A VLAHIDES

A native New Yorker living in San Francisco, John has contributed to 18 Lonely Planet guidebooks since 2003, ranging from *California* and *Western USA* to the *Dubai* guide. He is co-host of the TV series *Lonely Planet: Roads Less Travelled* (National Geographic Adventure).

Published by Lonely Planet Global Limited
CRN 554153
2nd edition – Feb 2018
ISBN 978 1 78657 356 8
© Lonely Planet 2018   Photographs © as indicated 2018
10 9 8 7 6 5 4 3 2 1
Printed in China